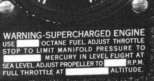

STAGGERWING!

STAGGERWING!

Story of the Classic Beechcraft Biplane

by

Robert T. Smith

The Private Press of
Robert Stephen Maney
Media, Pa. 19065 U.S.A.

Copy Number 717

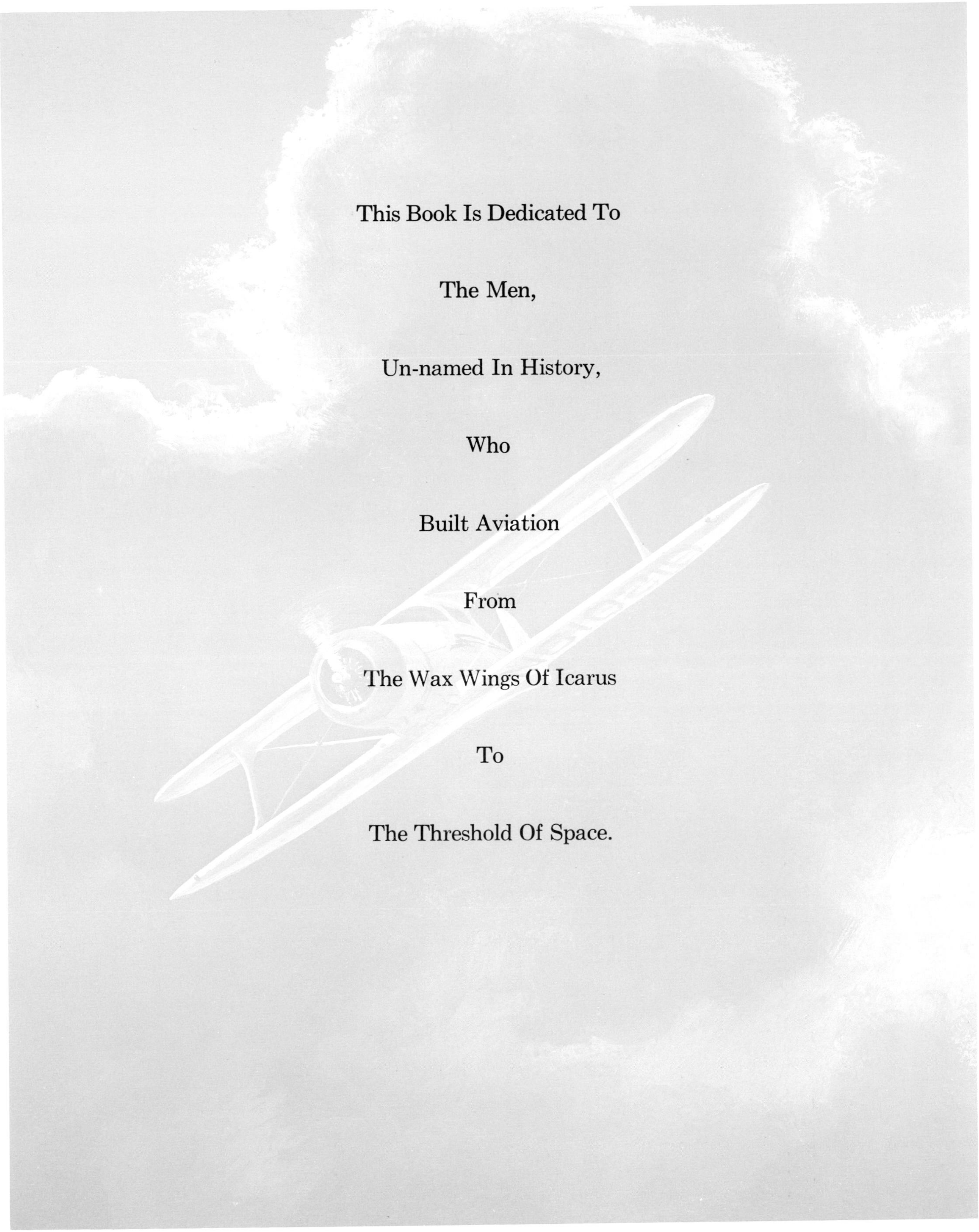

This Book Is Dedicated To

The Men,

Un-named In History,

Who

Built Aviation

From

The Wax Wings Of Icarus

To

The Threshold Of Space.

TABLE OF CONTENTS

Book Endpapers — Instrument panel of A17FS, s/n 11.
    (Photo from Henry B. DeSpain)

Frontispiece — G17S, s/n B-3, in flight over Atlanta, Georgia.
    (Color photo by Floyd Jillson)

PREFACE

This book really began in 1957 when I owned a Beechcraft model C17L. Of course, at the time I had no idea I'd ever attempt to write a book about the famed Beech Staggerwing. I just flew my C17L, and casually started gathering data on the history—first of my individual airplane, then on the entire Beechcraft 17 series.

In 1959 Bob Whittier challenged me to do a more comprehensive article on the Staggerwing for the Experimental Aircraft Association magazine SPORT AVIATION than he had done. He had written a very brief resumé —I wrote a two-part article for the magazine, and it appeared in the December, 1960 and January, 1961 issues of the magazine. It carried the sub-title "Condensed From a Forthcoming Book." So, here is the book!

William T. Larkins encouraged me to do a definitive work—to research the subject *completely*, and make the book historically accurate. It is easier said than done, as Bill Larkins knows from his books on the Ford tri-motor, and Navy and Marine aviation. I make no claim that this book is the *entire,* the *complete* history of the Beechcraft model 17 series airplanes. I *do* claim that it is as definitive, as accurate, as complete as seven years of intense research by myself and dozens of other interested people could possibly make it.

A book of this scope is never the product of one man—least of all the author. Many historians, researchers, photograph collectors, writers, and just plain airplane pilots contributed the information and photographs you will find in this book. About all I can claim is that I collected the data and photographs, and assembled them in what I hope is a reasonably sensible order.

It would be unfair to attempt to name every individual who made a contribution to this book—to do so would take many pages, and run the risk of leaving out the name of someone who sent me some extremely valuable information, or a rare photograph. The name of most contributors will appear, in one way or another, in the course of the story. Others will be in the credit lines of photographs. Some will go un-named. The point is, this book is hardly the product of my own efforts. It is the product of the efforts of many people. My thanks to them all.

It would be grossly unfair to omit mention of my wife, Louise. While she did not participate in the research and writing of this book (most of the time she was busy giving birth to a healthy son and a darling daughter), her strong support of this project made it possible, and her help as a secretary, sales manager, office girl, pepper-upper, and general assistant made the job much easier than it would have been otherwise. I might have done the book without her help, but I don't know how.

The publisher of a book is almost *never* mentioned. In this case he will be. Robert S. Maney is a printer by trade, and the reader can judge his skill from the quality of this book. He has spent his entire life in the printing business, with the exception of a short interlude a few years back when he steered a Republic P-47D around the skies over Festung Europa. He volunteered to do the book at prices no sensible publisher would consider. He spent hours of hard work taking old, poor photographs, and making them into usable reproductions. He did a great deal of the page composition and arrangement as well as making suggestions on the book's format and layout. No other publisher would have taken the personal interest in this book that Robert S. Maney did.

The excellent drawings in this book are the work of master draftsman and artist James M. Triggs who also did the painting of a D17S flying out of a thunderstorm that is used on the dust jacket and elsewhere in the book. He did the art work for this book on his own time, and without hope of compensation.

This book is the history of the Beechcraft Model 17 series airplane. In order to give the reader perspective, the story begins with Travel Air, and some brief notes on the early life of Walter Beech. There was a temptation, during the research of this book, to do a biography of Walter Beech. To a degree, this was done, but only where it directly pertains to the Beechcraft 17. It certainly is not intended as a definitive biography of the man, nor of any other individual—this book is solely the history of the Beechcraft 17 —the STAGGERWING!

Robert T. Smith
July, 1966

Walter Herschel Beech 1891-1950　　　　　　　　　　　　　　　(Beech Photo)

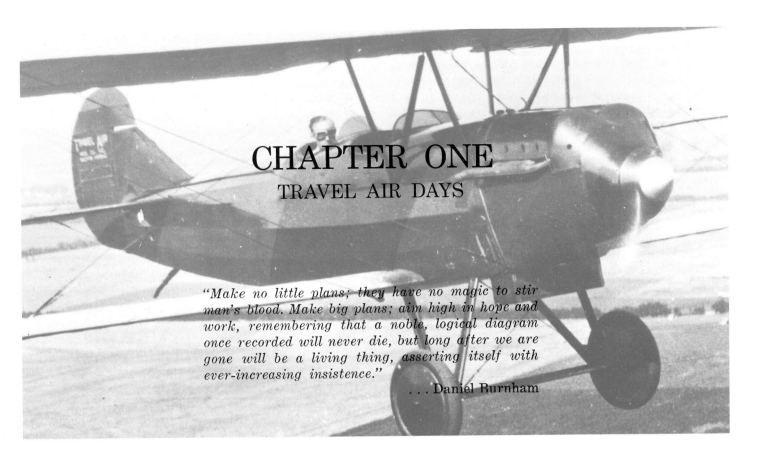

CHAPTER ONE
TRAVEL AIR DAYS

"Make no little plans; they have no magic to stir man's blood. Make big plans; aim high in hope and work, remembering that a noble, logical diagram once recorded will never die, but long after we are gone will be a living thing, asserting itself with ever-increasing insistence."

. . . Daniel Burnham

A noise like thunder broke the stillness of the Kansas plain as four hundred and twenty roaring horses thrust a sleek new biplane through the air at over two hundred miles per hour.

On the ground, a man with a pipe clamped in his teeth studied the airplane racing by overhead. The date was November 4, 1932. The airplane was the new Beechcraft 17R on its maiden flight, and the man was Walter Herschel Beech.

The first of a new and different breed of airplanes, the first 17R was to have a tumultuous life ending in disaster. Registered NC499N, it was the only Beechcraft airplane built in 1932.

Walter H. Beech was born to Cornelius and Tommie Hay Beech in Pulaski, Tennessee on January 30, 1891. What he did from then until he entered the Army in World War One I do not know. One source says he built and flew his own airplane, but there is too much evidence to the contrary. It is possible that he worked on or around airplanes, or more probably airplane engines, or maybe just engines because before the war ended he was promoted to the rank of sergeant and placed in charge of aircraft engine overhaul shops at Rich Field in Waco, Texas.

The same source that claims Walter built and flew his own airplane before World War One also claims he was a flight instructor during the war, but W. H. "Pete" Hill told me, "I met Sergeant Beech at the close of World War One", and that he was not a flight instructor, but was working in the engine shops at Rich Field.

Pete Hill offered Walter a job after the war, and when the war ended, Walter went to Arkansas City, Kansas where the Williams-Hill Airplane Company was in operation.

The war had moved aviation ahead several steps —not in economic and social acceptance, but in technical improvements. Aviation before the war had been little more than a circus-like oddity. When World War One ended, the Army made its Curtiss JN series trainers and DeHavilland DH series airplanes surplus. Every pilot who wanted to stay in aviation after the war did what Walter Beech and Pete Hill did—they bought a couple of surplus airplanes and started barnstorming—hopping passengers, and anything else they could think of to earn a buck.

To men like General William B. Mitchell, the war had proved the airplane's usefulness and potential as a weapon of war. To men like Walter Beech and Pete Hill, the airplane was a potential mode of transportation for business and pleasure.

What William B. Mitchell was eventually to prove

An oft-printed photo of the first Travel Air. It bore a marked resemblance to the WWI German Fokker DVII. With minor changes in the engine cowling, Hollywood used it for WWI aviation movies, caused it to earn the name "Hollywood Fokker". *(Beech Photo)*

First location of Travel Air. Look closely and you can see the name "Travel Air" painted over on the dark area at the top of the building. *(Beech Photo)*

A 1921 photograph of Walter Beech and his cronies shows the typical garb of an aviator in that era. The people are, standing, left to right, Unknown, Walter Beech, Unknown, Ted Moellendick, and Perry Hutton. Sitting, left to right, Dick Phillips, Charles Landers, and Francis "Chief" Bowhan. Bowhan might be "Bohan"; have seen it spelled both ways. This photo came originally from Lloyd Stearman who sent it to Matty Laird who sent it to Joe Christy who sent it to me. Notice the pipe in Walter Beech's mouth. A pipe was almost his trademark.
(Joe Christy)

This side view shot of a Travel Air 2000 shows the clean lines of the airplane, and explains why it was a favorite in the twenties. A few of these are still flying. *(Beech Photo)*

Mapping Course to Dayton Ohio

Lloyd Stearman on left, Walter Beech on right consult a road map before leaving for the Dayton Air Races. The airplanes are Swallows—compare them to the Travel Air 2000.
(Joe Christy)

in a Beechcraft later on.

The OX-5 engine was plentiful in the early twenties, but it only developed 90 horsepower in the best of condition. More power was needed to push airplanes to higher speeds. The Liberty and Hispano-Suiza of World War One provided more power than the OX-5, but they suffered from the same malady the OX-5 had; they were old, weighed too much for the horsepower they developed, and weren't as reliable as they should have been.

The basic Travel Air 2000 could be equipped with a number of engines, but the most expensive version carried the new Wright "Whirlwind" engine. The Whirlwind was a new design. It was a lightweight, aircooled, radial. It developed upwards of 200 horsepower, and weighed little more than the OX-5 or Hisso. But, it cost a lot of money, and barnstormers couldn't pay a lot for an engine.

It was not until the airmail routes started that people could really afford to operate the new Wright engines. At about the same time, oil companies began to buy airplanes. If it were not for oil companies, I'm convinced the aviation industry would have folded up in the twenties. Oil companies bought airplanes when nobody else would touch them.

An individual in the aviation industry in the twenties was caught between a rock and a hard place. On the one hand he wanted to sell the reliability and economy of flying as a mode of transportation, and on the other hand he wanted to stop the public image of aviation as a thrill-seeking episode at the county fair. But, to damn him before he started, the way to make money with an airplane in the twenties was to give the local citizens a few thrills at the county fair. Thus, aerobatics and wing-walking were very popular in the twenties. But, sensible men in industry realized the value of an airplane as transportation, and by the mid-twenties many companies owned airplanes, of which the name Travel Air was abundantly seen.

In 1926 Lloyd Stearman left Travel Air—the first of the famed trio (Beech, Stearman, and Cessna) to part company. He went to California where he built airplanes for a time, but eventually he returned to Wichita, and started the Stearman Company anew. It later became the Boeing—Wichita plant of Boeing.

Clyde Cessna had built many airplanes on his own before coming to Travel Air. They had been monoplanes. Cessna was a firm believer in the monoplane as opposed to the biplane, and in the mid-twenties that was like being against motherhood. But, Clyde was so determined to prove his point that, in 1926, he built a monoplane on his own time. Powered by a 120 horsepower Anzani engine, the highwinged monoplane seated a pilot and three passengers.

Although Walter Beech had openly opposed Cessna on the monoplane, Clyde convinced Walter he should build a monoplane, and told him he'd help him sell it. So, Walter agreed, and the Travel Air Model 5000 was built, and as Clyde promised, he went to Kansas City with Walter and sold thirteen of them to National Air Transport.

This first Travel Air monoplane used strut-braced monoplane wings. Not only did Clyde Cessna favor the highly controversial monoplane configuration, but he poured oil on the fire by advocating a *fully cantilever* monoplane. Walter had gone along with him on the strut-braced Model 5000, and later developments such as the famed "Woolaroc," but he put his foot down and said "No" to any darn fool idea about a cantilever wing.

So, in April of 1927, Clyde Cessna left Travel Air to build an airplane on his own. Setting up shop in a small building at 1520 West Douglas Street, Clyde mortgaged himself to the hilt to make his new "Comet" monoplane a success. With fully cantilever wings, and the 120 horsepower Anzani engine, the "Comet" of 1927 was the forerunner of many successful and famous airplanes bearing the Cessna name. And, through the years, Cessna never built a biplane!

Let's go back to the Travel Air 5000 for a moment. On July 14, 1927, Earnest Smith and Emery Bronte took off from Oakland, California in a Model 5000 named the "City of Oakland," and flew it to Molokai, Hawaii. They covered the 2340 miles in 25 hours and 36 minutes. Sadly enough, they were just about one month *too early* to win the California to Hawaii Dole Air Derby and $25,000 in prize money!

But, a Travel Air "Woolaroc," similar in design, but larger than the 5000, did win the Dole race.

Art Goebel and William Davis flew the "Woolaroc" from Oakland, California to Wheeler Field, Hawaii in 26 hours, 17 minutes, and 33 seconds on August 16 and 17, 1927 to win the Dole Air Derby and collect the $25,000 first prize money from the pineapple king.

Many airplanes were lost by entrants in the Dole Air Derby, but a Travel Air made it. Perhaps this is one reason sales made such an increase in 1927 and 1928 that Walter Beech sought help from Wall Street. The Hayden-Stone Investment Company in New York provided needed expansion money through a stock issue in the Travel Air name. This led, through many changes, purchases, sales, organizations and other financial razzle-dazzle, to purchase of Travel Air by the Curtiss-Wright Aeronautical Corporation in 1929. But, back to 1928.

The Travel Air Model 6000, a highwing, cabin

Above photo shows Walter Beech in front cockpit with Brice Goldsborough of Pioneer Instrument Company in the rear. This was about the time of the 1926 Ford Reliability Tour. Note early tape style instruments in rear cockpit. Photo at right shows the two in front of the airplane .

(Above, Beech Photo; at right Joe Christy)

Western movie hero Ken Maynard with his Travel Air biplane. Movie executives generally were leery of their valuable stars mixing with airplanes, but the safety record of the Travel Air eased their fears.
(Beech Photo)

monoplane, appeared in 1928. At the same time, the open cockpit, biplane Model 4000 was still being built.

As I have mentioned before, sales of airplanes in the twenties was enhanced by performance in air races. Many Travel Airs had entered races, air tours, and other competitive events, always with a good showing, and many times turning in a first place. But, in 1928, shortly after the National Air Races, Walter Beech bemoaned the fact that no airplane then in the Travel Air stable was a really hot, competitive racer.

Herb Rawdon, an engineer with Travel Air overheard Walter's lament, and went home thinking about the 1929 National Air Race, and a special racing machine to build and enter.

Herb knew that, if a really fast machine were to be designed and built for the 1929 race, it had to start then—late in 1928. He also knew it would have to be built by some enthused individual on his own time, at night and on weekends. Feeling that such a project was surely not a one-man job, Herb Rawdon approached Walter Burnham with the idea, and the *next evening* they began work on the project.

No messing around—no coordination with half a dozen project and program people—no work orders issued—no budget proposals to be approved by the comptroller—just go home and start to work.

Influenced by the 1928 Schneider Trophy racers, and the possibility of a six cylinder, inline engine, the two men laid out the preliminary drawings, and called the airplane the Model R.

The "R," Walter Burnham claims, did not stand for "Rawdon." He says it was only coincidental that they selected R and that it is the first letter of Rawdon and Racer. Perhaps so, but it did not fit the standard Travel Air numbering system which was Model 1000, 2000, 3000, 4000, etc. The Travel Air models used numbers, not letters. Anyway, the racer being designed by Herb Rawdon and Walter Burnham was the Model R.

They designed the airplane to carry a six cylinder inline engine that had not yet been built, but in their weight and balance calculations they used the Wright J4 radial engine of 220 horsepower. With this engine, the airplane would gross out at 1700 pounds.

The airplane was designed for 9 G's with an ultimate of 12 G's—fully enough for a military fighter airplane. Construction was to be welded steel tubing fuselage with wooden wings. The fuselage would be covered with sheet metal and plywood, and the wings were to use plywood covering. With the design completed, Walter and Herb waited for the opportune moment to approach Beech.

At about that time Beech had been approached with a new engine design capable of delivering 300 horsepower. Beech called Rawdon in to take a look at the engine design and give his opinion. This was it! While discussing the engine, Herb mentioned it might be a good engine for his new racer, whereupon Walter wanted to know more about the racer. So, while he was supposed to be evaluating an engine, Rawdon sold Beech on building the Model R for the 1929 Nationals. The idea was to use the new 300 horsepower engine.

But, time was short—it was already late in the Spring of 1929. As luck would have it, the 300 horsepower engine proved to be only a pipe dream, and not a working engine. They had to find a suitable engine for the Model R. And, in short order.

Curtiss-Wright had a new R-975 aircooled radial. Perhaps it was far enough along in its development for an engine to be shipped in time for the race. After many phone calls to the Curtiss-Wright engine factory, Guy Vaughn agreed to deliver an R-975, and to soup it up to 400 hp. By now, only ten weeks remained before the races. In those ten weeks, the Model R had to be built, tested, and tuned for the race. There were parts to be ordered, components to decide on, shipping schedules to arrange. Concerned, but not undaunted by the shortage of time, the Travel Air factory swung into action to build the racer.

While a select crew of 25 workers gathered behind closed doors to begin work on the racer, local Wichita newspapers begin to speculate that something was "going on" out at the Travel Air factory. No one denied it. But, no one confirmed it. For the first time, Travel Air was building an airplane without giving it any publicity. Actually, the real reason for building the airplane behind closed doors was probably to keep the public from wandering around bothering the workers with questions, and slowing work on the racer—after all, ten weeks is not a lot of time in which to build and test an airplane, especially a high-performance, racing machine.

As work progressed, the local aviation public began to refer to the special project at Travel Air as a "mystery ship." Which, in a way, it was. To Travel Air it was the Model R, but to the public it became the Travel Air Mystery Ship, and has been known by that unofficial name ever since.

In addition to the Model R project, Walter had the factory modify a standard biplane for the races, and when the Cheverolet brothers of Indianapolis announced their six cylinder, inline engine of 250 horsepower, he ordered another Model R built to use that engine! But, the prime project remained the first Model R.

Based on engine RPM, horsepower output, propeller blade angle, and expected airspeeds, the engineers decided on specific propeller models, and orders were placed. The standard biplane being modified for the races would use a Wright 240 horsepower engine, and the prop selected for it was 9 feet in diameter. The Model R prop would be only 8 feet in diameter although its engine was supposed to develop 400 horsepower—nearly twice that of the biplane.

When the two props arrived, Walter Beech commented that the small prop must be for the biplane, and the large one for the Model R. Walter Burnham, busy uncrating and checking them, assured him that just the *reverse* was true. This didn't seem at all logical to Beech, and a strong argument ensued—something that happened frequently at the Travel Air factory. Walter Burnham wouldn't back down, and Beech walked away muttering that engineers were a confused group of people consistently making bum decisions.

Six valuable weeks had been needed to order and receive the two props, and an error in engineering calculations would have been disastrous. As things worked out, the engineers had picked the correct propellers.

With the race so close, and money invested in the Model R, Walter Beech was understandably concerned about progress on the airplane, and such details as the size of the props wasn't likely to escape his eye. Luckily, the engineers knew more about props than he did.

With just fourteen days remaining before the race, the first Model R was completed, and rolled out the factory door. The NACA cowling was not yet finished, but it was decided to begin testing without it. There wasn't enough time to afford to sit around and wait for the cowling.

Design specifications for the Model R called for a top speed of about 205 mph. Without the NACA cowling, the airplane did 185 mph, and it was thought by the designers that the cowling would add the 20 mph necessary to reach the design speed of 205.

Several flight tests were made without the cowling, and no adverse flight characteristics were noted. Naturally, when the cowling was finished and installed, the anxious designers ordered the next flight be a maximum speed run to check the top speed. With everyone out watching, the Model R roared across the field on the test flight with the airspeed needle quivering on 225 mph—*twenty* mph faster than the original estimates. No doubt there

was a lot of jumping up and down and hollering when he landed and reported the speed he had made.

But, not without cost. The new NACA cowling had pulled forward into the propeller at high speed causing some damage to the cowling. After beefing up the cowling and adjacent structure, the problem was corrected.

With the exciting new racer tested and ready to go, and just bare days remaining before the race, Travel Air dealer Doug Davis from Atlanta, Georgia came to Wichita to check out in the Model R, and fly it in the race. It has never been made clear to me why a factory pilot was not selected. Perhaps none volunteered. Perhaps, in the process of selling Travel Air airplanes, Davis managed to secure a commitment from Walter to allow him to fly the airplane. Whatever the reason, Davis arrived at the factory a few days before the race to check out in the airplane.

Twice as fast as anything he, or anyone else, had ever flown, the Model R was responsive and solid in the air. Davis was enthused. So much so, that, on the day he left the factory for the races, he buzzed the field, and accidentally allowed the main landing gear to touch the ground at high speed.

Not knowing that anything was wrong with the airplane, Davis pulled up, and headed for Kansas City. On landing there, the wheels collapsed. Fortunately, the damage was minor. Repairs were quickly made, and Davis continued on to Cleveland, arriving in plenty of time for the race.

The Travel Air Model R was one of the first strictly racing airplanes the Nationals had seen, and it created quite a stir when Davis arrived. There was much speculation about the "Mystery Ship" from Wichita.

Event Number 26 at the 1929 National Air Races was the Free-for-all Speed Contest. This was the *big* one—this was *it!* Davis climbed into the cockpit, buckled his safety belt. On the sidelines, many anxious faces watched the souped-up Wright engine cough into life. Despite its obvious speed advantage, there was always the fear that some obscure mishap would pull the airplane out of the race—would the beefed up cowling hold for the grueling runs around the course? Would the engine overheat with the new cowling when being run wide open on a race course? Many questions and fears ran through the minds of the designers and builder as they watched Davis in the cockpit of the Model R.

They got off well, Davis easily pulled ahead. The racers streaked around the course, the Mystery Ship well in the lead. Well, the designers sighed, one point was clear—the Mystery Ship was definitely the fastest of the field. But, could she stand the

The Model R in flight. Reportedly this is the fifth one—the Italian Model R, and that may be one of the Wadlow brothers in the cockpit. *(Henry B. DeSpain)*

The famed "Woolaroc", winner of the 1927 Dole Air Derby. Note pilot's cockpit perched atop the fuselage. No doubt Lindbergh's flight from New York to Paris inspired such later events as the Dole race. *(Beech Photo)*

The Travel Air factory, circa about 1930. The flying field is in the foreground. The main plant of the present Beech factory is still at this location. *(Joe Christy)*

10

Frank Hawks being refueled on a transcontinental speed dash. Texaco No. 13 was the fourth Model R built. This photo was taken at Wichita, and Hank DeSpain remembers that Hawks didn't even get out of the airplane while it was being refueled. Of such attention to detail in the saving of precious time are air racing records set. *(Henry B. DeSpain)*

grind? Would she fail?

One of the most costly mistakes in an air race is to cut inside a pylon. The pilot must return and recircle the pylon immediately. Valuable time is lost, and fast ships have lost races on account of having to recircle pylons. On one lap, Davis cut inside one. He recircled it, but blacked out, and lost his orientation. When he eased up on the back pressure, and his vision returned, he wasn't sure he had circled the pylon.

Split seconds counted. If he *had* circled the pylon, he knew his lead would let him win the race, but he also knew he would be disqualified if he had *not* completely circled the pylon. Circling the pylon a second time might not only lose his lead, but place him so far back in the race that even with the superior speed of the Model R he couldn't regain the lead and win. One can imagine the fingernail biting that must have been going on on the ground as the Travel Air people watched Doug Davis circle the pylon, then begin a *second* circle around it! They too, knew the importance of not cutting inside the pylons.

Davis was not sure about the first circle, so he was making a second one to be sure. He had gambled. Now, could he make it? Could he still win the race?

With just seconds to spare the Travel Air Model R streaked across the finish line ahead of a Curtiss P-3A Army racer to win at an average speed of 194.90 mph. The Army P-3A chalked up 186.84 mph to take second place.

One consolation the Travel Air group had. On one lap of the race, Davis broke the world's record for a closed course race by clocking 229.8 mph on that lap. If it had not been for the extra pylon circling, the Model R no doubt would have turned in a much higher average speed for the race—probably something up around 215 mph.

As it was, the Mystery Ship's performance at the race caused many to comment that it was something of a break-through in design, and many challenged the Army and Navy to design fighters with the Mystery Ship's speed.

I had often wondered why the Model R was not offered to the Army or Navy as a military fighter. Ted Wells, Travel Air's chief design engineer at the time, said they did not want military business. Another factor might have been Walter Beech's knowledge that the Army and Navy in those days had, at best, a pittance for aircraft procurement. There just wasn't much of a future in military aircraft production. But, the Italians were interested, and purchased a Model R.

Five Model R's were built. The first one was the 1929 Thompson Cup Winner, NR614K. The second one was NR613K, originally powered with the in-line Chevrolair engine, it was later converted to a Wright radial. The third Model R was NR482N purchased by Shell Oil Company, and flown by Jimmy Doolittle and Jimmy Haizlip. Perhaps the most famous, over the years, of the Model R's, was number four—Texaco No. 13 flown by Frank Hawks for the Texas Oil Company. With this airplane Hawks set many cross-country speed dash records, both in the United States, and in Europe. The fifth one was purchased by the Italian government, obviously for military evaluation.

Beyond these five racing machines, nothing was done with the Model R as a commercial venture. Perhaps the times caused this—the stock market crash of 1929 slowed all business activity. Curtiss-Wright now owned Travel Air, and, in 1930, they closed the Wichita plant, and moved the operation to St. Louis, Missouri. Most Travel Air employees made the move to St. Louis. Curtiss-Wright evidently did not want to spend any time or money developing new commercial airplanes.

Or, it could have been that Walter was already thinking of leaving Travel Air (and Curtiss-Wright), and wanted to save any new designs for the future. When Curtiss-Wright moved the Travel Air division to St. Louis, Walter found himself in New York most of the time, performing "executive" duties. He was more at home roaming around an airplane factory where people were welding steel tubing, gluing wood, and doping fabric.

Some time during this period, the Travel Air numbering system changed. From the Model 1000, 2000, 3000, 4000, 5000, 6000, etc., they changed to simple numbers without the zeros. Thus, the Model 4000 became the Travel Air Model 4, the 6000, the 6, etc. Though many people still call the older models by the long number with zeros, the later models (up to Model 16) are generally referred to without the zeros. Curtiss-Wright produced airplanes up through Model 16 before closing the St. Louis plant altogether. Remember this last model number for later reference.

During 1930 and 1931 Walter Beech divided his time between New York and St. Louis. All of the old Travel Air employees (well, most of them) had moved to St. Louis. On his visits, Walter discussed a new airplane design. Ted Wells began to draw design sketches. The new airplane was to be a four-place, cabin biplane. Beech and Wells were *still* biplane men, still felt the monoplane was something of a hot rod. Perhaps that is another reason nothing was done toward developing the Model R into a commercial airplane.

In their spare time, Wells and other members of the St. Louis Travel Air design group worked on the new cabin biplane design. Such items as negative stagger wings were discussed, and finally decided on. They would use the reverse, or negative staggered wings for better pilot visibility. They would use one of the new Wright radials for good short-field takeoff performance, and a high cruising speed. At this point they didn't know if they were building a dream airplane on paper, or designing something that somebody would eventually build. They hoped to sell Curtiss-Wright on the design.

Their hopes were futile. Curtiss-Wright had no desire, in the middle of a depression, to attempt the design and development of a new airplane. Red Jackson had been killed in a Curtiss-Wright Teal amphibian, and about all that they wanted to do was continue production on the open cockpit series of Travel Air biplanes.

A pause here to note that, on February 24, 1930, Walter Beech was married to Olive Ann Mellor. They eventually had two daughters, Suzanne and Mary Lynn. Suzanne became Mrs. Thomas N. Warner; Mary Lynn grew up to marry John Edgar Hanson Pitt. Of course, this is getting 'way ahead of our story, but for the biographical buff who may obtain a copy of this volume, I thought it best to note these things in one spot rather than make him chase through all the pages trying to find it.

Walter Beech had an executive position with Curtiss-Wright. Why should he leave to return to the wind-swept Kansas plain to build his own airplanes in the middle of a great depression?

Curtiss-Wright had stopped Travel Air production entirely, the last model being the Travel Air 16. They made no attempt to develop the Model R "Mystery Ship" as a military machine, although it probably could have been successful as an Army or Navy fighter. Walter evidently also tried hard to get them to produce his new, four-place, cabin biplane. But, no soap from Curtiss-Wright. They just would not show interest in a cabin biplane design in the middle of a depression.

Beech must have been grossly frustrated with the situation. He had seen Travel Air grow from a group of three men to one of the major producers of general aviation airplanes in half a decade. It had been, to a large extent, his baby. Now it was just a toy in a giant corporation, and they didn't want it, evidently. They let it die. Later, of course, Curtiss-Wright did build airplanes, but never again under the Travel Air name.

Walter Beech made a decision—he would return to Kansas and build airplanes. How? He didn't know. With whose money? Some of his own from his sale of Travel Air to Curtiss-Wright, and some from men in Wichita who had the vision to back an airplane company in a depression. Where? He wasn't sure. Perhaps an old garage. Perhaps a cold, drafty hangar on an air field. The details he didn't care about—his *grand design* was to return to Wichita and build the four-place, cabin biplane that Ted Wells was so proud of on paper.

A ready source of experienced, trained people was the Travel Air factory in St. Louis. Luckily, they were all anxious for jobs. But, in the beginning, Beech couldn't take them all. Ted Wells, of course, was his chief designer. With the help of Cecil Barlow, Wayne Dalrymple, Harry Soderstrom, Willard Bashaw, and Jack Wassal, the cabin biplane was taking shape on paper.

Basically, it was a conventional biplane in every respect. It would have wings of equal span with a constant chord and elliptical tips. The spar would be a steel tube truss with fabric covering. The fuselage would be steel tubing with wood formers, and a fabric covering. The cabin would seat four people —a pilot and three passengers.

In bull sessions held in the engineering department at Travel Air in St. Louis the possibility of using something other than positive stagger for the wings had been discussed many times. Most biplanes of the period either had their two wings mounted directly above each other (neutral stagger), or the upper wing was forward of the lower wing (positive stagger). In neutral or positive stagger biplanes, the major problem was always pilot visibility upward. In many airplanes, he had none!

At least one person has claimed the biplane was merely a four-place, biplane version of the Travel Air Model R. Others violently disclaim this theory completely. I invite the reader to examine the side-view photographs of the Model R and the first Beechcraft Model 17, and note such items as the wheel pants, fuselage lines, wing planform (visible on other views), and empennage outline. To me there is a marked similarity between the two airplanes. It is possible that this would be so because the designers of the Model R, Walter Burnham and Herb Rawdon, daily rubbed elbows with the group of men working on the biplane. They would naturally be interested, and would make comments about the biplane. Just as naturally, Ted Wells and the others would be influenced by this contact with the Model R designers. So, in the final analysis, the similarity between the two airplanes may, indeed, be only a vague coincidence.

Travel Air Model R, the "Mystery Ship". This is the first one. A total of five were built.   (Beech Photo)

The dope and fabric shop at Travel Air. Airplane in the right, foreground is a Model 6000 with some model of an open cockpit variety in the background.   (Joe Christy)

Pretty (and newly married) Blanche Noyes receives congratulations from her husband and flight instructor, Dewey L. Noyes. This was in Cleveland, Ohio in December, 1928 in an OX-5 powered Waco 10. The couple had been married in July, 1928. He later flew the first Beechcraft; she participated in 1936 Bendix.   (Mrs. Blanche Noyes)

14

CHAPTER TWO
A NEW START

Clyde Cessna and Walter Beech had a falling-out over how many wings an airplane ought to have, but when Walter needed a place to start his own airplane company, Clyde was still his friend. He let the new Beech Aircraft Company set up shop in a corner of the Cessna factory. The depression had closed Cessna, but for only a few years. In the meantime, Walter Beech's determined group of himself, his wife, and eight other people gathered in a corner of the old Cessna factory to figure out how they could build Ted Wells' cabin biplane.

The Beech Aircraft Company was formally organized on April 1, 1932. During the next two years it would build only four airplanes. The road ahead would be rocky, and hard. To say that it started on a shoestring, ran on a shoestring, and made the grade on a shoestring would be something of an understatement.

Its first job, of course, was to build the airplane. The last model produced at Travel Air had been the Model 16, so Walter Beech continued the numbering system, and called his first airplane the Model 17.

During the summer of 1932 the tiny Beech crew welded tubing, cut plywood, and pounded aluminum. The biplane slowly took shape. A large chunk of their money went toward the purchase of the Wright engine for the ship, and the Smith controllable prop. The summer and early fall of 1932 was spent putting this new airplane together. All of Walter Beech's money was in it, and if it failed, he would fail too. He was gambling all he had on this new biplane.

As previously mentioned, it was a four-place, cabin biplane with negative stagger wings, and very conventional construction for the period—steel tubing with wood formers, pounded out metal fairings, and fabric covering.

The new biplane had many unique features. The wing spars were steel tubing in an era of wooden wing spars. The landing gear was heavily panted, and retracted into the pants leaving about six inches of the tire exposed in a day of fixed, strut braced landing gears. The empennage was attached to the fuselage in such a manner that the entire empennage moved up and down to provide pitch trim. An electric motor rotated a jackscrew to move the empennage.

Walter Beech wanted a fast airplane with a slow landing speed, and short landing roll. To obtain a fast cruise speed, Ted Wells used the thin Navy N-9 airfoil section, and careful streamlining on the entire airplane. Both he and Beech were biplane men —they regarded the monoplane as something of a "hot rod." To slow the biplane down on landing he used a split rudder. The rudder was split along its centerline, and the pilot could deflect it by pulling a lever in the cockpit. When split it still functioned as a rudder with left and right movement.

The engine would be a Wright radial of 420 horsepower, and to help the pilot with its torque, the tailwheel was rigidly mounted so that it would not steer left and right. With this tailwheel ground maneuvering was very difficult, and it was later changed on the number one airplane to a full swivelling tailwheel.

By late October, 1932, the new biplane was nearing completion. The specifications called for it to top 200 mph, land at 60 or less. In 1932 such performance was unheard of. If the airplane even came close to it, Beech would have set a remarkable record.

The man who started the real boom in aviation—Charles A. Lindbergh. On right is Walter Beech. Lindbergh flew this Travel Air 6000 to Mexico City to court Anne Morrow and later married her. *(Joe Christy)*

Famed motion picture actor Wallace Beery on left with director John Farrow. Beery owned a Travel Air 6000, probably the airplane in the background. *(Beech Photo)*

Typical Beech sales letter. Notice that Walter stressed the payload and landing speed rather than the cruising speed, and that the pilot's vision was a point to be emphasized. The Beechcraft offered better pilot visibility than contemporary airplanes of 1934, and Walter wanted to be sure the prospective customer noted this.

The Beech Aircraft Company
WICHITA, KANSAS
June 29, 1934

Mr. John H. Krueger
406 Elizabeth Road
San Antonio, Texas

Dear Mr. Krueger:

In answer to your letter of June 27 we are pleased to mail you under separate cover information on our new Beechcraft and would like to call your attention to the exceptionally high performance of this machine with a payload of 950 pounds and a landing speed of 45 miles per hour.

If you will compare this machine with competitive machines, we believe that you can easily see that it has superior performance, flying ease and also has the advantage of excellent vision and comfort.

The price of our 225 H. P. Jacobs powered Beechcraft is $8,000.00 with equipment that is shown in our catalogue.

If you desire any further information we will be pleased to hear from you.

Yours very truly

THE BEECH AIRCRAFT COMPANY

Walter H. Beech
President

WHB:gf

COMFORT-SPEED-VISION

View inside the Travel Air factory at Wichita with Model 6000's under construction. Notice the Model 4's in the left, background.   (Beech Photo)

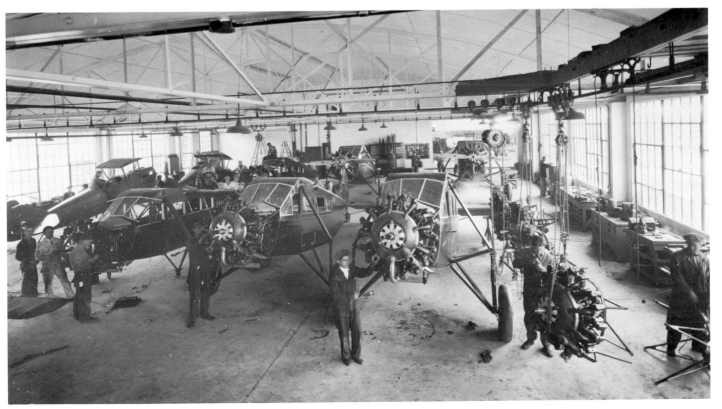

If the new Beechcraft biplane would do what Walter wanted it to, it would leave the competition behind. Its closet rival was the Waco cabin plane, and the Waco could turn in little more than 130 mph at cruise. In fact, 130 mph for the Waco was giving it the benefit of the doubt. But, the Waco did have a slow landing speed, and in those days, the landing speed was as important as the cruise speed of a ship.

Pete Hill claims he test flew the first Beechcraft. He probably did; no one else makes the claim. On the fourth of November, 1932, the new Beechcraft biplane made its first flight. A few days later it was clocked at 201.2 mph. It had made the top speed Walter Beech wanted. Tests showed it would cruise at about 170 mph which was easily 40 to 50 mph ahead of anything the competition had.

One thing bugged the new Beechcraft. With its narrow landing gear, and landing speed around 60 mph, the pilot had to be experienced, and capable, or he couldn't handle it. It was certainly not an airplane for old ladies. It could get up and go in the air, but on the ground, it was a tiger.

And, in the new Beechcraft, Walter had a tiger by the tail. He had all his money, plus other people's money, invested in the new Beechcraft, and it was a pretty hot machine. It wasn't something he could rush out and sell to *anybody*. In fact, he found that *nobody* wanted it.

Walter sent the airplane to Miami in January of 1933 to be seen at the All American Air Maneuvers, and pilot E. H. Wood reportedly flew it to first place in the Texaco Trophy event. Karl E. Voelter flew the airplane several times, and it may have been during one of his speed dashes past the stands that the announcer said, "Look at that negative stagger-wing Beechcraft go!".

Two things are important here. The name, and the event. First, the event. It brought the Beech-craft to the attention of a lot of people, probably led to its eventual sale. It *did*, without a doubt, establish the Beechcraft as a fast airplane. Second, the name. The announcer's use of the words "negative staggerwing Beechcraft" are credited with being the first time the airplane was referred to as other than a Beechcraft, and the first time it was referred to with respect to its wing arrangement. The name hung on. For some thirty-four years! So much so that few people today know the "Stagger-wing" is really a Beechcraft Model 17.

The new biplane came home from Miami with honors, but no sales! Beech Aircraft Company was now ten months old, had built one airplane and sold none!

One of the potential customers the airplane had been demonstrated to was Tom Loffland of Loffland Brothers Company in Tulsa, Oklahoma, an oil drilling outfit. Loffland had used Travel Airs, and was a close personal friend of Walter Beech.

Edwin F. Ross is a small man, he surely isn't over five feet seven inches tall. He smiles quickly, and you get the impression that, if it has wings, he can fly it, but he'll be the last one to say so. In the Fall of 1928 he was hired to take a Velie Monocoupe to Lovell, Oklahoma and teach Dude Camden to fly. At that time Camden was a tool pusher for Loffland Brothers Company.

While Eddie, as Mr. Ross is known, was teaching Dude to fly (using a pasture near the Camden farm house), Tom Loffland made several visits to the Camden farm. He and Grover Simpson, and the pilot of their 4000 Travel Air, stayed overnight several times while Eddie was teaching Dude to fly. Eddie recalls Loffland as a " . . . fairly big man . . . very rugged individual with a very direct speech, and you knew when you met him that he meant every word. . . ."

From that contact Eddie went to work flying for Loffland Brothers Company. Tom Loffland was the main ramrod of the company—his brother Jack lived in Fort Worth, left the company pretty much in Tom's hands.

During construction of the first Beechcraft, Tom Loffland made several trips to Wichita to see the new biplane, and watch its construction. He was very interested in it, and received one of the first demonstration flights. He was impressed—it was considerably faster than the old Travel Airs he was then using.

Now comes a controversial point. Remember, the company had been in business ten months, and no sales. Tom Loffland wanted one of the new Beech-crafts, and Beech was hurting financially. The easiest thing would have been for Loffland to have bought the first one, NC499N. But, that would have left Beech without a demonstrator.

So, a deal was made. One source says Loffland agreed to meet the Beech payrolls while the airplane was being built, but Mrs. Beech denies this. She does not admit that the company, at this point—January of 1933—was anything but entirely solvent, and financially flush.

She may be right, but several people who were there at the time agreed that Loffland probably was asked to put a substantial down payment on his airplane, and that he allowed Walter to build him an airplane rather than buying the demonstrator. In any case, it should be recorded that Tom Loffland ordered an airplane at the crucial moment in Beech history, and in so doing, probably saved the company.

The Beechcraft. Walter Beech and canine friend pose in front of the first Beechcraft.   (Peter M. Bowers)

Some enterprising individual posed the Beechcraft in level flight by elevating the tail. Compare this view to the side view of the Mystery Ship, the Travel Air Model R. In this view the rigid tailwheel is very evident.   (Joe Juptner)

Front view of the first Beechcraft Model 17. Note the cowling—this photograph was taken after the cowling with the individual cylinder openings had been installed. Also, this photo was taken after the landing gear had been widened, and the airplane repainted for Ethyl Corporation.   (Beech Photo)

Work was commenced on the second airplane early in 1933. Tom Loffland hoped to have it in time for Dude Camden's wedding down near Corpus Christi, Texas, but it wasn't ready, so he borrowed NC499N, and used it. That was near the end of June, 1933.

Ship number two was finished on June 19, 1933, but was not ready for delivery until July. Registered NC58Y it had the narrow landing gear, rigid tailwheel, and engine cowling with individual cylinder openings. George Hart checked Eddie Ross out in the new ship, and Eddie flew it to Tulsa.

It was a handful. With its narrow gear, rigid tailwheel, and torque from a 420 horsepower Wright engine, NC58Y was anything but a docile kitten on landings and takeoffs. Eddie freely admits he had one hundred hours in the airplane before he knew for sure where it was going on a landing.

On one of his first takeoffs he did a beautiful groundloop. Later he learned to hold the wheel back to keep the tailwheel on the ground until he had plenty of speed. Then, he would raise the tail slightly and allow the airplane to fly off.

The sale of NC58Y to Loffland Brothers Company was the first sale of a new Beechcraft airplane, and the only sale the company made during its first two years of existence.

It was during one of his many visits to the factory (which was now in the old Travel Air buildings) that Eddie Ross met what he calls a real artist in metal working, Jesse Chacón. Born in Durango, Mexico, Jesse Chacón went to work at the old Swallow company, and came to work for Beech in August of 1932. The beautiful wing root fairings on the Beechcraft 17's lower wing can be attributed to the skill of Jesse Chacón. He worked for the company continuously until his retirement in 1960. Jesse was the kind of man who made the Beechcraft biplane the great airplane it was and is.

Although he had made only one sale in two years, Walter Beech knew he had a good thing going—he just had to find a way to sell it. Except for its poor landing characteristics, every pilot who flew the airplane liked it. Ray C. "Skeets" Barker, George Hart, Eddie Ross, Bob Fogg, Sr. all had praises for the new Beechcraft—it could outperform all of its competition with ease. It was a pilots airplane, and those who had the good fortune to fly it, liked it.

During 1933 the Beech design staff headed by Ted Wells set about reworking the Model 17R design. The two most important changes were the engine and landing gear. The big Wright was replaced with a 225 horsepower Jacobs L-4, and the heavily panted landing gear disappeared—literally! Ted Wells worked out a method to fully retract the landing

gear, including the tailwheel. Luckily, the lower wing was in position to take the retractable gear— it wouldn't have been on an airplane with positive stagger wings.

Many small improvements were made in the design, but the basic outline, and beautiful streamlined shape was retained. The wing was changed to the Clark CYH airfoil, and standard wood spars and ribs. All of the changes made were to make the airplane lighter in weight, and less expensive to build and maintain. In other words, the redesigned airplane would be in direct dollar and cents competition with the Waco.

The letter L was assigned to the 225 hp Jacobs engine, and the new airplane was called the Model B17L. The first one was serial number three, and it was finished early in the Spring of 1934, in May.

In the meantime, something else was in the wind. Sales literature for the Model 17R had carried a note that the airplane was available with the Wright "Cyclone" engine. No such airplane had been built, and I suppose Walter just put that in to see what would happen. The 90 hp OX-5 engines had just barely been replaced with such engines as the 225 hp Wright and Jacobs radials, and these engines were very expensive. The price of a Wright Cyclone was literally astronomical for 1933. Surely no one would want an airplane powered with that engine. People could just barely afford the 225 hp engines, and the Model 17R with the 420 hp was not selling.

Despite all this, the Goodall Worsted Company of Sanford, Maine ordered a Cyclone powered Beechcraft. I can imagine the excitement this order must have created at the Beech factory.

The Cyclone model was assigned serial number 5, and work was begun on it right alongside the new B17L's being built. Starting with the basic 17R design, the Cyclone model featured a wider landing gear, and a full swivelling tailwheel. It used the same Navy N-9 airfoil, but did not have the 17R's split rudder.

The engine installed on s/n 5 was the Wright R-1820-F11 developing 690 horsepower and swinging a giant Hamilton Standard propeller. Warming up in the chocks the Cyclone vibrated and shook the Staggerwing so badly that frequent repairs were necessary to patch broken weld joints. But, once in the air she smoothed out, and roared along at an impressive 250 mph top speed—faster than any military fighter of 1934. The Goodall Worsted Company had themselves a *real* airplane.

Veteran barnstormer, Travel Air dealer, Edo float dealer, and now Beechcraft dealer Robert S. Fogg Sr. was selected, by Sanford Mills, as the pilot they wanted for the new Cyclone powered Beechcraft.

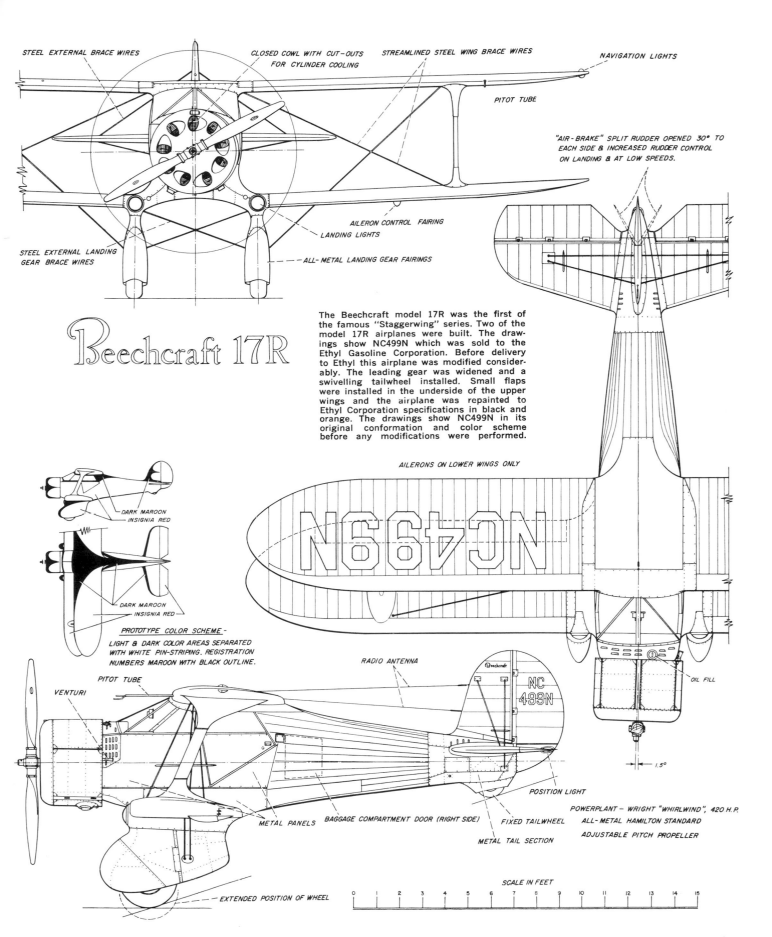

STEEL EXTERNAL BRACE WIRES

CLOSED COWL WITH CUT-OUTS FOR CYLINDER COOLING

STREAMLINED STEEL WING BRACE WIRES

NAVIGATION LIGHTS

PITOT TUBE

"AIR-BRAKE" SPLIT RUDDER OPENED 30° TO EACH SIDE & INCREASED RUDDER CONTROL ON LANDING & AT LOW SPEEDS.

AILERON CONTROL FAIRING

LANDING LIGHTS

STEEL EXTERNAL LANDING GEAR BRACE WIRES

ALL-METAL LANDING GEAR FAIRINGS

Beechcraft 17R

The Beechcraft model 17R was the first of the famous "Staggerwing" series. Two of the model 17R airplanes were built. The drawings show NC499N which was sold to the Ethyl Gasoline Corporation. Before delivery to Ethyl this airplane was modified considerably. The leading gear was widened and a swivelling tailwheel installed. Small flaps were installed in the underside of the upper wings and the airplane was repainted to Ethyl Corporation specifications in black and orange. The drawings show NC499N in its original conformation and color scheme before any modifications were performed.

AILERONS ON LOWER WINGS ONLY

DARK MAROON
INSIGNIA RED

DARK MAROON
INSIGNIA RED

PROTOTYPE COLOR SCHEME -
LIGHT & DARK COLOR AREAS SEPARATED WITH WHITE PIN-STRIPING. REGISTRATION NUMBERS MAROON WITH BLACK OUTLINE.

RADIO ANTENNA

OIL FILL

NC 499N

PITOT TUBE

VENTURI

NC 499N

1.5°

POSITION LIGHT

METAL PANELS

BAGGAGE COMPARTMENT DOOR (RIGHT SIDE)

FIXED TAILWHEEL

METAL TAIL SECTION

POWERPLANT - WRIGHT "WHIRLWIND", 420 H.P. ALL-METAL HAMILTON STANDARD ADJUSTABLE PITCH PROPELLER

EXTENDED POSITION OF WHEEL

SCALE IN FEET

0 1 2 3 4 5 6 7 8 9 10 11 12 13 14 15

21

Eddie Ross with NC58Y, the second 17R, at Rita Santa, Texas. You can clearly see the scoops added to the individual cylinder opening on the engine cowling. Notice the shiny, handrubbed finish on the wings. This, and all the photographs of NC58Y, were taken by Malcolm Hart. No other photographs of the airplane are known to exist. *(E. F. Ross)*

Front view of NC58Y. I think everyone will agree that the landing gear tread was narrow! *(E. F. Ross)*

Side view of NC58Y. Because of the film used, and the color of the numbers, they don't show on this black and white print. Expert William N. Fleming blew up this shot and found the numbers! *(E. F. Ross)*

Bob was a well known pilot in the New England area, and in the Spring of 1934 he went to Wichita to take delivery on the Sanford Mills airplane, and get checked out in it.

Only a few pilots ever flew the A17F, as the new Cyclone model was called. Most thought it had much too much horsepower, gave Bob Fogg one hundred days to live if he continued to fly it. He flew it for several months with no ill effects, said it was a pilots airplane and "very fast."

At about the time of the Cyclone sale to Sanford Mills, the first 17R, NC499N was modified to a wide tread landing gear, full swivelling tailwheel, repainted, and sold to Ethyl Corporation of New York. Dewey Noyes was their pilot. He flew the airplane (NC499N) for them until his death late in 1935. Dewey was killed in NC499N near Nunda, New York on December 10, 1935. NC499N, the first Staggerwing, was destroyed.

I don't know exactly how the second Cyclone model was started, but soon after the first one was built, construction started on a second one, to be flown by Bob Fogg and Louise Thaden in the 1934 MacRobertson race from London, England to Melbourne, Australia.

Competition was in Walter Beech's blood, and he dearly wanted the second A17F to fly the MacRobertson. He felt it could win, and it probably could have.

The airplane was finished in November 1934, and Bob Fogg came back to Wichita to fly the test flights on it. Unfortunately, not enough financial backers could be found, and the airplane was withdrawn from the race.

The airplane, s/n 11, was sold to the Bureau of Air Commerce. Beech had registered it briefly as NC12569, but the Bureau of Air Commerce changed it to NS68 and flew it until 1937. They reportedly dismantled it. Why such an historic airplane would be dismantled is beyond my comprehension.

Shortly after Bob Fogg left Sanford Mills, they sold their A17F to Howard Hughes. It was moved to the west coast, and later entered in several air races. We will hear more of it later on.

Now, a moment of review. The Beech company was founded in April, 1932. In November of 1932 they finished one airplane which they didn't sell until 1934. In 1933 they sold one airplane, the second 17R, NC58Y. Also, in 1933, they did design work on the B17L which did not go into production until 1934. The first B17L was sold in the spring of that year. So, 1934 was the first year of quantity production at Beech. Including the two A17 airplanes, a total of 19 airplanes were built in 1934, most of them the B17L.

The B17L and B17B models were identical and almost interchangeable. The B17L had the 225 hp Jacobs, and the B17B used the 285 hp Jacobs. Both engines had the same engine mount ring diameter, and it was possible to make a B17L into a B17B by removing the 225 hp Jacobs and installing a 285 hp Jacobs. Of course, the reverse was also true if one wanted to make a B17B into a B17L.

As 1934 opened, the only Beechcraft airplane in regular service was serial number two, the Loffland Brothers' 17R, NC58Y. To Tom Loffland an airplane was an oil drilling tool. And, the faster it could get from point A to point B, the better tool it was. Pilot Eddie Ross was kept busy logging time in NC58Y carrying Mr. Loffland, Grover Simpson, and other officials of the company around the country. From their Tulsa, Oklahoma office, the company flew regularly to almost every state west of the Mississippi and south of Oklahoma.

Many trips were directly into the oil fields where Eddie would put the 17R down on a dirt road, or a field especially cleared for use by the airplane. He found it tricky at first—the 17R required a special technique on takeoff, which Eddie discovered after he groundlooped on one of his first takeoffs. He learned to hold the tail on the ground until he had plenty of speed, then ease the tail up. Even so, the torque required full right rudder to hold the airplane straight, and on the narrow oil field strips holding a straight course on takeoff wasn't just nice piloting, it was a necessity to avoid hitting something.

A pilot's job in flying an airplane for a company isn't just to fly the airplane—he must "utilize" the airplane—he must use it as a tool to do a job. Sometimes that means doing things with an airplane the designer never thought would, or could, be done with it. And, in 1934 pilots like Eddie Ross were very anxious to prove the airplane could do the job—especially a nice-flying piece of machinery like the Beechcraft.

The measure of a man is never the number of feet and inches from the soles of his feet to the top of his head. It's what's inside that counts. Likewise, an airplane. It may be sleek and trim of line, but if it's not solidly built on the inside, it's not much of an airplane. Both a man and an airplane were proved of great value one day in the Oklahoma oil fields.

It was a hot day, and the strip was short, surrounded by oil pumps. The Wright engine roared, throwing up a cloud of dust, and the stubby red biplane began to crawl along the narrow, rut lined strip. Eddie's hands were wet with sweat as he gingerly held onto the wheel, nursing the Beechcraft

The only known existing photograph of a Beechcraft Model 17R in flight. This was at Rita Santa, Texas at the time the other photos of NC58Y were taken. In this photo, Eddie Ross hat not yet retracted the wheels up into the pants. On very close examination you can see Tom Loffland sitting in the back seat. *(E. F. Ross)*

NC499N, the first 17R, after its landing gear tread was widened, and it was repainted for Ethyl Corporation.
(Peter M. Bowers)

Rear view of NC58Y. Notice the trim tab installed on the left elevator. Eddie Ross didn't trust the electric trim, and had this manually operated trim installed. He never had to use it, the electric trim worked perfectly! *(E. F. Ross)*

24

The Ethyl Corporation Beechcraft. Both of the 17R's had wire braced empennage sections, but the wires had a tendency to break. Later, steel tubing was used.   *(Beech Photo)*

The big one! This is the first A17F, NC12583, before delivery. For 1934, this was an advanced piece of machinery.   *(Beech Photo)*

like a man caresses the face of the woman he loves. Like sentinels around a medieval fortress, oil pumps lined the end of the small strip. As the thundering Wright pulled the ship down the strip Eddie realized the folly of landing on short strips, then trying to get out in the middle of the day.

He wanted desperately for the Beech to make it— he hated the thought of this beautiful airplane mangled in a crash.

Slowly the wings began to take hold, to develop lift; the Beechcraft became light on its spinning wheels. The time is now, he thought, the oil polish rods are too close for comfort. He eased the wheel back, full right rudder—that torque was still there! Slowly NC58Y eased into the air, leaving a swirl of dust on the ground beneath her.

He was upon the polish rods now—they were going beneath the wings.

There was a loud Whump! A careening motion, something snapped. The Wright was still thundering, but motion seemed to be lost, the Beechcraft had hit something. There was no time for conscious thought. A tiny open field lay in front of him, then trees. The field was not really suitable for landing, but there was no choice. Out of the corner of his eye, he had seen the right wing bend backwards, the Beechcraft was no longer safe for flight.

He seemed suspended in space, his hands moved as if they were in slow motion. In a way he was relieved, the ordeal of the polish rods at least was behind him. All that remained was to make a forced landing in that grubby field directly ahead. He closed the throttle, cut the switch. His mind called upon all his training, all his years of flying Travel Airs and Wacos to move his hands and feet to bring the beautiful Beechcraft down softly, then hard braking with the hand brake lever, and boy, how those trees are coming up!

She stopped. Somehow, she stopped. Just short of the trees. His shirt was drenched with sweat, the Wright was stopped, the propeller immobile. He thought, it's over with, and we're not hurt.

The lower right wing had hit a polish rod about even with the I strut. The strong, steel spar had buckled, but had not given 'way. The I strut held the wings together, and the spar kept the tip from bending backwards. The Staggerwing was not only a lovely ship, she was strong—when the chips were down she could take it, and keep going.

A new lower right wing was built for the airplane, and within a short time NC58Y was back in the air. And, Eddie Ross was convinced that, if a better airplane were built, Beech would likely build it!

NC499N had originally been built with an NACA cowling. This was later changed to the closed cowl with the individual cylinder openings, and NC58Y was delivered with this type cowl. After a few flights Eddie noticed oil streaks on the outside of the cylinder opening for the number one cylinder. The cylinder head temperature also appeared too hot. On one of his trips to the factory at Wichita, Eddie mentioned this to Ted Wells, and Ted suggested putting the scoops on each cylinder opening.

But, the scoops didn't help. The engine continued to run hot. When NC58Y had about 100 hours on her, the reliable Wright blew the number one cylinder head. The engine was repaired, an NACA cowling installed to replace the closed one with the individual cylinder openings, and on the next flight, the head temperature ran 100 degrees cooler than before! There was no more trouble after that.

You will remember the 17R's had a moveable empennage operated by an electric motor and jackscrew for pitch trim. In a day of bailing wire and glue, Eddie Ross didn't trust the sophisticated electric trim. He asked that a manual trim tab be installed, and it was done. Naturally, the electric trim never had the first minute's trouble!

Most flying in airplanes is done straight and level going some place, especially business flying. While serenely engaged in going some place, Eddie was hit in the foot by a slap from the rudder pedal—one of those moments of stark terror pilots like to talk about. It was all over in a split second, and NC58Y kept droning right along. After the original fright was over, and Eddie realized he was still in one piece, he started figuring out where the nearest airport was. He wanted to get down, and take a look. *Something* had happened. It undoubtedly would make good conversation in the bar later on, but right now Eddie had to find out what was ailing the lady.

She had hit him in the foot with her rudder pedal, and something was amiss. Pilots in that situation normally close the throttle, hold her nose up until airspeed dissipates, then let her lose altitude slowly, keeping the speed down. They know that, if something is wrong, high speed generally makes it worse. Eddie eased NC58Y into a nearby flying field.

The "moment of start terror" proved to be nothing worse than a broken flying wire on the empennage. On later flights two more wires broke in a similar fashion.

Eddie asked Ted Wells if it wouldn't be possible to remove the wires and replace them with steel tubes. Ted said he thought it would do just as well, and the change was made. The steel tubes proved to be entirely satisfactory, and the extra drag of the streamlined tubing over the thin wires wasn't enough to notice on the airspeed indicator, so Ted Wells designed steel tubes for the empennage on all

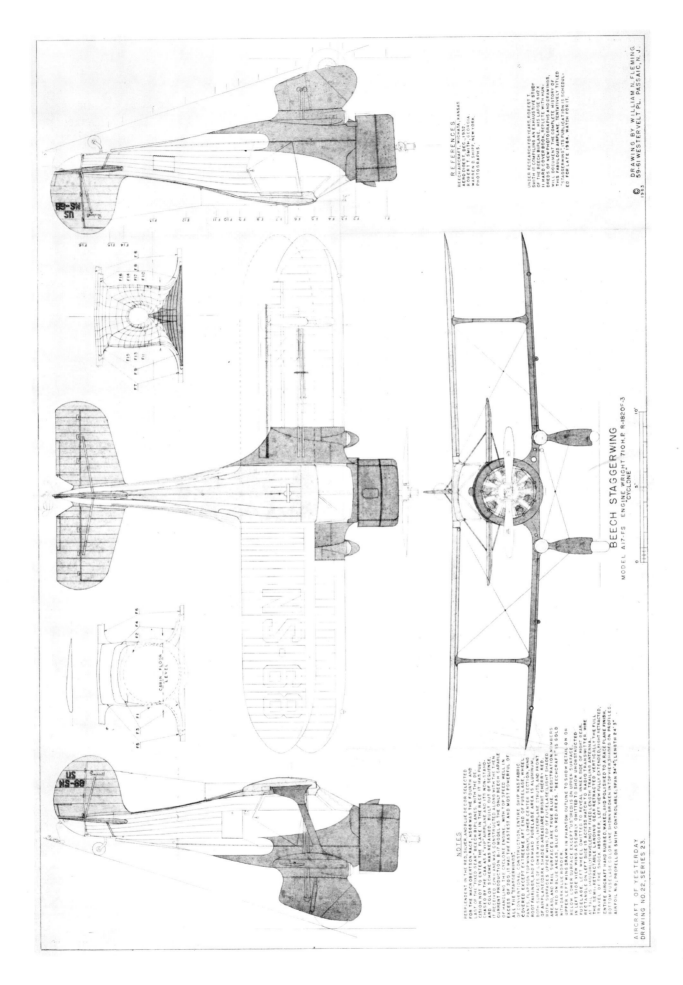

BEECH STAGGERWING
MODEL A17-FS ENGINE WRIGHT 710 H.P. R-1820F-3
"CYCLONE"

REFERENCES:
BEECH AIRCRAFT, WICHITA, KANSAS
AERO DIGEST, DEC. 1932
ROBERT T. SMITH, GA.
WARREN D. SHIPP, NEW YORK
PHOTOGRAPHS.

DRAWING BY WILLIAM N. FLEMING.
59-61 WESTERVELT PL. PASSAIC, N.J.
1963

AIRCRAFT OF YESTERDAY
DRAWING NO 22, SERIES 23.

27

Three views of A17F, N12583, the Goodall Worsted airplane. Critics gave Bob Fogg "One hundred days to live" if he flew this airplane regularly. He managed to survive considerably more than that—no doubt the airplane was tricky, but in the hands of a competent pilot it was safe enough. Isn't it a massive looking thing? Kind of like a graceful bulldog. Eddie Ross called it the closest thing to a pursuit ship he was in up to that time. Wouldn't it look impressive on an airport today?

(Top, Beech Photo; Lower Left, Warren D. Shipp; Lower Right, Robert Esposito)

Three rare views of A17FS, NS68, from Warren D. Shipp, printed by expert William N. Fleming. Notice in these photographs, and in those of NC12583 the short, stubby fuselage. Bumps on the bottom surface of the lower wing just inboard of the I struts are the aileron hinge fairings. These were found on all of the fixed gear models on account of the thin Navy N-9 airfoil used.　　　　　　　　　　　　　　　　　(All Three, Warren D. Shipp)

subsequent Model 17's that used a braced empennage.

One quick word about the split rudder on the 17R. Eddie says it didn't slow you down much on landing, but splitting it did improve rudder control, so he normally used it. Only the two 17R's had the split rudder, the A17 and subsequent models didn't use it.

Since the day that Wilbur and Orville Wright got an airplane around the pea patch, weather has been the pilot's chief bugaboo. To a pilot, when the weather is good, there *is* no weather. To him, "weather" means *bad* weather. So, when a pilot says he has weather, he means bad weather, not clear weather.

Flying Travel Airs for Loffland Brothers, Eddie Ross found weather held him up as much as anything. He decided to find a solution to that problem by learning to fly instruments. He made up a cloth "hood" for the Model 6000 Travel Air, and with Grover Simpson as safety observer (on trips when he carried Mr. Simpson), Eddie started learning how to control an airplane with reference to instruments.

There was very little written about instrument flying in those days, and even less *said* about it. The few pioneering pilots who tried it seriously were pretty much on their own. Eddie had a devil of a time with it, especially when he got vertigo. But, he managed to figure out what was going on, and after a while he considered himself a pretty good instrument pilot.

Until one day in the 17R. One of the marks of a real professional pilot is that he doesn't try to cover something up when he goofs. Eddie freely admits his overconfidence on instrument flying, and gave me permission to reprint, verbatim, his own account of his first experience flying instruments in NC58Y.

"My first actual experience of instrument flying happened in Louisiana," he told me. "Simpson (Grover Simpson . . Author) and I departed LaFayette for Houston on a drizzly, rainy, low overcast day. I was flying the highway in to Lake Charles—in fact, we were only about ten miles east of Lake Charles."

"It was raining fairly heavy, and I was looking out the side window watching the highway on my side when Simpson asked, 'Did you see that oil derrick that just went by on the right?'. I said, 'No, I didn't see it.' Grover said, 'Well, one just went by, and it's higher than we were! So, immediately I made a left hand turn around the highway and started back out."

"Simpson said, 'Well, if we can't go to Houston, how about going to Tulsa?' This airplane had a receiver, but no transmitter, and I'd just listened to a

weather broadcast."

"Shreveport was in good shape, so I told him we'd try to go back by Shreveport, and on to Tulsa. I picked up the highway that led to Alexandria, planning on going towards Alexandria and then maybe up the river to Shreveport. Approximately 35 to 40 miles out of Lake Charles on the way to Alexandria, the road made a fairly sharp turn."

"At that time I was probably flying about 50 feet above the treetops in fog that was dipping down into the trees, and visibility wasn't over a quarter of a mile. Not being able to make the turn in the highway we skidded out through the treetops, and when I got turned around, no highway anymore! Only one thing to do, and that was go on instruments and climb."

"We topped the clouds at 3500 to 4000 feet. I took up a compass heading for Shreveport, and after about thirty minutes flying, a top layer and a bottom layer came together. My bravery quit me, and I decided I'd rather not fly any more instruments. I was just a little on the touchy side then, so we decided to turn around and head back towards LaFayette."

"Simpson asked me where I was going. I told him if we couldn't find a hole to get down, I was going to New Orleans and make a range approach because they should have around a thousand foot ceiling, and try to get on the ground there."

"About 35 to 40 minutes later a hole broke through with a town underneath it, so I pulled the throttle back, spiraled down, broke out, circled the town, and it was Opelousas. So, I followed the highway from Opelousas on back to LaFayette, and landed about two hours and forty minutes after takeoff at the point of departure!"

"This experience made a Christian out of me, and I took up instrument flying then with a vengeance, practicing every minute I could. After about 25 or 30 hours under the hood with Simpson watching me, I became expert enough that I could make a range approach, and stay in there and fly."

"We started flying instruments then, whenever we needed to. Of course, at this time of the game, we had no clearance—we had no transmitter to tell anybody where we were. The only thing I had was a receiver. I always hoped that nobody was working an approach or flying the same airways we were. I guess they didn't—we never hit anyone."

Later, Eddie had a transmitter installed, and talked to the airliners to coordinate altitudes. There was no Air Traffic Control at the time, and the only "control" was between the airlines and the few executive pilots flying instruments who had sort of a gentlemen's agreement about who did what.

Eddie said the worse trouble he ever encountered

One of the A17F's under construction. I believe it is serial number 5, NC 12583.

(Beech Photo)

on instruments was when the flying wires iced up once, and nearly shook the airplane apart. After that, he avoided flying in forecast icing conditions.

Of such stuff were the pioneers made. Like the forty-dollar-a-month cowboy, they thought it was all in a day's work. They didn't complain, and they didn't say anybody owed them anything. They just went out day after day and did their job, and thankfully, men like Eddie Ross had ships like the Beechcraft to fly— airplanes of integrity and honesty capable of sticking with the gutty men who flew them.

During our many frequent contacts over the past few years, Eddie emphasized one thing again and again. When a customer visited the factory, he was given the "royalty" treatment. NC58Y made many trips to the factory for maintenance, and Eddie remembers that, on a Saturday morning when he arrived, a crew would be there to meet him, headed by Walter Beech. He remembers that Walter would stay there with the men until the ship was ready to go.

Eddie Ross Flew NC58Y for Loffland Brothers until the Spring of 1935—around March—when it was traded in on a newer model. Walter Beech offered to give NC58Y to Eddie, less engine and instruments, if he would keep it, and never let anyone else fly it. Being a young man with his eyes on the far horizon Eddie declined, and NC58Y passed into oblivion. I personally consider it unlikely that the airplane was broken up for spares, or even that it became part of a later machine, but history does not record what its eventual fate was, and the present factory disclaims any knowledge of it.

Beech's first real production year was 1934. In the spring of that year the first B17L was completed and sold, the two A17's were built, and the original 17R was sold. Things were looking up! Beech was at last in the business of building airplanes, and the future looked good. But, the B17L's had a couple of minor problems.

A peculiar feature of the 225 hp Jacobs engine in the B17L was a magneto for one set of spark plugs and a battery distributor for the other set. The ship's electrical system was 12 volts, but the battery distributor ignition was only 6 volts, so a resistor had to be used to drop the voltage from 12 to 6 volts. If the resistor burned out (which sometimes happened), the distributor ignition went out leaving only the magneto operating. Eventually Jacobs designed a 12 volt distributor which cured the problem.

The first B17L's used an air starter, and on these airplanes, the gear was retracted with air. It operated very rapidly, and in some cases so fast that it damaged the gear mechanism. Probably about the

first 20 airplanes used the air system. Later models had electric starters and electric landing gear, and the older air operated models were changed over to electric operation.

With the small 225 hp Jacobs engine, designer Ted Wells didn't expect much performance, especially not anything to compare with the 200 mph top speed of the 17R. He figured 170 mph top speed would be doing real well for the B17L. Initial flight tests turned in a top speed of 175 mph with a cruise of around 150 mph. Quite respectable for 1934!

Try to visualize yourself moved back in time to 1934. You visit the local air field, and you find mostly old, OX-5 powered, open cockpit Travel Airs, Eaglerocks, American Eagles, Wacos, and other assorted types, a very few of which have later model engines like the 225 hp Jacobs or Wrights. A friend tells you that, out in Wichita, Kansas Walter Beech has built a new, retractable geared cabin biplane with reverse stagger wings.

It will do, he says, "nearly 200 mph". (Of course, it will only top 175, but a few hangar flying sessions can easily push 175 to "nearly 200 mph").

You're impressed—the hottest thing you've been in was a 90 mph OX-5 job, and the fastest thing you've ever *seen* was a 300 Wright powered Travel Air that stopped by for gas one afternoon when you were at the airport.

The new Beechcraft's negative stagger wings don't bother you much, but you've always favored an open cockpit with the wind roaring by—that open cockpit gives you the "feel" of flying. You aren't sure about the closed cabin of the Beechcraft. But, maybe that's okay. The new Wacos are closed cabin ships, and you know of several others.

But, retractable landing gear? On commercial airliners it may be okay—those guys are paid to remember to put it down before they land. But, you aren't sure about a private airplane—will the owner remember to put it down?

Even some of the military jobs have fixed gear, and maybe Walter Beech is a little crazy putting retractable wheels on his new biplane. The negative stagger wings are okay, and the closed cabin isn't too bad, but wheels that fold up into the ship's belly may be carrying things a little too far.

Does this kind of thinking sound strange to you today? Well, it was normal for 1934. The Beechcraft, as an airplane, was okay, but those folding wheels were a drawback to some buyers. So much so that Beech designed a skid that could be mounted under each lower wing to protect the airplane's belly and lower wings if the owner forgot the landing gear. And, later on, Beech was to demonstrate gear-up landings at the National Air Races.

George J. Pearson of Ward-Pearson, Inc. at Roosevelt Field, Long Island, New York took delivery of B17L s/n (serial number) 8, NC12590. He used it as a demonstrator. George was an aggressive salesman. Once, flying in a prospective buyer's new Waco (the fact that the man had just bought a Waco didn't deter George from trying to sell him a Beechcraft), the prospect landed his Waco short of the runway—in a lake! The occupants (George among them) climbed out onto the top wing of the sinking Waco as a nearby boat paddled over to rescue them. After thinking about the situation for a moment, George pulled off his shoes and dived back into the water. In a few seconds he emerged with some wet papers in his hands—his Beechcraft sales literature!

"Customers loved the performance of the plane," George told me, "But were dubious of such a new-fangled idea as a retractable gear on a private plane. Also, the inability to get the tail down on landing with a light load was a deterrent. I found that with plenty of practice this was not too difficult, but the potential buyer, of course, didn't have the time. Selling had to be based entirely on efficiency of operation, speed, and cruise-landing speed ratio."

Bill Lear of radio and LearJet fame was one of George's early Beechcraft customers. George said he traded in a beaten up Waco. Lear was working on perfecting the ADF set and had designed the Lear-O-Scope, an early version of the ADF (Automatic Direction Finding) radio.

George left Beechcraft sales in 1936, barnstormed a Waco Straightwing on floats in Maine that summer, then headed west for Corpus Christi, Texas where he ran an air charter service with a Waco YKC until mid-1937. In 1938 he married and moved to San Francisco to do charter work for Mouton and Clyde, Inc. in their Beechcraft E17L. Later he went with Eastern Air Lines, and is now retired.

Late in 1934 Beech started working on a modified B17 model. The tall landing gear on the B17L and B17B made the aircraft difficult to land, and on this modified B17 model, the main landing gear would be shortened, and a 285 hp Wright engine installed. Known as the B17E, Loffland Brothers Company ordered one. While waiting for it to be delivered they borrowed B17L number 7, NC12589, from the factory. They later purchased it.

Eddie Ross, who was still flying NC58Y, the 17R, also flew the B17L. He liked it, but came near to disaster with it. Being a young man, and full of vim and vigor, he liked to take off, and immediately retract the gear. With the air retraction, the wheels snapped up rapidly giving the appearance of jerking it out from under the ship while it was still on the

ground. When he did this one time in Tyler, Texas, the gear came up okay, but he found the ailerons jammed tight!

Using rudder to control the bank, Eddie climbed to a safe altitude and returned for a landing. After he put the wheels down, he checked them down with the hand crank. They felt as if they were down.

In those days paved runways almost didn't exist. The field at Tyler was mostly sand. With little difficulty, Eddie lined up and started his approach, ailerons locked, and using the rudders to keep the ship level. Easing the Beechcraft onto the sandy field, Eddie thought his problems were over.

Then, after rolling about 500 feet, he thought he was going into a hole in the sand. The ship dropped gently down, the prop started hitting the ground, then Eddie realized something was wrong and cut the switches. The gear had collapsed!

The airplane was hoisted, and the landing gear inspected. They found that the cable going back to retract the tailwheel had a split pulley which caused its cable to jam the aileron cable. When Eddie put the gear down, the tailwheel cable jammed between the split pulley and the guide, making him think the gear was fully down when he checked it with the hand crank. But, it wasn't all the way down—the only thing holding it was the small tailwheel cable. When enough weight was on the gear, the tailwheel cable broke allowing the main gear to retract. The gear was wired in the down position for a ferry flight to the factory.

Eddie borrowed a Hisso powered Eaglerock and flew to Dallas to buy a new prop for the Beechcraft. Upon his return, the new prop was installed and he flew the Beechcraft to Wichita where repairs were made.

The Loffland Brothers B17E was delivered early in 1935, and might have been the airplane NC58Y was traded in on. The most important change in the B17E was the shorter main landing gear—landing characteristics were greatly improved. Speed of the B17E was about the same as that of the 285 hp Jacobs powered B17B, about 160 mph cruising.

As 1935 opened Beech was in production on three airplanes, the B17L, B17B, and B17E. Eddie Ross was flying the Loffland Brothers B17E. Tom Loffland liked speed. In the B17E he had less speed than he had become accustomed to in the old 17R, NC58Y. So, on one of his many trips to the factory Eddie Ross asked Ted Wells if it would be possible to install a 420 hp Wright in the B17E, and only use 285 hp for cruise.

It may be that Beech was already planning to up the horsepower to 420, but in any case it had not yet been done, and now Beech had a customer asking

The cockpit of A17F, serial number 5, NC12583.

(Beech Photo)

34

for it. So, approval was obtained for installation of the 420 hp Wright with the stipulation that 420 hp would be used only for takeoff with 285 hp the maximum otherwise.

The 420 Wright was installed in the Loffland airplane. A fixed pitch prop was used, and the static RPM was 1500. This guaranteed that not over 2000 RPM would be available at cruising altitude, to prevent exceeding the 285 hp restriction. Eddie says the airplane did fair with this fixed prop, but he was not really pleased with it. He knew he was not getting all the performance he should. So, he asked about installing a two position Hamilton Standard.

Ted Wells told him the Hamilton Standard would weigh too much—would put the CG too far forward for safe flight.

Undaunted, Eddie asked about putting weight in the tail to counterbalance the prop, and Ted said this would be possible, providing the Bureau of Air Commerce approved it. With his foot now in the door, and not wanting to waste payload carrying dead ballast weight, Eddie advanced the idea of carrying his tool kit in the tail fairing cone, and wanted to know it this would counterbalance the prop. After some calculations, Ted said it would, so this was approved providing Eddie would agree never to fly the airplane without his tool kit in the tail fairing. He agreed, and the two position Hamilton Standard replaced the old wood prop.

The fixed pitch wood prop, turning 1500 RPM in the chocks, had not allowed the Wright engine to put out its full 420 hp. The new Hamilton Standard, in low pitch for takeoff, revved up to full power on the Wright, and Eddie had to hold the nose well up immediately after takeoff to keep the engine from overspeeding. On his first takeoff at the factory with the new prop Ted Wells told him later that he thought Eddie had pulled the airplane off too early, but remarked, "It really went, didn't it?".

That remark fitted not only the new B17R (as the 420 Wright powered B17E came to be called), but also the entire Beechcraft factory in 1935 for "it really went" also. As near as I can determine about 36 airplanes were built in 1935. Most were the B17L, but a substantial number of the new B17R models were built and sold, and two or three B17E's were built.

The 17R of 1932 and the A17F of 1934 were in the 200 mph plus class. Going back to 225 hp in the B17L had dropped the Beechcraft down to about 150 mph at cruise, but the 420 hp B17R of 1935 put Walter back where he really wanted to be—building a private airplane capable of over 200 mph—the B17R was advertised at 202 mph true airspeed for cruise. It probably indicated about 170 mph which,

at around 10,000 feet, should turn in a true airspeed close to 200 mph.

1935 was also the year of the first Staggerwing on floats. B17L serial number 40 was ordered with floats, and was designated an SB17L, the "S" denoting "seaplane". Perhaps the construction of this airplane helped a certain Englishman to decide he needed a float plane for a trip 'round the world.

In 1934, serial number 10, a B17L, had been sold into Mexico, to one Harold Farquhar of Mexico City.

Harold Lister Fraquhar was born April 15, 1894, just three years after the birth of Walter Beech. Though born an ocean apart, and destined to lead lives widely separated in both manner and occupation, they were brought together in 1934 by a common bond, the Beechcraft Model 17 biplane. The airplane was B17L-10, registered in Mexico as XB-AIZ. At the time Harold Farquhar was First Secretary to the British Legation in Mexico City, hence the Mexican registration. Captain Farquhar was evidently much impressed with the Beechcraft, and no doubt the personality of Walter Beech helped convince him the Beechcraft was the airplane for a First Secretary to own.

In 1935 Captain Farquhar brought XB-AIZ back to the factory to trade in on B17R-50 (serial number 50). This time he registered the airplane in his homeland as G-ADLE. The airplane was destined to become one of the few Beechcrafts to make a name for herself. With the exception of the Atlantic Ocean, she would girdle the globe westward from New York to England.

The trip, made with Herr Fritz Beiler (a German national living in Mexico) as copilot and general helper, would involve great endurance, considerable flying skill, and some danger. To Captain Farquhar and Herr Beiler, the danger was not important. Herr Beiler had reportedly served with the German Air Force in World War One, and was an experienced aviator. Captain Farquhar entered World War One with the famed Life Guards, later transferred to the Coldstream Guards.

Captain Farquhar entered the British Diplomatic Service in 1922 serving as a Second Secretary as early as 1925, then became the First Secretary in Mexico City in 1934.

When Captain Farquhar purchased B17R-50, he obviously had the 'Round The World trip in mind. The aircraft was displayed at the Detroit show from July 19th through 28th, 1935, and it was known at that time that it had been fitted for Edo 39-4000 floats in College Point, New York. The plan, which worked well, was to retract the landing gear, then install the floats. Thus, while floats were

36

Instrument panel of A17F, NS 68.

(Henry B. DeSpain)

A17F, s/n 5, at the factory. After a hectic career, she disappeared at the beginning of WWII. Now (1966) there are strong rumors that she's in somebody's garage in California.
(Henry B. DeSpain)

Second Cyclone job (s/n 11, NS68) pours on the coal for takeoff. *(Henry B. DeSpain)*

William H. "Pete" Hill, early aviator and friend of Walter H. Beech. He helped Walter enter post World War One aviation, later test flew the first Beechcraft. *(W. H. Hill, Sr.)*

37

fitted, the airplane's landing gear would remain retracted. Then, when the vast expanses of water they would cover between New York and China were behind them, they could convert to the landing gear merely by removing the floats.

Extra equipment stowed on G-ADLE included an extra propeller, reserve oil, an anchor, ropes, tackle, a rubber boat, and nearly one hundred pounds of spare engine and airframe parts. The gross weight with floats was 993 pounds over the normally approved maximum weight.

With this overload, the two flyers found they could make water takeoffs only under ideal conditions.

From the Detroit Show, the airplane was evidently flown back to Mexico City. Captain Farquhar kept a diary during the trip, and Peter Berry obtained that diary from Captain Farquhar's son Adrian. The following description of the flight is based on the diary.

On August 16, 1935, Farquhar and Beiler left Mexico City for New York to get the floats installed. They arrived at North Beach Airport on the 22nd after having flown 1382 miles.

The floats were installed, and the extra equipment carefully stowed on board the airplane. Four days later (on August 26th) at 1:40 pm, the Wright engine roared, and the heavily laden Staggerwing slowly increased speed, and finally lifted off the water. Climbing slowly she turned northwestward. Within minutes the sound of her engine had faded, and she was but a speck on the western horizon.

The weather was good, but the Beechcraft made poor time on account of strong headwinds. Pulling 26.2"Hg (inches of Mercury, absolute engine manifold pressure), and 1800 RPM (engine revolutions per minute), the B17R made the trip from North Beach, New York to Toronto, Canada (420 miles) in 3 hours, 40 minutes.

Remaining over night in Toronto, the two young men were up early the next morning for the next leg of their long flight. The weather wasn't bad—2000 feet and rain, but the water was glassy, and there was no surface wind. After several attempts to take off, it became apparent they would have to lighten the load. So, 58 gallons of fuel was drained, and a successful takeoff made. Following the north shore of Lake Huron past Georgian Bay and North Channel, they set down at Sault St. Marie for fuel. This time the wind was up some, and the water was choppy. They decided to try full fuel tanks.

With the dependable Wright straining, and spray flying back from the floats, the overloaded Staggerwing made it into the air, and Captain Farquhar headed for Lac du Bonnet via the north shore of Lake Superior. The weather was good, but cold. At Lac du Bonnet they were met with an enthusiastic crowd, and the RCAF gave them excellent maps for their journey west and north across Canada's vast expanses.

The next day, August 28, 1935, started in gloomy and very cold weather across desolate country to the RCAF station at Cormorant Lake where they refueled.

Even with the RCAF maps, the navigation was difficult—there were few good checkpoints in the wilds of Canada across Lac da Range, the Churchill River, and on in to McMurray, their next stop.

Staying overnight at McMurray, the chief pilot of Canadian Airways told them of the many dangers of their next leg, and helped them understand the problems of operating an airplane in Canada's desolate northwestern regions.

Departing McMurray on August 29, 1935, they met the terrible loneliness and desolation of the country between McMurray and Norman. Captain Farquhar noted that they seemed to be doing about 130 mph at 26.4"Hg and 1800 RPM. This was about the performance designer Ted Wells had told them to expect in their overloaded condition with the floats installed.

On August 30, 1935, the two flyers left Norman to fly beyond the northern tip of the Rockies, thence into Alaska, and on to Fairbanks where they set down on Harding Lake, fifty miles out of Fairbanks. Captain Farquhar left Canada with a certain feeling of relief at having behind him the thousands of square miles of northern wastelands, but with a distinct knowledge that, in the help and aid he had received from the inhabitants of that land, he had incurred a debt no man could ever repay. At every landing in Canada, he had been met with smiles and helping hands. He could not but admire the men and women of those northern Canadian outposts, especially the Royal Canadian Mounted Police, for whom he had the most praise.

In Fairbanks, he found Joe Burrows of Pan American Airways very kind, and willing to take over and do all that was needed to speed the flyers on their way. But, bad weather intervened, as it would many times on their long journey, and they were not able to leave Fairbanks until September 1, 1935. Even so, the weather wasn't the best, and they had to fight low ceilings and rain all the way. They stayed overnight in Nome, and the next day the weather worsened, making conditions ahead doubtful. Herr Beiler wanted to try it, but Captain Farquhar insisted in not flying that day (September 2, 1935), so Beiler "sulkily" (in Captain Farquhar's words) agreed to remain grounded for the day.

B17L, s/n 12, NC12592, photographed on September 2, 1934, just about two weeks after it was built. The main gear strut fairing is plainly visible in this photograph.   *(Emil Strasser)*

The second B17L, s/n 4, NC12584, later painted in Aero Mobiloil's insignia, and sold to them. This photo was evidently taken immediately after the airplane was built.   *(Beech Photo)*

The first B17L, Beechcraft s/n 3, NC270Y. This airplane still exists, in basket case condition, and is owned by Air Force Lieut. Colonel James T. Winkler who plans to rebuild it to original condition. Notice the landing gear fairings. The main gear strut has no fairing. Look closer. There is a small, barely visible, spanwise door on the bottom of the wing, a fraction of an inch forward of the main gear strut that swung backward and upward to close the opening the main gear strut retracted into. On later models this was removed, and a fairing was put on the main gear strut. Notice also, this airplane has a fixed pitch, wood propeller. Some of the first few airplanes did. Later models used the Hamilton Standard counter weight constant speed prop.   *(Beech Photo)*

The next morning (September 3, 1935), the weather was no better, but by noon had improved so that Captain Farquhar thought Beiler justified in insisting that they make an attempt to cross the Bering Straits to Siberia. Though his notes do not reflect it, the flight from Nome across the Bering Straits must have been one for the book.

It was not until 3:30 in the afternoon that the weather improved enough for Captain Farquhar to agree with Beiler that they ought to try it, and even then, much low clouds and fog abounded. Of the flight, Captain Farquhar says only that they crossed the Diomede Islands (covered in fog), and landed at Uelen in Siberia as dusk fell.

At Uelen they found an amazing change from the comparative modern civilization of Canada and Alaska. Two wooden communial dwellings housed the communist authorities. The local natives (Chungehis) lived in huts. They found no one who spoke English, and only the political chief understood German, but Beiler was not convinced he understood *much* German. There appeared to be plenty of chiefs at Uelen—there was a local, native representative of the local communist party; the head of the settlement; the military representative who checked their passports and credentials; and the political chief who supposedly understood German.

The soviets claimed their arrival was unexpected, but gave them beds, gasoline, and food, and would not hear of payment. Which was handy as Captain Farquhar notes they had no rubles anyway.

They lost a day by crossing the International Date Line so they departed Nome on September 3rd and landed at Uelen on September 4th, the same day.

A few hours after their arrival at Uelen, the barometer dropped steadily, and a thick mist descended. On September 5th, the fog was right down on the ground. The two flyers began to feel low—their morale was not good, and the desolation of the country around Uelen was getting on their nerves.

The next day, September 6th, they took off in spite of the fog, and after much deviating from course on account of low ceilings and fog, they made it to Anadyr, the next outpost of human life on that desolate continent.

They were met with an enthusiastic welcome from all the authorities including a Mr. G. Lanu, an Intourist representative who spoke English. They visited the salmon and caviar cannery at Anadyr, and found the factory head spoke German.

The military commander of Anadyr advised the two pilots to try the inland route via Markovo to Yamsk, and on the 7th of September, they left in weather that was none too promising. In rain and a 2500 foot ceiling, they flew across the artic tundra along the Anadyrk River to Markovo. On arrival they decided it would be impossible to takeoff if they landed, so reluctantly turned around to fly back to Anadyr.

On the way back, by an extraordinary coincidence, they flew directly over the remains of Jimmie Mattern's Lockheed Vega, resting quietly on the desolate Arctic tundra.

A southeasterly gale on September 8th and 9th kept the two men grounded at Anadyr though their nerves got on edge deciding whether they should go or not. On the 10th the weather showed faint signs of clearing, but the engine backfired on starting, and caught fire in the carburettor intake. They put the fire out, and Beiler decided to dismantle the cowling and take a look. With the help of the local soviets, he spent all day looking for the trouble, finally traced it to a shorted distributor cable. It was quickly repaired, but too late in the day to take off.

The next morning, September 11th, the weather lifted a little, and they left Anadyr heading overland for Olyutorski on the coast. Flying under a 200 to 300 foot ceiling with visibility sometimes down to one-quarter mile, and unpleasant moments of zero-zero, they arrived at Olyutorski at 3:50 p.m. Since leaving Alaska they had been plagued with bad weather, fog, low ceilings, and rain.

The next morning dawned bright and clear. For the first time since leaving Alaska, Captain Farquhar climbed up to 10,000 feet in the clear, cold air, and made an uneventful trip to Nogaevo. After the usual good treatment—free gas, quarters, and food—they left the next noon for Okhotsk. The clear skies were gone, replaced by low, scuddy ceilings, and now, high winds. They landed at Okhotsk in gale force winds, and anchored the airplane. By the late afternoon the winds had increased and G-ADLE was in danger of turning over. Beiler and Farquhar waded out to her (Beiler nearly drowned, but Farquhar's rubber boots filled with water, weighing him down), and with the help of local authorities, tied her to two small boats loaded with rocks.

Day after day of fighting bad weather, sleeping in unclean quarters with rats running about (despite the helpfulness of the Russians, they didn't keep things clean), and eating tinned foot caught up with Captain Farquhar and Herr Beiler at Okhotsk. The next day, September 14th, the weather cleared, but neither felt like getting out of bed, and Farquhar was quite ill. The 15th was beautifully sunny, and though still tired, and out of sorts, the two flyers decided it best to take advantage of the weather and press on.

They had to wait until noon for the tide to come

in before they could leave, but they finally made it off with 135 gallons of fuel—more than they normally carried. Since Russian aviation gasoline was only 73 octane, they kept the fuselage tank of 80 octane for takeoff, then switched over to the 73 octane for cruising. They had purchased the 80 octane in Alaska where normal aviation gasoline was 80 octane, and luckily had not used it up. The engine would cruise on the Russian gasoline, but at full power would detonate.

They made a quiet, uneventful flight over uninhabited wastes to Nikolaevsk where they again received an enthusiastic welcome, and the usual donations of fuel, a place to sleep, and food. September 16th (the next day) they left Nikolaevsk in poor weather, and flew around for several hours before landing at Mascrisk, 100 miles south of Nikolaevsk! They refueled at Mascrisk, and pushed on to Niune Tambovskoie.

Now the country was improving—wooded slopes replaced the desolate tundra of the Arctic, and on the 17th they made a flight in good weather to Khabarovsk where they received a grandiose welcome followed by a four hour dinner, and a free offer to check the Wright engine over. Farquhar accepted, and the mechanics did a good job considering they had never seen a Wright engine before.

The next morning, the flyers awoke to find the Soviet authorities evidently hung over and still sleeping, and the weather awful. They finally left the following morning in heavy rain and visibility of about one-quarter mile.

An hour out the weather cleared, and Captain Farquhar climbed G-ADLE to her correct cruising altitude, 10,000 feet. Next stop, Harbin, Manchuria, and the first real touch with civilization since leaving Fairbanks, Alaska. They arrived at 4:30 p.m., and a Japanese Air Force Colonel rescued them from an encounter with what Captain Farquhar called "an impertinent little junior customs official", and they went to the hotel to get a much needed bath, and sleep in clean beds.

The next morning, Captain Farquhar decided it might be wise to remove the floats, and continue on wheels. Not knowing exactly how to do it, he put the problem to the Japanese Colonel who quickly turned out his detachment plus 60 coolies. They very cleverly built a sand wall around the airplane in the river, carefully removed the floats, and made a runway on the mud flat in the middle of the river. The wheels were lowered, and the airplane took off from the mud flat easily, and was flown to the airport.

They stayed four days in Harbin, and left on September 23rd in the usual bad weather. After about an hour the weather cleared, and they climbed

to 10,000 feet. They crossed the Chinese frontier at Changchun, and landed at Peking at 3:30 p.m. The Chinese were obliging, and the two pilots stayed at Peking until September 29th. On that day they flew to Shanghai where they found a most friendly and courteous greeting from everyone—especially from China National Aviation Company who gave their engine a complete check, polished the airplane, and did a general inspection of the machine—all free of charge. The Shanghai Royal Air Force Association gave a luncheon in their honor.

September 30th the two men flew down to Hong Kong, their first encounter with the British, and from Captain Farquhar's notes, it was an encounter he would have enjoyed avoiding. The first thing that happened was pained surprise and indigation that he had flown from Mexico to the United States, and across Canada, Alaska, Siberia, Manchuria, and China without a "log book". The next thing they did was take Captain Farquhar's Certificate of Airworthiness for Export, and the British Air Ministry's telegram validating it, and lose the telegram, the first words of which were "This telegram *must* be carried on the ship as evidence of validation."

The British aviators in Hong Kong ignored Farquahar and Beiler, and G-ADLE when the two were about, but carefully inspected G-ADLE when they were away from her. They were unable to obtain maps from any of the airport officials, but finally got some information from an outfit who trained Chinese students to fly.

Weather reports were non-existent, but the Director of the Royal Observatory made great efforts, and finally turned up with an excellent weather summary made up by the French observatory at Phu-Lien near Hanoi in French IndoChina.

For the first time since leaving Mexico, Captain Farquhar had to pay a landing fee and hangar rent (in a practically empty hangar), but nothing was charged for the wireless "expert" who supposedly cleaned up the Lear radio—Captain Farquhar commented in his notes, "It hasn't worked since."

On October 2nd they left Hong Kong, and after three hours and thirty-six minutes landed at Hanoi in French IndoChina. Everyone was very nice, and the flyers noticed the French had developed a ground communications system, and excellent weather reporting facilities.

Flying around thunderstorms, they flew down to Saigon on October 4th, and again received a most friendly welcome. They stayed in Saigon, making an automobile side trip to Angkor, through October 7th, and left on the 8th for Bangkok, Thailand. Most of their flying was at 10,000 and 11,000 feet where, in the tropical climate, the temperature of the air was

60° to 70° F which caused the oil to run hot. Captain Farquhar resorted to flying at reduced power for some periods on each flight in order to keep the oil temperature down.

They spent October 9th and 10th sightseeing in and around Bangkok, and left on the 11th to fly all the way to Calcutta, India. At Calcutta they found a bumpy, dusty field, and being under British control, they naturally were charged a landing fee, their first since Hong Kong.

October 12th they flew to Jodhpur where they found the Maharaja of Jodhpur, an excellent pilot, had built his own airport—an excellent one with a paved runway, lights, etc. Captain Farquhar wondered why the Indian government couldn't follow his example.

On the 14th they flew to Poona, and stayed as guests for two days with the Governor of Bombay.

Leaving Poona on October 16th, they next flew to Bombay, then to Karachi, Basra, and Baghdad, arriving at Baghdad on October 18th. Experienced difficulty keeping the oil temperature down in the heat, and found Shell gasoline produced higher cylinder head temperatures than Stanovo gasoline.

They found excellent facilities at Baghdad, but the entire field was sand—no paved surface to run up on, and Captain Farquhar observed that they must want as much sand and dirt as possible in their engines.

En route to Cairo they toured over Jericho, Jerusalem, Bethlehem, and the Dead Sea. On October 22nd and 23rd they flew to Luxor and return, and found the airfield there "quite awful."

October 24th Beiler fell ill with some tropical bug, and was hospitalized. But, he was better the next day, and able to travel, so they flew to Benghasi for refueling, thence on to Tripoli. On the 26th they flew on to Tunis, then to Marseilles, France, and on to Lyons, France where they landed at 4:35 p.m. Captain Farquhar's notes end here. They must have done some sightseeing in France as they did not arrive at Heston airport in England until 2:46 p.m. on October 29th, which completed the flight.

Peter Berry compiled some interesting statistics on this flight. From New York to Harbin, Manchuria, the two flyers covered 8,658 miles in 71 hours 55 minutes for a speed of 120 mph. Changing to wheels (floats removed) at Harbin, they flew on to Heston covering 12,674 miles in 80 hours, 58 minutes for a speed of 156.5 mph. The total trip mileage was 21,332 miles covered in 152 hours 53 minutes for an overall average of 138.2 mph. For 1935, that was an outstanding achievement, and well worth the accolade, "The world is small when you fly a Beechcraft."

After this historic flight, Captain Farquhar was transferred to the British Foreign Office in 1939, serving in Warsaw and Bucharest. In 1950 he was made a Knight Commander of the Order of St. Michael and St. George, and is therefore known as Sir Harold Farquhar. He died on January 31, 1953. In World War One, Sir Harold was awarded the Military Cross, an award given to officers for gallantry in the field of battle.

Little is known of his traveling companion, Herr Fritz Beiler except that he was a German subject living in Mexico, and supposedly flew for the German Air Force in World War One. His widow and son still live in Mexico.

As for G-ADLE, the airplane was sold to L. G. Siro in June, 1936, and crashed on the Danish Island of Lialand on January 20, 1939, and was destroyed.

* * *

All of the Beechcrafts produced through 1935 (the 17R, A17F, B17L, B17B, B17E, B17R) were plagued with poor landing characteristics caused by a nose heavy condition, and inadequate up elevator power. In the B17E and B17R this had been remedied to a degree by shortening the main landing gear legs. As the company moved into production for 1936, the B17 series was replaced by the C17 series. The C17 series was identical to the B17 series except that all of the C17 airplanes had the shorter landing gear leg on the main gear, and the angle of incidence of the horizontal stabilizer was changed to improve landing characteristics. The same airfoil, the Clark CYH was used, and the C17 was available in the same models, the C17B, C17L, C17E, and C17R. Serial number 67, built in March, 1936 was probably the first C17 model, and it was a C17B.

Going back for a moment to 1934-35, Richard G. Beeler said he was one of the early pilots around the factory in that period. Remember, it was in the middle of a depression, and most pilots were out of work. Even if they were not employed by Beech, they might hang around the factory hoping to pick up five bucks for a test hop, or delivery flight. Dick Beeler hung around the factory for a while, then was put on the payroll. The work, he said, covered everything from sweeping the floor to test flying airplanes.

On September 16, 1934 he test flew B17L, s/n 14, NC12597. On September 24, 1934 Dick set an unofficial speed record between Wichita and Lincoln, Nebraska covering the 217 miles in one hour and five minutes which is a speed of 200 mph! This was accomplished, he said, by taking advantage of good tailwinds, and accounts, in his opinion, for the saying in aviation that the Beechcraft was a "200 mph airplane." The plain fact is, the B17L with its 225 hp

Jacobs, cruised a little over 150 mph, but a 50 mph tailwind would make it a "200 mph airplane."

Dick said it was common practice in those days to set intercity records. He would go out in the morning, and notice the direction the clouds were moving. If they were moving northwest, he'd pick a city to the northwest, then take off. Checking his groundspeed frequently, he would change altitude as necessary to get the best groundspeed. He told me that Western Union clocked their takeoff and landing to establish a semi-official time for the flight.

On October 5, 1934 Dick took NC12597 to Chicago, and demonstrated the airplane at the Chicago Air Races plus entering a few races with the airplane.

Spending most of his time demonstrating the airplane, he took time out to carry Herb Fisher around the Indiana Air Tour which started June 16, 1935 and ended June 24, 1935. Dick would take off from the airport last with Herb Fisher, the tour director, and reporters, then have to be the first to arrive at the next airport! The speedy Beechcraft always made it, he said.

During the summer of 1935, he spent most of his time at air shows and contacting prospective buyers for the airplane. The airplane was finally sold on August 25, 1935 to a Mr. Williams of General Motors. Dick said he spent a week with Williams before he was ready to fly the airplane himself.

In the summer of 1936 the negative stagger Beechcraft was gaining fame around the world. Sir Harold Farquhar's flight had certainly not hurt the airplane's excellent reputation, and several foreign buyers had purchased Beechcrafts. In the summer of 1936 buyers from an oriental country ordered a C17E airplane. Today the Beech factory, if you can find anyone who remembers it, is reluctant to talk about this particular buyer although there is no reason for this.

Nippon Koko Yuso Kaisha (Japan Air Transport Company) ordered a C17E, serial number 77. On June 10, 1936 the factory changed s/n 77 and s/n 78 so that C17E-77 became C17R-77 and C-17R-78 became C17E-78.

C17E-78 was completed for Nippon Koko Yuso Kaisha, and shipped, dismantled, to Japan. We will hear more about it later.

In the meantime, C17R-77 was finished in Sherwin Williams blue with white striping, and was to be a demonstrator. It made its first test flight on July 1, 1936.

During the first week in August, 1936, Blanche Noyes (widow of Dewey Noyes), and Louise Thaden were in San Antonio, Texas working with the State of Texas on a project to put airmarkers on 600 Texas towns.

Late one night they had a phone call from Olive Ann Beech. She wanted to know if they'd care to fly in the Bendix Trophy Race, a grinding flight across the United States from New York to Los Angeles against the stiffest competition the genius minds of Jimmy Wedell, Benny Howard, Art Chester, and other racing greats could muster. Louise's first reaction was that they wouldn't let women enter. "Well, they are this year," Mrs. Beech told Louise, "and furthermore, Mr. Bendix has posted a special award of $2,500 for the female pilot who finishes first regardless of her position in the race itself. I think we might as well have that money, don't you?" To this Louise agreed.

But, she considered winning in the money very unlikely in view of the special racing planes that would be entered.

When Mrs. Thaden arrived at the factory in Wichita she found things in somewhat of a hectic uproar. To begin with, factory pilot Bill Ong was upset because he wasn't going to pilot the airplane in the race, and Louise Thaden found the airplane they were going to fly (C17R-77) had an old model radio receiver, no transmitter, and no directional gyro. After a lot of running around, pulling stuff out, and putting stuff in, probably some cussing and name calling, C17R-77, NC15835 was pronounced ready for the race, and the two girls, Louise Thaden, and Blanche Noyes, departed for New York, the starting point.

On August 28, 1936 Walter Beech addressed a letter to Colonel William C Brooks, Director, Escuela Militar de Aviation, Honduras, Central America telling him that he regretted the loss of the Colonel's first Beechcraft, and to show him their good faith, Walter agreed to sell him C17R-77, NC15835 at a reduced price. The price on a new C17R was $14,500. Walter Beech gave the Colonel $4,100 for his crashed airplane, a discount of $2,900, and agreed to disassemble the engine in NC15835, and have it overhauled before delivery. The total cost to Colonel Brooks was his crashed Beechcraft and $7,500, and he would have a nearly new C17R valued at $14,500. I would say that Mr. Beech was giving the man a "deal" he could hardly pass up.

Contestants for the 1936 Bendix gathered in New York, to depart from Floyd Bennett Field. For some reason, there were a number of commercial airplanes in the race, including a Douglas DC-2, but few special racers. Colonel Roscoe Turner had cracked up on a New Mexico mesa in his Wedell-Williams racer which put him out of the race, and Benny Howard in Mister Mulligan was top contender. Louise and Blanche just hoped to come in second or third and win the $2,500 for the first female pilot to finish.

The men and the machine. Upper left, G-ADLE on wheels. At right, Captain Harold Farquhar. At left, Herr Fritz Beiler. Below, G-ADLE on floats, the wheels retracted.
(Upper Left, Robert Esposito, Right, Peter Berry, Left, Adolfo Villaseñor, Below, Robert Esposito)

On the morning of the race, both girls were nervous and apprehensive—a natural condition before an air race, especially one like the Bendix. At 1:37 a.m. a Vultee V1A flown by William Warner departed, and at 2:03 a.m. the Douglas DC-2 took off followed by Amelia Earhart and Helen Richey in their Lockheed at 2:47 a.m. At 3:12 a.m. Joe Jacobson left in Gar Wood's Northrop Gamma. These airplanes represented stiff competition, and as the girls taxied out they passed Benny Howard's "Mister Mulligan", illuminated by their landing light. The Bendix was a timed race, so contestants could depart when they desired, with a cutoff time to arrive in Los Angeles.

Fighting storm conditions over most of the eastern United States, the girls had a rough time navigating, and flying instruments, but they broke out into the clear about 200 miles east of Wichita. Louise had been cruising at 65% power, and when she told Walter Beech this while refueling at Wichita, he stormed, "What the hell do you think you're in, a potato race? Open this damn thing up!"

Louise said "Yes sir.", making a mental note to continue to cruise at 65% power. Louise remembered the days when she flew Travel Airs in races that a race is not always won by the fastest airplane —that good common sense in taking care of the engine and equipment sometimes proves the winning factor.

As in any race, problems plagued the contestants. The Northrop Gamma blew up, and Joe Jacobson parachuted to safety. Amelia Earhart and Helen Richey had an escape hatch come open. They fought with the hatch two hours, finally tied it closed with a rag. They lost precious time. Laura Ingalls, flying the race on her own with no ground help to plot courses, check the weather, and be waiting to refuel her Lockheed, lost the race on the ground putting 450 gallons in the airplane herself after trying to get someone to do it for her.

Climbing to 16,000 feet over the Rockies, and over clouds, the Beechcraft C17R droned on westward to Los Angeles at 65% power.

Unknown to the girls their chief contender, Benny Howard, had crashed, with serious injury to himself and Mrs. Howard.

Letting down into the late afternoon sun, the two girls in NC15835 found it difficult to pick out landmarks. There was considerable haze to add to their troubles. They could only see things clearly behind them, looking down-sun. Straining to find the airport, they flew past it, had to reverse their course, and pass the finish line in the wrong direction!

Certain that they had lost any chance of placing in the race, Louis landed and taxied toward the parking ramp. A stream of automobiles roared out onto the field, headed for the Beechcraft. Men were waving their arms excitedly. The two girls exchanged glances, what had they done now?

There were shouts of you've won the Bendix!, and people swarmed around the airplane. Louise cut the switches, and got out.

They *had* won! Not only the $2,500 for the first female pilot across the finish line, but the entire Bendix Trophy Race. Their time was 14 hours, 55 minutes, and 1 second for an average speed of 165.346 mph. Laura Ingalls, in her Lockheed Orion, came in second with 157.466 mph.

Now, Walter Beech had a problem. He had just promised to sell the airplane to Colonel Brooks at a cut rate price, and now it was a valuable Bendix Trophy winner! To add to his problems, Colonel Brooks had already sent him the check for $7,500 for the airplane, and indicated he was anxious for delivery immediately, if not sooner!

To further complicate matters, on September 5, 1936, writing from Hollywood, California, Walter told Col. Brooks that he had just received an offer of $20,000 for the airplane, and would sell it for him at that price if he so desired. Not only had Walter Beech sold the airplane to Brooks at a reduced price; now he was willing to pass on the $20,000 offer to Brooks for his benefit. Be hard to find a man honest enough to do business that way today. Be a refreshing thing though, wouldn't it?

Unfortunately, Brooks valued the Beechcraft so highly, and was so anxious to get it that he turned down the offer, and asked that NC15835 be delivered to him as soon as possible. It was returned to Wichita, cleaned up, the engine overhauled, and delivered to Colonel Brooks.

This left Beech in a peculiar situation. He had just had a stock airplane win the toughest cross-country race in the world, and the airplane was in Honduras, sold to a Colonel. The normal procedure at this point, if the airplane had not been sold, would be to fly it around the country on demonstration flights advertising the fact that it had won the Bendix, and identical models were in production at Wichita for sale to anyone who could afford one.

Not to be outdone, Walter Beech hurried home to Wichita, and ordered C17R-81 finished identically to C17R-77, the airplane that won the Bendix. He even obtained Department of Commerce approval to use the same number, NC15835 as it had been released when the original NC15835 left for Honduras.

Early in October, 1936, the new NC15835 was test flown, and delivered to Louise Thaden who flew it on many demonstration flights around the nation. On March 18, 1937 the airplane was sold to Albert

A vaud
beside B1

Oops! B
during Ma

H. Stackpole, a publisher, who had published a book of Mrs. Thaden's.

Since 1936, the entire aviation world has been led to believe that C17R-81, NC15835 won the 1936 Bendix, when in fact, the airplane that really won it was C17R-77, then designated as NC15835. From the evidence I have, Walter Beech did not intend for this to happen, but the public never paid much attention to an airplane's serial number, and it wasn't considered such a big thing that everyone at the factory would carefully note it, so, over the years, the assumption was made that s/n 81 won the 1936 Bendix when, in fact, s/n 77 won it.

At this writing, 1966, C17R-81 is still flying.

Recently rebuilt on the west coast, it was purchased by William C. Yarbrough of Atlanta, Georgia. He sold it to Lieutenant Colonel James T. Winkler who plans to use it extensively after his retirement from the Air Force.

One moot point that historians have generally evaded about the 1936 Bendix is that, if he had not had troubles, Benny Howard would probably have won. Hands down, too. But, part of the Bendix is the endurance factor—the ability to fly across the continent at high speed. Benny's luck ran out at an inopportune time, and the Beechcraft kept going. There are always a lot of "ifs" in an air race, and Benny just happened to be a victim of one of them.

* * *

B17L-16. This was standard paint scheme on the early B17Ls.
(Warren D. Shipp)

B17R-54 running up. This paint scheme was common in late 1934, early 1935. *(Richard C. Seeley)*

SB17L-40, the first Beechcraft on floats. *(Beech Photo)*

50

Instrument panel on an early B17L.

Another Oops! Beechcraft B17L-58 landed gear up at the 1939 National Air Races. Note that the tail wheel had just started to extend. *(Emil Strasser)*

Upper right wing from B17E-49. *(Dwight Addington)*

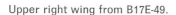

Serial number 22. It may have been the first B17E. *(Beech Photo)*

B17L-15. This photo shows the lower wing root treatment. On later models this was metal fairing without the longitudinal lines. *(Beech Photo)*

This late B17L or early C17L instrument panel has only one gyro instrument—the turn needle. Later Staggerwings had full gyro panels. Note uncluttered arrangement of panel at left, compare to modern instrument panels. Lever coming up from floor on left is flaps; one on right is brake lever.

(Howard A. Jones)

CHAPTER THREE

THE WORLD IS SMALL

In 1936 Beech's design staff began work on something new and different. Departing radically from the single engine biplane theme, the new design was a twin engine monoplane. The first one built was assigned serial number 62 although it did not fly until January, 1937. To say that it became a success would be an unkind understatement. The Beechcraft Model 18 is still in production—*thirty years later!* No other airplane that I know of can equal that record.

In addition to designing the Model 18, Beech's engineers spent time in 1936 working on improvements on the Model 17. It was generally realized that the Model 17 had some handling characteristics that were undesirable. It was nose heavy, and was difficult to flare for landing on account of the nose heaviness, and inadequate elevator power. An attempt had been made, in the B17E and B17R, and the entire C17 series to remedy this problem by shortening the landing gear legs and changing the horizontal stabilizer angle of incidence.

But, the remedy did not work completely, as any Beechcraft pilot, including yours truly, can testify. When being flown solo, the C17 series was almost impossible to three-point on landing. I always made wheel landings when flying solo. However, with a full load of passengers and baggage, the airplane landed as easily as a J-3 Cub.

The D17 series, to be introduced in 1937, had several improvements. First, the fuselage was lengthened 13-5/16 inches—this moved the horizontal stabilizer and elevator back giving more elevator power to flare the airplane for a three-point landing.

The ailerons were moved to the upper wing, and standard flaps were installed on the lower wing. The wheel brakes were changed from the lever actuated type to toebrakes on the rudder pedals. *That*, I can assure you, was a great improvement. I flew an old C17L with the lever type brake, and on landing you had one hand holding the control wheel back, one hand on the brake lever, one hand on the throttle, one hand trying to unlock the tailwheel so you could turn off the runway, and just as things were getting interesting, the tower always called to inquire if you were "having difficulty". It was *fun!* But, I haven't flown an airplane, before or since, that I liked better than that old C17L. I sold her in 1959 and have been mentally kicking myself since.

Another interesting event was happening as 1936 closed, and 1937 came into being. On November 14, 1936, one Virgil H. Adamson went aboard the good ship *Empress of Japan* at Vancouver, British Columbia, and two weeks later stepped ashore at Yokohama, Japan.

His purpose in Japan? To assist Tokyo Hikoki Seisaku-Jo (The Tokyo Aircraft Works) in building

Instrument panel of a late B17 airplane.

a Beechcraft C17E.

Virgil Adamson had his hands full. In a country foreign to him in customs and language, he must assist in the very complicated job of building a Beechcraft C17E. The Japanese realized they would have a problem in this regard, so the first man to meet Virgil when he stepped ashore in Yokohama was Yogi Iida, an English speaking official of Nippon Koko Yuso Kaisha (The Japan Air Transport Company) who would buy the C17E airplanes that Tokyo Hikoki Seisaku-Jo planned to build.

Mr. Iida became Virgil's shadow, helping him get settled in the famed Imperial Hotel in Tokyo, the most elaborate hotel in Japan, and getting him started on the project of building the C17E. Of slight build, and of youthful appearance, Virgil Adamson ran into trouble the first week. The airline company called him in, and through Iida, questioned him at length about his education, background, and experience. They were afraid they had an inexperienced novice on their hands who would not be up to the tremendous task ahead. After a few minutes of the questions, Virgil realized why they were concerned. He asked that the blueprints for the airplane be brought in, and when they arrived, he pointed out his name on them—the name Adamson appeared on almost every sheet. The Japanese were satisfied. They never again questioned his professional ability.

The first job was to assemble C17E-78 when it arrived from the United States. In the meantime Mr. Iida toured Virgil around Tokyo, showing him the sights, and allowing him an opportunity to study the Japanese people—something the tourist didn't often have a chance to do.

When the airplane arrived, the difficult job of uncrating and assembling it began. Work began in January, 1937, and it was not until April that the airplane made its first flight. So much time was required because the Japanese were unfamiliar with the Beechcraft, and because assembling the airplane was used as training for workmen who would later build them from scratch.

When the airplane was completed, the test flight was made by a Japanese pilot and mechanic who flew without parachutes over Adamson's protests, to demonstrate their complete confidence in the airplane.

On June 11, 1937, Adamson sailed from Yokohama aboard the *Chichibu Maru*. Many banquets were held in Adamson's honor before he sailed, and as the ship steamed out of Yokohama harbor, the C17E circled overhead—a final salute to the American who taught them how to build the Beechcraft.

According to Richard M. Bueschel, an expert on Japanese aviation history, Tokyo Hikoki Seisaku-Jo built 14 C17E's in 1938, 5 in 1939, and 1 in 1940 for a total of 20. From all evidence, none of them survived the war.

Few people are aware that some 20 C17E's were built in Japan, and almost no one at the Beech factory today likes to talk about it. And, you can get *very* little information on the A17J design sketch. From all I can find out, the A17J was a Japanese proposal for a biplane fighter based on the Cyclone powered Beechcraft A17F. Nothing was done beyond a design sketch.

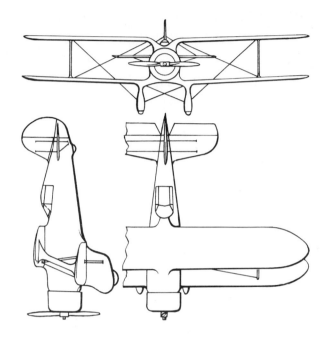

A17J drawing redrawn from a Japanese aviation magazine by James M. Triggs. Compare with 17R and A17F three-view drawings.　　　　　　　　　　　　　　*(James M. Triggs)*

Late in 1936 Beech tried to put amphibian floats on a C17B. Selecting serial number 99, the floats had wheels located about where the normal main wheels were on the landplane. No tailwheel was used—the aft end of the floats acted as a tailskid.

The airplane, NC16440, had a short career as an amphibian. Skeets Barker told me it handled okay as a float plane, but was definitely a "bear" on land. The airplane made only a few flights before the project was abandoned. In recent years Cessna has successfully installed such floats on their Model 180 aircraft, but the wheels are located aft with nose wheels in the floats. It would seem that the tricycle configuration, if Beech had tried it (especially with the nose-heavy tradition of the Beechcraft), would have been ideal. But, in those days tricycle landing gear was unheard of—probably considered "sissy".

C17E-78 registered in Japan as J-BAOI after assembly by the Japanese with the help of Virgil Adamson .
(Richard M. Bueschel)

Japanese officials examine the Beechcraft.
(Richard M. Bueschel)

C17R-75 in flight. *(Leo J. Kohn)*

C17B-110, equipped with special skids, and a brake to stop the prop horizontal, made intentional belly landings at the 1937 and 1938 National Air Races to demonstrate safety of the Beechcraft when landed gear up. *(Beech Photo)*

The noble experiment—amphibian floats. *(Warren D. Shipp)*

Unusual flight shot of C17B-110. *(Joe Juptner)*

C17R-73, the first C17R, on takeoff. *(Beech Photo)*

So, the noble attempt to build an amphibian died on the vine. But, as a pioneering effort it cannot be ignored. And it speaks well for the vision of the Beech design staff.

Speaking of vision, remember that Travel Air was not interested in a military version of the Mystery Ship? Beech did not, evidently, place much confidence in military orders.

But, in late 1936, C17R-115 was purchased by the United States Navy. It was Beech's first dealing with the military. Details of this purchase are not known to me, and it was only by remote chance that I found out what the serial number of the airplane was. The airplane was designated a JB-1 by the Navy, and carried Navy Bureau Number 0801. As war clouds gathered over Europe in 1937, 1938, and 1939, Beech became more and more interested in military business, as we shall see later on.

The Beechcraft 17 models scheduled for production in 1937 were considerably modified over the C17 series of 1936, as we have already mentioned. The first one was an experimental model, the D17W, s/n 136. Pratt and Whitney Aircraft had designed and built a geared version of their 450 hp R-985. Known as the R-985-SC-G, the engine developed 600 hp at 2850 RPM using 100 octane fuel. Beech elected to build the first D17 airplane using this experimental engine. The airplane was s/n 136, NC17081, later modified to a 420 hp Wright engine. It was known as a model D17W.

I have heard that NC17081 was built for Frank Hawks, but have not be able to substantiate that he ever actually owned the airplane. In World War Two the airplane was given to the Navy by a Mr. Ralph E. Myers of El Centro, California.

The second airplane using the souped up R-985 was serial number 164, and had a much more spectacular career. Registered NR18562, it went to Jacqueline Cochran who used it in several air races.

On July 26, 1937 Miss Cochran set a 1,000 kilometer speed record with the airplane at 203.895 mph. It was entered in a number of other races, sometimes being flown by Max Constant. In 1939 Miss Cochran set an altitude record of 30,052.43 feet at Palm Springs, California with NR18562.

When World War Two came along, Miss Cochran sold NR18562 to the U.S. Army. The special P&W engine was removed, and a 420 hp Wright installed. It was cracked up at Sweetwater, Texas during the war, and never repaired.

The D17W was a fast airplane—at 13,500 feet it cruised at 235 mph. One big problem with it though was that the airplane could not be fitted with a propeller large enough to really absorb all the engine's power. So Beech did not press P&W to develop the

engine, and the R-985-SC-G of 600 hp never became a production engine.

Three D17 models were built, the D17S, D17R, and D17A. The D17S, by far the most popular of all of the Beechcraft 17's, used the 450 hp Pratt and Whitney engine. The D17R used the Beech standby, the 420 hp Wright, and the D17A had the 350 hp Wright.

The first D17S was s/n 146 built in June, 1937. In 1937 the biplane was almost out of the picture—few manufacturers were building them. But, the Beech company put into production an airplane, the D17S, destined to become the standard the world over in single engine, four/five place airplanes. Despite its biplane configuration, it was then, and is now, a hallmark in aviation. It is the standard against which all others are judged.

The D17 series was designed as a heavy horsepower group of airplanes. Simultaneously Beech introduced the E17 series consisting of two models, the E17L and E17B. They replaced the C17L and C17B, and had all of the improvements of the D17 series including longer fuselage, upper wing ailerons, flaps on the lower wing, and toebrakes.

Now, let us go back, for a moment, to the A17F, s/n 5, NC12583. Sanford Mills sold it to Howard Hughes, and it is shown registered to him for the first time on January 1, 1935. Either he or Bob Perlick (also spelled in one book, Perlich) lengthened the fuselage 18 inches, which is apparent in photos taken before and after the modification.

Hughes kept the airplane on the west coast, in California. The last registration to Hughes was on January 1, 1937. Either Hughes hired Perlick to fly it, or Perlick purchased the airplane from Hughes.

In either case, Perlick entered the growling, Cyclone powered A17F in the 1937 Bendix which was to be flown from Los Angeles to Cleveland. Top contender for the race was the military Seversky P-35. Perlick could not hope to beat the Seversky's 300 mph speed in the 250 mph A17F, but he reasoned that a non-stop flight, eliminating costly (in time) refueling stops might place him in the money, or even win the race.

With her cabin filled with fuel tanks, the A17F taxied out in the pre-dawn stillness, her Cyclone rumbling. The day was Friday, September 3rd, 1937.

Blue exhaust flame licked downward from the Cyclone's cowling as Perlick eased the throttle open. The big Hamilton propeller sliced through the air. The heavily laden Beechcraft strained under the weight of nearly three and one-half tons of fuel. Something happened out there is the pre-dawn quiet. The big Staggerwing, grand-daddy of them all, crumbled slowly to the ground, her landing gear no longer able to support all that weight. Perlick saw what was happening, cut the throttle, and switched off. She came to rest with her prop tips slightly bent, but with Perlick's hopes tossed to the winds—he was out of the race even before he started.

For the 1937 Bendix the A17F carried number 64, and "Ring Free Red Streak" painted on her fuselage side. In 1938 this was removed, and the number 85 painted on with no mention of "Ring Free Red Streak".

In 1938 the big A17F made a better showing. Perlick got her off the ground, and climbed high into the sky, into the air where men must breath oxygen from a pipe or mask. His idea was to take advantage of high altitude winds to give the Cyclone Staggerwing the advantage she needed to win the Bendix.

In 1937, Perlick had not even started good when the big Cyclone Staggerwing let him down with a collapsed landing gear. In the 1938 race, sure that he would place in the money, maybe even, through some stroke of luck, win the race, Perlick must have felt elated as the thundering Cyclone carried him across the Sierra Nevada, the Rockies, then across the Great Plains into Illinois.

With success almost in his hands, the big Cyclone coughed in the air high above humankind, and with the relentless capacity of an aircraft engine to fail at just the wrong moment, the Cyclone quit. Perlick made a landing at Woodriver, Illinois, his dream smashed a second time.

Details end here. I know the A17F was flown back to the west coast, but have not been able, in six years of research, to turn up anything more beyond a photograph taken by B. B. Deatrick at Grand Central Air Terminal in Burbank in May, 1940 showing NR12583 in a hangar. I am convinced the airplane is still in existence, but where? Some place, in some remote spot, in California?

Early in 1938 D17S-199 was built, and sold to one Ross Hadley of Los Angeles, California. It had a most unusual paint scheme, the theme of which appears to have been the United States—it had stars all over it. An excellent idea—we could use a little more patriotism at this time (1966) in America's history.

Hadley entered the airplane in the 1938 Bendix, and turned in a speed of 181.842 mph to win fifth place. In the 1937 Bendix Jacqueline Cochran had taken third place at 194.74 mph in the D17W, and Max Constant, flying the D17W in the 1938 Bendix, came in fourth at 199.330 mph.

Hadley gave D17S-199 to the U.S. Army during World War Two. It survived the war, served a tour with the CAA, then ended up with Robert V. Williams of San Antonio as a high altitude photo ship.

After the war Hadley acquired D17S-4900, an ex-military airplane, and had it painted similar to his old D17S-199. It (D17S-4900) was last registered in Hadley's name on the 1955 registration list I have.

It can be said that Ross Hadley's Staggerwings were the most spectacular Staggerwings ever in existence so far as their paint schemes were concerned. I must say that I have a great deal of respect for anyone who will paint his airplane up to so represent his country, particularly when it is *this* country—the United States of America.

In 1938 Beech added another model to the D17 and E17 series already in production. The new model was the F17D powered by a 330 hp Jacobs engine. The D17 series had introduced the longer fuselage, and cantilever empennage, but both the E17 and F17 had the strut braced empennage. The E17 and F17 did, of course, have the longer fuselage, upper wing ailerons, and lower wing flaps similar to the D17 series.

The F17 series was produced only in the F17D model. Along with the D17 and E17, the F17 continued in production until the beginning of World War Two.

In 1939 the Army conducted a test for a personnel transport capable of carrying three to five people. Naturally interested in selling airplanes, several manufacturers entered the competition. The Beechcraft D17S won, and the Army ordered three D17S airplanes for Air Attaché service.

One of the airplanes, designated a YC-43, was sent to London where Frank O'Driscoll Hunter was serving with the U.S. Embassy. I don't know what his rank was then, but he retired from the United States Air Force as a General officer, and I met him in his home town of Savannah, Georgia in 1957. A World War One ace, Hunter Air Force Base is named for him—it was originally the municipal airport for Savannah. General Hunter enjoyed the Beechcraft, said it was one of the finest airplanes the Army had ever purchased. He remembered the speed restriction imposed in the late thirties or early forties which he thought was because some civilian airplanes had lost wings in flight. We will return to this subject later.

In 1939 the Army purchased three YC-43 airplanes, serial numbers 295, 296, and 297. Immediately thereafter the Navy bought serial numbers 298 through 304 (all D17S models), and designated them the GB-1. Later the Navy purchased more D17S models and gave them the designation of GB-2, and before the war ended a GB-3 was ordered, but cancelled when the war ended in 1945. Army models purchased during the war were designated the UC-43.

CHAPTER FOUR

IT TAKES A BEECHCRAFT

Beechcraft advertising in the 1930's claimed "It takes a Beechcraft to beat a Beechcraft." Air racing results of that period certainly bear that out, as we have seen, in part. I did not compile a detailed list of Beechcraft wins in air racing for one simple reason. The airplane was not designed as a racer.

But, many of them were raced—some by Beech, and some by private owners. And, the fact remains, a Beechcraft won the 1936 Bendix. Jacqueline Cochran flew her D17W to third place in the 1937 Bendix, and Max Constant took fourth in 1938 in the same airplane. He repeated this in 1939 while William Maycock flew a D17S to sixth place. Ross Hadley's D17S came in fifth in the 1938 race.

At the Miami All-American Air Races of 1936, held on December 10th through 12th, 1936, a Beechcraft C17B nosed out another Beechcraft to win the Colonel E. H. R. Green Trophy Race at 185 mph. This led to the Beech advertising slogan that "It takes a Beechcraft to beat a Beechcraft."

At the Mile-High Air Races held in Denver, Colorado on July 4th and 5th, 1936, Bill Ong flew C17R-77, NC15835, to first place for the Frank E. Phillips Trophy. This same trophy was won again in 1937 by a Beechcraft flying in the race at St. Louis, Missouri. The airplane was a D17R, and it turned in a speed of 192.4 mph.

Official race results show the various Beechcrafts turned in speeds in the 200 mph range. Some were well over 200 mph, none were far under it. This did not slow the reputation, and growing legend that the Beechcraft was a "200 mph airplane".

With speed one has problems. Remember, the Beechcraft was designed in an era of strut and wire braced biplanes.

The Beechcraft was the ultimate in biplane streamlining with its heavily faired wing-to-fuselage juncture, its single I strut, and its lack of interplane wires. It did, of course, have interplane wires, but only two landing and two flying wires.

The Beechcraft had retractable landing gear which fully retracted with nothing left hanging. It had an engine capable of pulling it to speeds in the 200 mph range. Despite its age, it is still regarded today as a fast airplane. In the 1930's, it was considered the ultimate in airplanes, and the ultimate in speed.

Speed sometimes means trouble. It did for the Beechcraft 17 as it has for a lot of airplanes.

The airplane lost a wing in flight. An inexperienced pilot trying to fly on instruments? Too much turbulence? Or, was the Beechcraft at fault? I do not know. One thing I know—the present Beech factory is very touchy on this subject, for no reason

Frank Andrews checks fuel on C17B-84 before a charter flight. Lady is the charter passenger. *(Frank G. Andrews)*

Photo given to Eddie Ross by Don Teel who then flew for Loffland Brothers. Teel later went with United States Steel as their pilot. *(E. F. Ross)*

C17L-108 at Bankstown, Australia on October 26, 1963. *(John Hopton)*

Cockpit photo showing the T control column available as optional equipment. *(C. L. Elwell)*

This photo of C17L-100 shows the landing gear in the retracted position. *(Franklin A. Higgins)*

Close-up of C17L-100 shows details of the landing gear truss. This view is of right side, looking aft. *(Franklin A. Higgins)*

that I can easily determine. A Beechcraft 17 lost a wing in flight. That is a fact, easily documented. Because of its impact on the historical side of this thing, I did considerable research on the loss of Beechcraft 17 wings in flight.

First, as near as I can document it, there were three wings failures in flight. They occurred on models with upper wing ailerons. The Beech factory blames the failure on VFR pilots flying into IFR conditions, a common occurrence today in high speed airplanes. Two of the wing failures resulted in fatalities, and I cannot rule out the VFR pilot in IFR weather theory on those two. But, the third one was in VFR weather, and I have a detailed account of it by the pilot.

Also, I have read a detailed NACA report on flutter tests on the Beechcraft 17, and it points out that flutter could, under some conditions, occur in the upper wing. Induced by the aileron, the flutter would spread to the wing, destroying it. Walter Beech himself admitted that flutter could have been the cause of the wing failures.

A discussion of flutter is outside the scope of this book, but in simple terms, flutter is a condition imposed on a structure which has too much elasticity to the point of failure of the structure, if not checked. Normally, a reduction in airspeed, if accomplished rapidly enough, will stop the flutter, and prevent destruction of the structure. The problem is that the average pilot would not recognize flutter until too late.

To prevent the possibility of flutter on the Beechcraft 17, Models D, E, and F had plywood added to the wingtips for additional stiffening, and the ailerons and flaps were balanced. Models B and C required only balancing of ailerons. After these modifications, no more flutter occurred.

On the case that I have the pilot's detailed report, the entire upper, left wing was reduced to splinters, but the wing held together. The excellent covering contained the wing structure long enough for the pilot to make a safe landing. Obviously, an excellent fabric job on an airplane isn't just for looks!

I cannot prove the wing failures were due to flutter, but so much evidence exists to support flutter as the cause of failure that I cannot entirely *buy* the VFR pilot in IFR weather theory although it must be added that a high speed spiral certainly could exceed the design limits of *any* airplane and cause wing failure, and many accidents have been attributed to this.

I don't understand the touchy attitude on this subject at Beech today. The Beechcraft Model 17 was the finest biplane ever designed and built, and was so superb an airplane that it was not until about

1960 that current models exceeded its speed and weight carrying capability. And, there are those who claim NO airplane will EVER be designed that can beat a Beechcraft 17. If I had to take sides, I would lean in this direction—it is a pilot's airplane, an airplane that a pilot likes to fly, and it turns in enough speed to satisfy anybody.

During the 1930's the Beechcraft 17 was regarded as *the* airplane—the Rolls Royce of the aeronautical set. The ability of the airplane to get in and out of small fields and still cruise at high speed made it a real workhorse as well as being a speedy showpiece.

Mr. Henry B. Hanson of Minera Frisco, S.A. in Mexico City bought an F17D in 1939. Named "El Minero" the airplane was used to make trips to the smelter at Torreon and the refinery in Monterrey, and was flown into mountain fields at elevations up to 8,000 feet regularly.

Mr. Hanson liked the airplane so well that he flew it regularly until 1946. He wrote me that he considered the Beechcraft 17 far ahead of its time, and one of the most efficient airplanes ever built.

George E. Fisk grew up in Binghamton, New York. While a boy he saw a side-show with a wild man of Borneo. The plight of the man touched his heart and he decided on the spot to become a missionary when he grew up. A Presbyterian, George Fisk became The Reverend Mr. Fisk, and joined the Christian and Missionary Alliance, at that time a body not directly affiliated with any specific church.

The CMA (Christian and Missionary Alliance) sent The Reverend Mr. Fisk, at his request, to northeast Borneo. Controlled by the Dutch, northern Borneo was a land of dense jungle, fierce rivers, and the Dyaks, native headhunters.

Travel in Borneo was by dugout canoe—overland travel through the jungle was next to impossible. But river travel was slow and dangerous. Swift currents and bone crushing rapids abound. Much portaging around dangerous water was necessary. An upriver trip of 240 miles might take two months. Downriver the trip still required nearly two weeks.

Reverend Fisk realized he could make more converts among the headhunting Dyaks if he could visit them more often. Too, his mission was called on to administer to the health of his prospective converts, and many times he would bring an ailing Dyak downriver to his base at Tandjongselor for medical treatment only to have the poor fellow die en route.

A man of determination, George Fisk hated the time consuming upriver trip to visit the Dyak villages in the interior of Borneo, and fretted at the slow portaging around fierce rapids. He felt frustration at the difficult trip downriver with a dying man. Surely, he thought, there must be a better way.

The Lord gives man solutions to his problems in various and sometimes strange ways. Completing a difficult portage on the river one day, Reverend Fisk sat down on a large rock to rest while the Dyak boys he had converted brought up the dugouts.

For no reason that he remembers now, George looked through the jungle growth to the sky. Silently and gracefully a large bird slid across the jungle opening. High above the steaming jungle and fierce rivers, the bird made his way across miles of Borneo real estate with relative ease. Suddenly, it hit him— *the sky! That was the way to travel!*

Leave the jungle and rivers to those who cared to travel slowly, and take to the sky. It *could* be done. It *had* to be done.

Elated with his new idea, George began to plan a course of action to get himself airborne. The Lord's Word, he thought, must travel on man-made wings. He must learn to fly, and bring an airplane to Borneo.

On his next furlough home, George set about the task of getting a pilot's license. It was common practice for him to go on lecture tours on his visits home to raise money for CMA and his mission in Borneo. While on these tours, George visited the local airport in each town, getting a flying lesson here and a flying lesson there. It was difficult jumping from one airplane to another—one lesson might be in an OX-5 Travel Air, the next one in an Aeronca C-3. But, George made it. Flying, to him, was just a means to an end. He attacked the problem directly and scientifically. Studying at night, he learned all he could about airplanes, engines, navigation, all that was known about the skill of flying airplanes.

Reverend Fisk spent several years getting his pilot license. It was difficult, but he was completely sold on the practical aspect of an airplane in Borneo.

There were no landing fields in the interior of Borneo, but he reasoned a seaplane could land on the infrequent smooth runs of water on the rivers. So, his training included a seaplane rating, and because of the weather Borneo had, an instrument rating. George Fisk wanted to be well prepared.

Reverend Fisk did not approach flying because of its romantic aspect, but as a practical businessman.

Unfortunately, the directors of CMA did not share his enthusiasm for air travel. On the first go-'round they turned thumbs down on the idea. Except for Dr. A. C. Snead. For many years the foreign secretary for CMA, Dr. Snead saw merit in the idea of air travel in Borneo.

But Dr. Snead alone couldn't get an airplane for George Fisk. George himself went to work on the board of directors. Fortunately he had movies and slides showing the difficulty of travel in Borneo. He

told me that these, more than anything else, helped turn the opinion of the board from one of opposition to one of reluctant tolerance. They told George he could have an airplane if he could raise the money on his lecture tours.

George had decided on the Beechcraft SE17B as the most desirable airplane for his mission in Borneo. He knew that raising enough money to buy one would be next to impossible. Dr. Snead came to his rescue, promised to help finance the airplane. So, George set out on his lecture tour, and raised half the price of the airplane. Dr. Snead provided the other half.

Airframe serial number 280 was set aside as an SE17B, to be registered as NC18778, and after its factory test flights, to be crated and shipped to Borneo.

"Borneo!" Walter Beech was fierce. What idiot had sold a Beechcraft to another idiot in Borneo? He didn't want a Beechcraft in the hands of an amateur in the jungles of Borneo. After a few hurried phone calls to CMA headquarters in New York, Beech agreed to send pilot-mechanic Ralph Smith with the crated Beachcraft to Borneo.

When the airplane arrived, Smith helped Reverend Fisk pull it out of the crates and begin the assembly.

The arrival of the airplane in Dutch controlled Borneo, a part of the Netherlands East Indies, brought on another problem—that of dealing with a firm jawed Dutch government.

First, George held a U.S. pilot license, and the Dutch had no reciprocal agreement with the United States on pilot certificates. Second, the Dutch had no other civil aircraft in Borneo, and no one to test Reverend Fisk for a Dutch pilot certificate!

George insisted he be allowed to fly the airplane. The Dutch officials just as bull-headedly said he couldn't. There appeared to be no solution until someone suggested the Dutch Navy pilots fly with George to determine if he could fly.

After the Beechcraft was assembled, George demonstrated his ability as a pilot to the Dutch Navy, and they passed him with no problem at all.

With the Dutch pilot license in his pocket, Reverend Fisk began to make trips upriver in Sam, as Beechcraft PK-SAM was called. His dream was at last realized—he was finally soaring over the jungles of Borneo like a bird.

But, unlike the birds, he still had to deal with the treacherous river. He had to select quiet runs of the river between rapids, and near to Dyak villages. The river was wide enough in most places, but high ridges and mountains followed the river so that a landing meant making a one-way, no-

The Reverend Mr. George E. Fisk, his ground crew, and "Sam". Registered in the Netherlands East Indies as PK-SAM, the Beechcraft was known to George Fisk as Sam. This shot was taken at the home base at Tandjongselor.   (Rev. George E. Fisk)

Sam at an upriver run in flood stage.   (Rev. G. E. Fisk)

Sam's ground crew.   (Rev. G. E. Fisk)

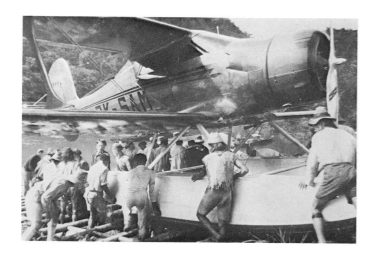

Putting Sam in the water for a trip upriver.   (Rev. G. E. Fisk)

Reverend Fisk and ground crew with Sam.   (Rev. G. E. Fisk)

return descent between the ridges to the river.

It was not like the flying he had done back in the states! There were no navigation aids, no maps, and no other civil aircraft in Borneo. Reverend Fisk had the entire skies to himself.

Going into the interior he had to remain VFR beneath the clouds, but going out he frequently climbed up through the clouds, and flew a DR (Dead Reckoning) heading until he knew he was at sea, then let down over the water. When he saw the water, he would fly underneath the clouds back to the island of Borneo, and upriver to his base at Tandjongselor, about 30 miles inland.

The first arrival of Sam at a Dyak village on the river created great consternation among the natives, and they hid in the bush. George tied Sam up along the river bank, and went out to see the Dyaks. Slowly he was able to persuade them to come see his "new dugout" that could fly like a bird. In time the airplane lost its strangeness to them, and to a people who had never seen an automobile, train, or indoor toilet, the Beechcraft became as accepted to them as their poison darts and head trophies.

Reverend Fisk remembered one old chief who held out, and would not go near the Beechcraft. After many trips to his village, George was able to get him down to the river, where Sam was tied up to a dock of logs. Slowly the old man stepped up on Sam's lower wing, peered into the cabin. "Where is the stove?" he asked. George said there was none. The old chief snorted and stepped down, "This house is no good without a stove!".

To his mind the Beechcraft was George's house, and no house was complete without a stove. His Dyak mind, filled with the theory of headhunting and poison darts, could not comprehend the airplane.

At his regular stops on the river the natives built primitive ramps to pull the seaplane ashore. Where the ground rose too steeply from the water, they built docks by tieing logs together.

The Beechcraft was blamed for everything. If a Dyak got the itch, it was on account of Sam. If the rice crop failed the year George flew over it, it was his fault. The Dyaks lived under a canopy of fear. They couldn't move without consulting spirits. They were afraid to go out in the morning without looking to see which direction a chicken hawk was flying. If it was the wrong direction they had to go back inside for three days, and couldn't fish or work in the rice fields. George's teaching of Christianity changed that. Of some sixty thousand Dyaks in the northeast section of Borneo, about five thousand were converted to Christianity. Christianity freed them from the old beliefs, and helped them accept George and his airplane.

In Dutch controlled colonial Borneo, the Dyaks had a sultan, paid by the Dutch. They felt satisfied they ran their own country. Reverend Fisk told me the colonial possessions in all of southeast Asia fared well under colonial rule, and in fact had many advantages they do not have today. For example, eligible natives were sent home to Holland to attend college at Dutch expense. The idea was to train them to eventually run Borneo and the Netherlands East Indies by themselves. But, not in too much of a hurry—not until they were completely capable of it, and that would have been about 100 years—certainly not by 1966.

PK-SAM was built in May, 1939; probably was delivered to Borneo and flying by August of that year. Since the early thirties, the Dutch on Borneo had been expecting some sort of war or attack from the Japanese. Japanese were all over southeast Asia, ostensibly to study the habits of fish to expand Japan's fishing industry. But everyone knew better. The Japanese were getting information to help them in World War Two.

Late in 1941 the CMA sent Fred Jackson out to Borneo to relieve Reverend Fisk so that George could take a furlough. Jackson was a pilot, and George checked him out in Sam, and turned the airplane over to him just days before Pearl Harbor. George got on a boat, and made it back to the United States, but Fred Jackson did not fare so well.

Just before the Japs moved into Borneo, Fred flew Sam to the interior with the last bit of gasoline on hand, then returned to the coast by dugout. The Japanese captured him, but promised to set him free if he would bring the airplane out of the interior. They gave him gasoline, and he set out for the interior.

Fred returned to Pudjungan with the gasoline to fly Sam back to Tandjongselor as the Japs had ordered him, but the Dutch seized the airplane at Poedjoengan. Rather than let Sam fall into Jap hands, the Dutch burned her. Fred took refuge at an interior Dutch outpost. Not long afterwards, the Japs took the outpost, and killed Fred and all the missionaries in the area.

Today the memory of Sam and Borneo are clearly etched in the mind of Reverend Mr. George Fisk. He says he never had any desire to fly beyond helping him travel in Borneo, and he tries to indicate that airplanes were, to him, just machines like the dugout canoes of Borneo. But, his references to Sam are far too personal not to have felt some respect for the airplane, and some closeness to flying beyond its being just a mode of transportation. Airplanes are inanimate objects. All of us know that. But, sometimes they take on a character and a person-

ality we cannot easily explain — sometimes they appear to have souls. We know they cannot. Yet, we fly with them, and we survive turmoil and strife with them, and we feel close to them, and we leave them in a war and they are burned, and we call them Sam.

* * *

Ephraim Watkins Cleveland was born on November 5, 1889 at Naples, New York. He learned to fly in the years before World War One. After the war he settled in Cleveland, Ohio, became a vice president of the Cleveland Pneumatic Tool Company making landing gear oleo struts.

Known by almost everyone as "Pop" Cleveland, he was active in aviation circles, and flew several airplanes in pursuit of his business with Cleveland Pneumatic Tool. Known as "Miss Aerol," the first four were an open cockpit Waco, a Ryan B1, a Travel Air, and a Stinson. "Miss Aerol No. 5" was a Beechcraft F17D, serial number 230. Pop Cleveland flew this airplane until after World War Two, when he purchased "Miss Aerol No. 6," a Beechcraft Bonanza.

In August, 1952 veteran of the skies Pop Cleveland left us. His Bonanza slammed into fog shrouded Mount Baldy, 30 miles southeast of Seattle, Washington, and an aviation pioneer died. With him were his wife Lucille, and his secretary of many years. Annabelle Elmslie. He did little to further Staggerwing history—his being and existence are noted here because he flew a Beechcraft, and because he was a pioneer. He belonged to a breed that we have too few of today.

"A buck well spent on a Springmaid sheet" was an advertisement of the Springs Cotton Mills of Lancaster, South Carolina. The ad pictured an Indian maid lying on a hammock made of a Springmaid sheet, and an Indian buck getting off the hammock. Such advertising was sponsored and pushed by young Elliot White Springs, an ex-World War One fighter pilot, and publisher of the famed "War Birds," a moving story of the fighter pilot's life in World War One.

Like Pop Cleveland, Colonel Springs is mentioned here only because he flew a Beechcraft (F17D-225, NC285Y). And, like Pop Cleveland, he was a pioneer.

Beechcraft D17A, s/n 357 was sold to the Research Foundation of Armour Institute of Technology in Chicago, Illinois. It was flown on their Antarctic expedition, and is the only Beechcraft known to have visited that continent. Operated on skiis, the airplane performed satisfactorily, and little else is known about its use on that expedition. It was later sold to E. J. Connellan of Alice Springs,

Central Australia for use in charter work. Before Mr. Connellan got it, World War Two intervened, and the airplane was used in RAAF service, returning to Mr. Connellan after the war.

A lady named Edna Whyte purchased a C17B in the late 1930's, and from the logbook entries, she flew it almost daily. Her area of operation was in Louisiana and Mississippi with occasional trips into Texas. One time she couldn't get the gear down. Circling the airport, she retracted the gear, then extended it again. No soap, it wouldn't go down. After several cycles, she finally got it down and locked.

Once on the ground, another Beechcraft 17 owner told her to clean the gear slide tubes and put graphite on them. Which advice she followed and never had any more trouble with the landing gear. But, she said, "I was always covered with graphite!".

Later, when Edna sold the airplane, she checked out the new owner by riding the right seat, and reaching over to his side to make corrections on the throw-over control wheel. She said it wasn't easy, but it could be done if you were agile, and very fast with your corrections. Before, she added, the neophyte tore the airplane up.

In 1965 I visited the Columbus, Georgia airport, and met Edna. She was flying a Beech Musketeer. It was our first meeting, and we immediately began to chit-chat about old airplanes. She had a scrapbook along, and told me the short tales I have just related to you. Then, she opened the scrapbook, and showed me a photo of the Beechcraft. It was NC17072.

NC17072 was the Beechcraft I owned in the mid-1950's. When I had it, it was a C17L with the 225 hp Jacobs engine. *Why did I ever sell that airplane?*

In the turmoil of the late 1930's, when half the world was preparing for war, Beechcrafts were selling to far-off India, and down-under Australia. Two C17 models went down-under, and Indian National Airways purchased several E17B models for passenger and cargo hauling over their difficult routes. Painted silver and trimmed in Consolidated Blue, the Indian National Airways Beechcrafts were purchased primarily because of their ability to operate into the small, rough fields in India. Carrying capacity loads on most of their runs, the Beechcrafts were favored by Indian pilots.

In the year 1936 one William H. Clyde bought out Bob Six's interest in the San Francisco, California aviation firm of Mouton and Six. It therefore became Mouton and Clyde. They sold Beechcrafts in northern California and Nevada, and later added the Luscombe line.

Monte Mouton was an Army pilot in World War

E. E. "Monte" Mouton on left with radio inventor Henry Wolff.
(William H. Clyde)

Neal Monroe with one of the Staggerwings sold to him by Mouton and Clyde. He is pointing to the wooden skid on the underside of the wing which was designed to protect the belly of the airplane in a wheels-up landing. (William H. Clyde)

Shirley and Bill Clyde in front of a Mouton and Clyde demonstrator. (William H. Clyde)

SD17S, CF-DTF, photographed at anchor. Staggerwing on floats made a good bush airplane. (Leo J. Kohn)

Mouton and Cylde D17R (s/n 405) with a special paint scheme. (William H. Clyde)

E. W. "Pop" Cleveland, a dapper man.
(Cleveland Pneumatic Tool Co.)

One, and was one of the first airmail pilots. He was one of the early pioneers flying the DeHavilland DH-4 on the transcontinental air mail routes. By the time he operated Mouton and Clyde, I would describe him as quite the dapper fellow, wearing a moustache, and dressed sharply in the very latest fad. Always the salesman, he was a colorful figure on the west coast in the 1930's.

Bill Clyde was more the quiet type. He described some of the Beechcraft owners in California to me. Will Tevis, he said, was the man who bought Bill's favorite demonstrator. A well known polo player, he used the Beechcraft to fly to matches, often startling the spectators by landing right on the polo field. He owned a ranch north of San Francisco with a short, narrow landing strip.

Bill said Carl Johnson's strip at Zephyr Cove on Lake Tahoe in Nevada was real tricky. With a dog-leg run, you were operating at 6,200 feet above sea level on a field just barely large enough for a fly. Landings were made towards the mountains; take-offs towards the lake, regardless of the wind. As Bill said, "This could make it pretty interesting." Though Bill didn't say so, I would imagine the sale of a Beechcraft to Carl Johnson involved a demonstration flight into Johnson's airstrip to see if the Beechcraft could make it. By then, high altitude, short field operations were a moot point with a Beechcraft.

Two other well known Beechcraft owners that Mouton and Clyde sold airplanes to were Fred Talbot and Neal Monroe. Talbot was in the lumber and shipping business, and Monroe originally came from Quincy, Illinois, and used his Beechcraft to visit his business interests in Quincy. One might say he commuted from San Francisco to Quincy in his Staggerwing.

Bill Clyde sent me some old factory sales literature which included a price list dated April 1, 1940. I thought it might interest the reader to see what Beechcrafts were selling for back then;

E17B ......$12,380 ($9,190 less engine and prop)
F17D ......$13,980 ($9,190 less engine and prop)
D17A $16,350
D17S ......$18,870 ($12,900 less engine and prop)
D17R ......$18,870 ($12,900 less engine and prop)

Seaplane versions sold for about $4,000 more than the landplane. The price list contained information on finish and colors available, and on interiors. The standard finish was a solid color fuselage with a contrasting or complimentary Beechcraft bird striping.

Parachutes, built into the seats, were available at prices from $290 to $325. It is interesting to note, on the optional equipment list that almost all prices were rounded off to the nearest dollar with only one or two items showing a fraction of a dollar.

Standard interior was Chase or Laidlaw upholstery fabrics plus genuine leather lower sidewalls. Genuine leather on seats, sidewalls, and ceiling (the entire cabin) was available for only $60.

One of the items of sales literature contained a testimonial letter from a Beechcraft owner which I think is worth quoting here. He was flying from Cincinnati, Ohio to Paducah, Kentucky. After passing Owensboro he was caught by darkness. He had no previous night flying experience, and the airplane was not equipped with landing lights. He wrote, "I was able to locate Paducah airport from the Department of Commerce description and from a car's flashing lights which we found to be our nephew waiting to meet us. . . . To keep from losing sight of the hangar I pulled into a tight turn and cut the gun to make the approach in a *full power stall* (italics mine . . Author) high enough over the hangar to avoid any possible unlisted pole lines. . . . We hit the ground solidly, but not too hard, and I instantly gave it all the brakes it would take and as soon as our speed was sufficiently lessened, turned sharply just in case there might be fences or trees ahead that I could not see. . . . I went out the next morning to see where we had landed and found that from the point where the wheels touched the grass until we turned was 135 feet." A *short* landing, wouldn't you say?

Frank G. "Jerry" Andrews told me the Mouton and Clyde organization was one of the few business-like aviation sales companies during the thirties. Jerry worked for them for a while. When he sold NC15841 to Charles Hooper Crosby, Jerry went with the airplane as Mr. Crosby's pilot.

* * *

World War Two brought an end to civilian production at Beech—just as it did to most other industries. But, it did not end Beechcraft 17 production. Army and Navy versions of the Beechcraft 17 were produced through 1944.

Known to the Army as the UC-43 series and to the Navy and Marines as the GB-1, -2 series, their principal use was transporting personnel. Navy and Marine models were normally assigned to station commanders. Colonel Karl E. Voelter remembers that, as the Commanding Officer of Marine Corps Air Station (MCAS), El Centro, California during World War Two, he had four of them assigned. You may remember he was one of the pilots

Beech factory about 1937. Flat area in upper right is the flying field.   (Beech Photo)

F17D-392, NC12922, on takeoff.   (William T. Larkins)

Pilot Ray W. Brown poses in front of General Tire's Beech. Both the airplane and Brown went into the Navy in World War Two. Neither survived the war.   (General Tire and Rubber Co.)

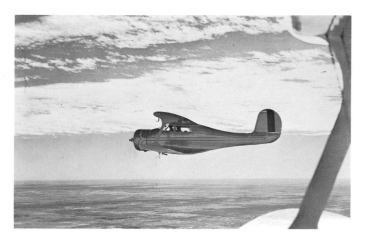

Two photos of a Staggerwing in flight. This was a D17S airplane sold to Brazil.   (C. L. Elwell)

Walter Pidgeon and Myrna Loy on the wing of an SB17L on Hollywood movie set. The airplane was used in a number of movies made by MGM. *(Beech Photo)*

E17B instrument panel showing the optional T control column. Though typical of the original E17B instrument panel, this one has much modern equipment added by Ed Burger in the early 1960's. Wheel on the vertical part of the T column is the elevator trim tab. *(Ed Burger)*

Cockpit photo of the first Model 18. Notice similarity of instrument panel and control wheels to Model 17. *(Howard A. Jones)*

74

Yes, this is a Beechcraft 17. The pilot took off with the baggage door open. When he returned to land a student in a Porterfield taking off from a crossing direction barged right in front of the Beechcraft. The pilot slammed the power on to go around, torque took over, the Beechcraft dug a wingtip, and here is the result. No injuries!   *(Earl C. Reed)*

SD17S going into the water. Note the ventral fin which the lower powered seaplanes like the SB17L did not require. Also, this airplane has the optional paint job.   *(C. L. Elwell)*

Workers assemble the Beechcraft 17. The job was one of expert hand crafting which resulted in a tough, unbeatable airplane.
(Beech Photo)

An E17B (s/n 336) sold to Indian National Airways.   *(Beech Photo)*

D17W-164, Jacqueline Cochran's airplane.   *(Leo J. Kohn)*

Ross Hadley with his D17S, s/n 199, on right, and taking off, above. Both Hadley and his airplane were colorful characters, participated in many air races in the late 1930's.

(Peter M. Bowers)

who flew NC499N (s/n 1) at Miami, Florida in January, 1933.

Colonel Voelter said the Marine Corps had few restrictions on their use by qualified pilots. However, one of the four assigned to MCAS El Centro was considered Colonel Voelter's own airplane.

Military pilots who flew the UC-43 and GB-1, -2 airplanes remember them as fondly as though they were their own privately owned machines. William C. "Dub" Yarbrough (see G17S, s/n B-3 in Part II), a Navy pilot in World War Two, told me he flew a high ranking Navy officer around in one, vowed he'd someday have his own. Today he owns G17S, N44G, s/n B-3.

Lieutenant Colonel Charles D. Moore remembers flying one as a First Lieutenant in the Philippines. He said they were regarded as fast airplanes, and were used for administrative flights mostly.

Many of the Beechcraft 17's were sold lend-lease to such countries as Brazil and England during the war. Prince Bernhard of the Netherlands had one assigned to him as his personal airplane, and was very fond of it.

When World War Two ended in 1945, the military Beechcraft 17's, like other airplanes and equipment, became surplus to military needs, and were sold. A large number of the Beechcraft 17's were turned over to the Civil Aeronautics Administration, and were not sold surplus until as late as 1948-50.

Beech built more 17 models for the military in World War Two than they built for civilian sale from 1932 through 1941. For this reason the largest number of Beechcraft 17's remaining in service today are ex-WWII D17S airplanes.

As World War Two came to a close, two things happened at Beech. First, a small group of designers worked at night and on weekends designing a post war replacement for the Beechcraft 17.

The war had focused attention on the air—some of the most spectacular exploits of the war had been in the air. This, and the technical improvements made in aviation during the war, caused many to speculate that everybody would want an airplane after the war. There was much talk about a "family" airplane . . . a family "flivver of the air." The men at Beech were more practical.

They realized that no such development was likely to take place—that a suitable replacement for the model 17 had to offer basically the same things the 17 had given its customers, i.e. speed, comfort, and economy. Therefore the new airplane was designed to carry four people as fast as was thought economically feasible. Great speed is possible if one is willing to pay for it in fuel consumed, but a businessman is more likely to look for reasonable economy with reasonable speed. The Beech designers felt a little less speed than the model 17 had would be acceptable if there was an accompanying amount of increased economy of operation.

Thus, the new design was to have a 165 hp engine (185 hp for takeoff), be a low-wing monoplane, and use a radical new empennage section. Tests with the Beech AT-10 military trainer had proven the feasibility of a "V" tail with no horizontal or vertical surfaces, but two surfaces arranged in a wide "V" which would function as both a horizontal and vertical control surface.

Henry B. Hanson's F17D, "El Minero". The airplane was s/n 334, XB-AGO. Mr. Hanson used the airplane in his mining business for seven years, 1939 to 1946. When I wrote to him in 1963 he was very helpful, and supplied four excellent photographs of "El Minero". I regret that space doesn't allow the reader to see the other three. *(Henry B. Hanson)*

The first Army Staggerwing, D17S-295, known to the Army as YC-43 s/n 39-139.   *(Beech Photo)*

CHAPTER FIVE
A LEGEND REBORN

During World War Two Beech production centered on military versions of its model 17 and 18, the special military (Army) AT-10, and subcontracting on such projects as building Douglas A-26 wing sections, and the fabulous XA-38 proposal near the end of the war.

As peace loomed on the horizon at the end of 1945, civilian aviation prophets forecast new aviation engines, new propellers, new radios, and new airplane designs. Everyone would want an airplane —the world had just experienced the war to end all wars, and everything would begin all over again, and brand new.

(Most people, in 1945, forgot one thing — the Communists. As we ended World War Two, the Communists in Moscow quietly began World War Three. It has been going on ever since.)

While Beech worked on a new single engine monoplane for the postwar market, and revised their model 18 for civilian production, a small group at the Beech factory took D17 s/n 424, and began certain modifications to it.

First, they removed the engine cowling, lengthened the engine mount, and installed an engine cowling similar to the new model 18 cowl. Next, they redesigned the vertical fin and rudder to have a slightly different outline—almost like the D17S,

but changed just a hair. The third major change was to the landing gear wheel fairings. Everything else on the airplane remained identical to the D17S.

This new model 17 was known as the G17S, and would be produced, mainly for nostalgic reasons, only on specific customer order. The new Beech single engine monoplane would be their production airplane, the G17S would be offered only as a custom built machine.

Miners call a gold or silver strike with a high ore yield, a "bonanza." The word has come to mean anything with a high monetary yield. Certainly a gold or silver ore with a high yield would bring in lots of money.

It is difficult to predict, in the early life of an airplane, that it will bring in a high monetary yield to its builder. Nevertheless, the new Beech single engine monoplane was named the "Bonanza," and assigned model number 35.

The big jump in model numbers from the models 17 and 18 to the 35 can be taken up, in part, from military contracts during the war, and from the experimental model 34. But, it is likely that some numbers were skipped. Whatever the case, the new Beech design was the model 35, introduced in 1946, and still in production twenty years later! That it has proven a real "Bonanza" to Beech would be an the 59th Street bridge. If he was heavy, he had to go under it. He said he has seen passengers turn green before reaching 125th Street!

Bill said, "This wonderful airplane took that abuse year after year and never gave any trouble, and the maintenance was less than one would expect." Bill's Staggerwing had a payload of 1273 pounds, cruised at 130 mph indicated, and had six hours range.

He never worried about the load he had. If he didn't happen to have any scales along, his only concern was ". . . can I get the doors shut?" If he could, he went, and he claims the load or weight never seemed to make much difference.

Bill operated the Staggerwing until 1956. He felt that the present day all metal airplanes on floats aren't up to the standards his Staggerwing set.

Two brothers in California owned Staggerwings in the post-War period. They were Strafford and Hampden Wentworth. They both owned several, and flew them all over the United States, into Mexico, Central, and South America.

Hampden, a Navy fighter pilot in World War Two, made one 18,000 mile trip into South America, and his brother Strafford sent me the figures on it. I thought they would be interesting to those of you who might be thinking of buying a Staggerwing. The trip was made in June, 1951, so any cost figures are prices charged in 1951. The airplane was a D17S.

Total miles flown 18,133
Total flying hours 109.5
Average speed . . . . 165.6 mph
Total fuel consumed . . . . 2484 U.S. gallons
Total oil consumed . . . . 234 quarts
Fuel and Oil cost/hour $8.26
Fuel and Oil
    cost/mile . . . . . $0.0499 (about 5¢ per mile)

Strafford made a similar trip with a fuel and oil cost/mile of 5.3¢, and an average speed of 150 mph.

In July, 1954 Hampden made a flight across the North Atlantic to Europe on a combination business and pleasure trip in his D17S. At the time he was president of Longren Aircraft in Torrance, California, and the business part of the trip was to further sales of Longren's products in Europe. On July 29th, after his arrival in London, he wrote a letter to the executives at Longren about the trip across the North Atlantic. I will quote some from it—not so much to show how wonderful the Staggerwing is as to record the tremendous faith young Hampden Wentworth had, not only in the Staggerwing, but in aviation in general.

Hampden was concerned that the officials of Longren, and the public, might consider his flight a "dare-devil" stunt. He wrote, "The greatest deterrent to the modern, small aircraft's growth is that all of us like to think of ourselves as pioneers, veritable Lindberghs. This adds charm and drama to the daily flight accomplishments, however, it creates an aura of danger which is nonexistent."

On the trip across the water Hampden felt he had many advantages over a similar trip in some parts of the United States. He reminded the Longren executives that he had survival gear, that the airplane would float on the water long enough for he and his wife Christina to inflate their rubber boat, that the Air Force rescue airplanes would be out looking for them within one hour after they became overdue, and that they were wearing clothing to protect them in the cold North Atlantic. But, he considered an engine failure remote. He wrote, "We were behind the most reliable engine ever built, and had three hours of fuel to spare."

Hampden was anxious to have the flight considered a routine general aviation flight; that such flights could be made by any pilot of average intelligence who took the time to plan carefully, and who carried adequate survival equipment.

Both of the Wentworth brothers were tremendous boosters of general aviation, and the Beechcraft model 17. It is tragic and ironic that a Staggerwing should take the life of one of them. On the afternoon of February 2, 1960, Hampden Wentworth and his wife Christina attempted a takeoff from a short, muddy field at mile-high Reserve, New Mexico. Despite the tremendous power of the Wasp engine, the Staggerwing could not clear a juniper tree on the end of the field, and crashed into a canyon wall just beyond the end of the runway. Hampden and Christina were killed instantly, and Beechcraft s/n 284, NC19468, was demolished.

Hampden Wentworth had flown Staggerwings for 3,440 hours. He was a strong general aviation enthusiast who believed there was no end to the ways in which an airplane could be used to further one's business, and increase one's pleasure. He proved this on his flight to Europe and on his several flights into the southern hemisphere. He was only thirty-nine when he lost his life—his greatest potential was yet to come.

The Hacienda de Carretas is in the state of Chihuahua in old Mexico. It is a cattle ranch operated by Quinn G. Boyd. Mr. Boyd lives in El Paso—he uses a D17S built in 1944 (s/n 6904, registered in Mexico as XB-PAN) to commute between the Hacienda de Carretas and El Paso. He bought the airplane in 1955, has been using it continuously ever since.

The Hacienda de Carretas airstrip is 2,000 feet in

length with an elevation of 5,000 feet. Fortunately it has clear approaches. But, Quinn says, there are many strips with high hills on one end which means the pilot can't change his mind once committed.

Quinn had one comment about the Staggerwing's landing characteristics that I'd like to quote verbatim, "The Staggerwing has a reputation among some people as being prone to ground loop easily. I have never even had a close call with mine. An old timer gave me a piece of advice that I imagine holds true with any aircraft. (It certainly does . . . Author) This advice was simply to hold it straight during the complete landing roll as well as the take-off roll."

Operating into unimproved fields presents certain hazards, as Mr. Boyd found out on one occasion when he returned home with a vesicular volcanic rock stuck through the fabric of the horizontal stabilizer. Being of light weight, the rock had been thrown into the stabilizer by the prop blast.

He also found out that an open baggage door causes severe empennage buffeting when he took off one time with it open. Keeping the speed down to 100 mph, he returned and landed. There was no damage to the airplane.

As I have mentioned before, the Staggerwing is widely quoted as being a "200 mph airplane." It might be, but an average pilot flying an average D17S, D17R, or C17S is going to have a lower true airspeed than 200 mph. Mr. Boyd sent me some performance figures based on a load of pilot, two passengers, and 60 gallons of fuel. The abbreviations are: Alt. is altitude. Temp. is temperature in degrees centigrade. MAP is manifold pressure in inches of mercury absolute. RPM is engine RPM. IAS is indicated airspeed, and TAS is true airspeed.

Alt	Temp	MAP	RPM	IAS	TAS
5000	+20	26	1950	164	182
10,000	+5	25.5	1925	157	186

Mr. Boyd says his fuel consumption runs about 24 gallons per hour for most cruising power settings. Which seems to be about right for the 450 hp P&W.

Quinn G. Boyd's Staggerwing, like many, is still a working airplane. Unlike many airplanes built in the 1930's, the Staggerwing still serves its owners as a method of fast transportation able to get into and out of, small airports at high elevations.

Going back for a moment to the performance of a D17S, Robert H. Bell wrote me that his D17S indicates about 150-155 mph with 27" Hg manifold pressure and 1950 RPM and burns about 22 gallons per hour. Which is in line with Quinn Boyd's figures. Bob Bells says, "As for flying, the plane has no equal. Stall is beautiful. Landing is *no* problem if

you forget the military manual. I fly final at 75 and slow her down to 65 over the fence and three-point everytime. The landings are so smooth that sometimes it is difficult to tell touchdown. And there is *no* tendency to ground loop. Most pilots bring these planes in too fast and wheel land. But, as you know, this plane was designed in the days of short, grass strips. Fly it that way, and you'll have no problems." I concur! !

Jack K. Crall has been with Western Airlines twenty-six years. He has the Three See Ranch in Elizabeth, Colorado. His proudest possession is a Beechcraft D17S, s/n 4829, N1255N. Like many of the old timers, Jack Crall feels the Staggerwing is a pilot's airplane. He uses it primarily for cross country flying and for checking pastures on the ranch.

Jack says the Staggerwing's high altitude performance makes it an ideal airplane for use on his ranch's 6500 foot high strip, and crossing the Great Divide is no problem with the Staggerwing.

"The Old Man of The Mountains", Bill Woods of Boise, Idaho put in 5,000 hours flying Staggerwings into Idaho's primitive area where the fields are short, one-way level spots on the side of a canyon wall. Bill liked the Staggerwing because of its excellent short field performance on strips four and five thousand feet above sea level. Bill owns a D17S, originally owned the D17S, and a D17A. He sold the D17A to Bill Humphreys of Mackay Bar on the main Salmon River in Idaho.

Bill Humphreys lives and works at a hunting and fishing lodge at Mackay Bar. He uses the D17A Staggerwing to haul hunters and fishermen into the lodge, and has even used it to bring building supplies in.

Bill Humphrey's friend, Jack Hoke of Boise, Idaho, a former Staggerwing owner, used his airplane in his real estate business, and for fishing trips into Idaho's primitive area. He said, "There are few ships that will out-perform the Staggerwing." And, he should know—he flew into 1,000 to 1,500 foot strips 4,000 feet above sea level in his Staggerwing.

Another pilot who regularly uses a Staggerwing for back country work in Idaho's primitive area is L. G. McCarley of Blackfoot Flying Service in Blackfoot, Idaho. He says, "The Beech is a dependable workhorse on fields of high elevation and short length."

Back in 1940, earning flying time was difficult, and time consuming. Robert H. Woodard went to work as a lineboy for Mountain States Aviation in Denver earning six hours of flight instruction per month. Wonder how many young boys today would work a month just for six hours of flight instruc-

The first G17S (ex-D17S, s/n 424) in final configuration.

(Beech Photo)

Left to right, Mr. Manning of Manning Drilling Company, Mr. Hardison, and Bob Woodard with G17S NC80306 on May 15, 1948, the first day Bob flew for General Petroleum.
(Robert H. Woodard)

Bob Woodard poses beside empennage of G17S NC80306, the airplane he flew for General Petroleum.

(Robert H. Woodard)

Mackay Bar airstrip on the Main Salmon River in Idaho.
(Bill Humphreys)

The silence of winter in the Sawtooth Range, broken only by the thundering of a Staggerwing. This is Bear Valley where the headwaters of the Middle Fork of the Salmon lie.
(Bill Humphreys)

Bill Humphrey's D17A and grandson at Mackay Bar on the Main Salmon River. *(Bill Humphreys)*

Typical mountain airstrip. This is Pistol Creek on the Middle Fork of the Salmon River in Idaho. *(Jack Hoke)*

Sally Sweetbriar II, a G17S, s/n B-2, NC80303. *(C. L. Elwell)*

G17S s/n B-12 delivered in Stearman Vermilion and Insignia Blue to Furrow and Company. *(C. L. Elwell)*

guess I've already had too much!"

Bob had been thinking of going into business for himself as the operator of a small airport, and around April, 1948 he resigned from the Sweetbriar company. Ray C. "Skeets" Barker, who was then flying Manning Drilling Company's Beechcraft 18, asked Bob if he would like a job flying a G17S out of Casper, Wyoming for General Petroleum Corp, the west coast affiliate of Socony Vacuum Oil Company. Skeets was helping General Petroleum get their aircraft fleet into operation.

Bob never got his small airport—in May of 1948 he went on the General Petroleum payroll flying their G17S, NC80306. Bob flew around the west for several years in the Staggerwing, and flies the DC-3 today for Mobil International out of Tripoli, Libya.

Bob flew the Beechcraft, as he prefers to call it, over three thousand hours, and considers it one of the best airplanes he has ever flown. He said one of the fastest speeds he ever recorded was on a cross-country trip from Denver, Colorado to Lynchburg, Virginia in Sally Sweetbriar II. They covered the 1400 miles non-stop in six hours flat, an average speed of 233 mph. Flying at 13,000 feet on a cloudless November day, he averaged an astounding 285 mph from abeam Kansas City to Louisville.

Bob liked the name Beechcraft, said it always sounded more dignified than Staggerwing, and I agree. Any old timer will know what airplane you're talking about if you say "the Beechcraft", but today Beech builds so many models that the name Staggerwing is more often used when referring to the Model 17.

All 20 of the G17S models were built in 1946, but not all were assembled and sold that year. The last one was put together and sold in either 1948 or 1949. When the last one rolled out the factory door it marked the end of an era—the era of biplanes, of flying wires, struts, flying off grass fields, leather helmets and goggles, castor oil, and a glint of sun off hand-rubbed, fabric wings doped to a drumhead tightness. The growl of the last Staggerwing's 450 Wasp engine signalled the end of the romantic period in aviation history.

For almost a decade—until near the end of the 1950's—about the only Staggerwings flying were those flown by businessmen, aerial photographers, mountain charter pilots, and an aerial applicator in Australia who used his to put out grass seed.

Then, in the late 1950's a few antique airplane fans began finding old Staggerwings and restoring them. Unlike the average antique whose usefulness was generally confined to pleasure flying, the Beechcraft 17 was an antique that could serve as a fast, comfortable, cross-country airplane.

Lt. Tim Grier of the United States Navy owned B17L-8 for a little over a year—he purchased the airplane because she was both an antique, and an antique that could turn in acceptable cross country performance. His wife tells the story of how Lt. Tim Grier purchased "Windsong", as they called B17L-8, much better than either he or I could do it. She wrote, "One evening my husband came home with a yellow paper full of airplane advertisements (Trade-A-Plane . . . Author), and proceeded to sit in his chair all evening reading it." Some weeks later, she explained, Tim announced they would go look at an airplane on the coming weekend.

Came the weekend, "When we reached our destination, a dusty old hangar outside a dusty little Texas town, I was almost afraid to look as the hangar doors were opened. The whole airport had an air of the early days of flying about it. As I looked into the open hangar time might just as well have slipped back thirty years. There stood a lovely big, old biplane in all of her majesty. Her sleek lines gave her a dignity transcending the dust which covered her wings and fuselage. She was so sleek in her design that she seemed to be misplaced in time."

That was early in 1961, and in that dusty old hangar began a year-long romance between Tim Grier, his wife Jean and Windsong, the B17L. Because of transfers in the Navy, and other commitments, they only owned the airplane a little over a year, but in that year they pretty well covered the United States on weekend flights.

Ed Burger of Sidney, New York is another antique airplane lover whose E17L Staggerwing provides fast cross-country transportation. Ed bought his in poor condition, spent some time rebuilding it. He has flown it now for about seven years on trips all over the United States. He said he normally cruises his between 60 and 65% power on the 225 Jacobs engine, and gets around 150 mph TAS (True Airspeed) with a fuel consumption of about 15 gallons per hour.

Ed says he likes the way a Staggerwing feels in flight, and considers it a good instrument ship although he doesn't do much IFR flying in it.

Unlike a lot of Staggerwing owners, William C. "Dub" Yarbrough owns his for the simple joy of owning a beautiful thing. He flew a GB-2 in the Navy in World War Two, bought a D17S in the late 1950's. Today he owns G17S s/n B-3, N44G. Painted a deep maroon and red, N44G is the most beautiful Staggerwing in existence. I have not seen John Church's G17S, nor L.B. Maytag Jr.'s G17S, but they'd have to be something to outdo N44G on looks, inside and out.

Dub Yarbrough's airplane is obviously beautiful

Dr. Roy G. Larson in his D17S (s/n 6670, N947OH) makes a takeoff over the photographer just for our benefit. *(Dr. Roy G. Larson)*

G17S (s/n B-2) cabin interior. *(C. L. Elwell)*

D17S-424 converted to a G17S was actually the first G17S, but airplane pictured here was first production G17S, s/n B-1, NC80302. Called in Part II of this book, the Cuban Dominican Beechcraft, the airplane actually went to the Cuban Dominican Sales Company, a sugar company. Man standing in front of the airplane is their pilot, Ed Burgin. *(C. L. Elwell)*

The first G17S (s/n 424) in flight. *(Joe Juptner)*

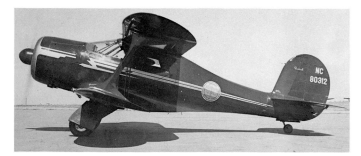

G17S s/n B-11 turning up. This airplane went to the Nebraska Department of Aeronautics. *(C. L. Elwell)*

Factory personnel inspect G17S s/n 424 after a wheels-up landing. *(Henry B. DeSpain)*

G17S s/n B-3, at the factory before delivery. Today the airplane carries the same paint trim although it has been recovered since original delivery. *(C. L. Elwell)*

D17S s/n 4922 in Australia. *(Richard C. Seeley)*

Bill Mellor's SE17B tied up at the dock. *(William Mellor)*

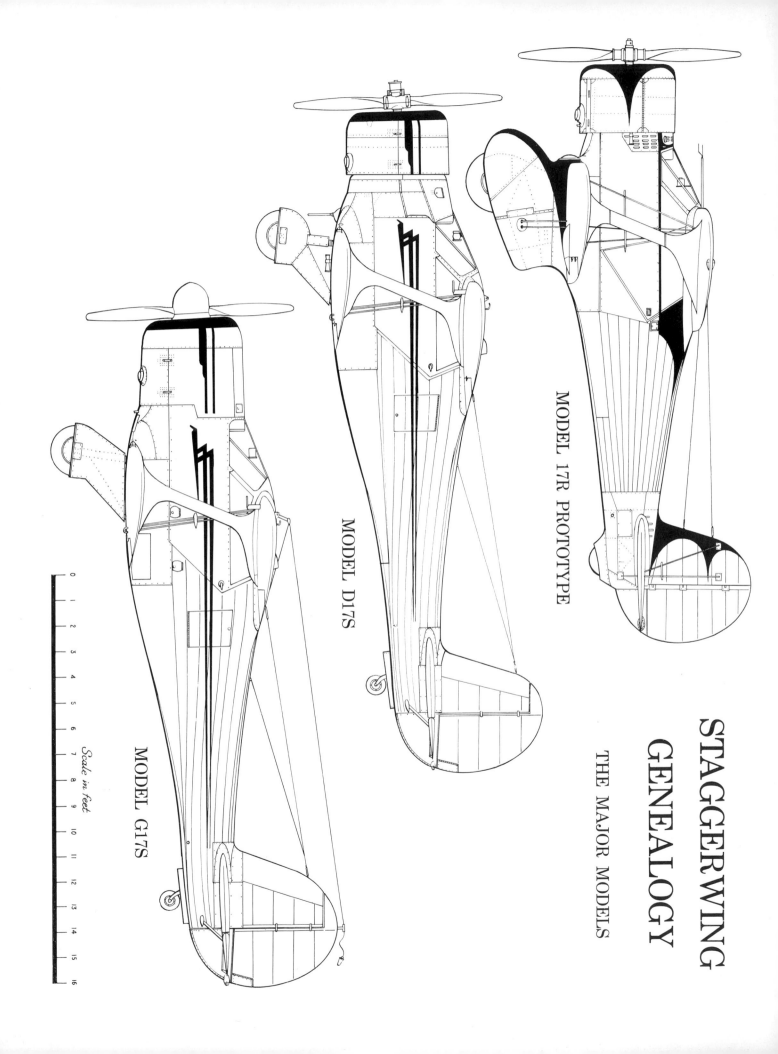

STAGGERWING
GENEALOGY
THE MAJOR MODELS

MODEL 17R PROTOTYPE

MODEL D17S

MODEL G17S

Scale in feet

0 1 2 3 4 5 6 7 8 9 10 11 12 13 14 15 16

G17S, s/n B-1, the first production G17S.

on the outside with its highly polished finish, but the cabin interior is even more impressive. The seats and cabin are done in expensive cloth and real leather. Even the control column and wheel are leather covered. The instrument panel, with eyebrow lighting on the instruments, and a full set of radio gear, is finished in a yellowish gold crackle finish.

Dub is president of the National Staggerwing Club which had its first annual convention in Wichita, Kansas in September, 1965. The second convention was held at Wichita in July, 1966. It promises to be an annual affair, with Staggerwings flying in from all over.

Robert C. Ellis, a veteran of the famed Bloody Hundredth, owns an ex-Navy Staggerwing which he uses for business and pleasure travel in South America. Bob works for a bank in Cartagena, Columbia, has flown his Staggerwing all over South America, and uses it for vacation trips to the United States. Recently, he had a narrow escape when a landing gear truss member partially collapsed on a remote mountain air field. Making temporary repairs from his tool kit, Bob successfully flew the airplane back to Bogota where permanent repairs were made. Already an expert in long-distance, over water flying, Bob plans to fly his Staggerwing 'round the world in the near future.

So, we are at the end—of the story, not the Staggerwing. I walked by one sitting in an open hangar the other day, alongside all the modern, shiny, all-metal jobs. She is a rare sight—less than 250 of her sisters exist today—the possibility of seeing one at any given aiport is fairly remote.

When you see one, you know you are in the presence of one of the Great Ones. We all know she has no soul—she is an inanimate object made of steel, plywood, and spruce. But, in a dark, silent hangar, surrounded by tricycle landing gears and sleek aluminum, the Staggerwing sits in profound majestic grace. For an instant, you are a part of the past—you hear her low-pitched, rumbling Wasp engine, you see her wingtips trembling in the gray light of an early dawn—she is a Queen, ruling quietly over her domain, and like all royalty, she has no need to speak to prove her claim to the throne—it is a fact accepted by all who see her. People walking through the hangar idly glance at the other airplanes, but when they pass the Staggerwing, they stop, and their eyes go slowly over her—from the big radial cowling down the rapidly tapering fuselage to the rounded fin and rudder, then back to the negatively staggered wings with their graceful I struts, their steel brace wires, and their elliptical tips. They walk around her slowly, one asks, "What is it?", the other replies, "I never saw one before." They speak in hushed tones, as one does in the presence of a Queen. They stay one minute, or perhaps five, then they leave, walking slowly. Outside the hangar, in the sunlight, they turn for one last look, their faces serious and filled with awe. They have been in the presence of one of the Great Ones.

—THE END—

CF-EKA

Ron Uloth's D17S, (s/n 4813) in flight.

Ed Burger's E17L in flight above the Susquehanna River near Sidney, New York.   (Ed Burger)

D17S s/n 6890, XB-HAY landing in Mexico City.

(Adolfo Villaseñor)

D17S s/n 4891 in flight over California.   (M. E. Park)

Fred Johnson of Atlanta, Georgia at work with the water hose. Fred flies his D17S (s/n 4865) in his business, says nothing built today can replace it.   (Photo by Author)

The late Jim Phillips at Ottumwa, Iowa in his D17S.

(William P. Kupka)

"Wall to wall airplanes" is how Mrs. Freeman describes Delta Airline Captain William E. Freeman's basement project to rebuild G17S s/n B-5. Built with a sturdy steeltubing framework, the Staggerwing achieved its graceful fuselage lines from generous use of wood formers, stringers, and fairings.
(William E. Freeman)

G17S s/n B-3, N44G, with pilot-owner W. C. Yarbrough at the controls. Frequently offered large sums of money for this airplane, Yarbrough refuses to sell—he feels this is the airplane he has always wanted, and for that reason, it has no real monetary value to him. Nothing could replace "Big Red." (Floyd Jillson)

Cockpit shot of partially completed G17S instrument panel during rebuilding. This is Bill Freeman's s/n B-5. It has many deviations from standard G17S panel, most resulting from Bill's experience as an airline captain. Wheel and bicycle type chain on left is the hand crank for operation of landing gear by hand.
(William E. Freeman)

E17B-157 photographed by its owner, Hays Maxwell, at Clover Field in California in 1957. Mr. Maxwell uses the airplane for both personal and business transportation. (Hays Maxwell)

D17S, s/n 6871, with unusual paint trim was owned by Clarence Baker and Richard Marvin in Trona, California in 1964.
(Clarence Baker)

Photographed in Van Nuys, California in July, 1965, this G17S, s/n B-19, now belongs to L. B. Maytag, Jr., president of National Air Lines. Recently rebuilt, it is said to be immaculate inside and out. (B. B. Deatrick)

D17S s/n 6935 after a bad landing at the Detroit City Airport, July 12, 1962.
(Robert F. Pauley)

D17S s/n 4898 getting an all-metal fuselage. Fuselage formers were replaced with metal ones, and entire fuselage was covered with aluminum.
(Robert L. Horner)

Wearing a tired, worn look, SF17D, s/n 227, sits forlornly by a Canadian hangar. Staggerwing on floats served well in the Canadian bush, had reputation of being able to haul any load the pilot could put in her and still close the door.
(William T. Larkins)

Interior view of G17S s/n B-1 showing the special, all-leather upholstery. Notice the interior of the airplane reflecting off the highly polished fabric on underside of the upper wing just outside of the door.
(C. L. Elwell)

E17B s/n 160 in flight over Kansas during the summer of 1961. Wingtips and I strut in right foreground belong to D17S s/n 4823, N9113H owned by Air Force Capt. Don Quinn.

(Donald R. Quinn)

Don Quinn's D17S in Panama, 1965. The airplane, s/n 4823, has been completely recovered, and is now a beautiful white with red trim in standard Beechcraft bird marking.

(Robert A. Maiden)

E17L s/n 196. It should be obvious why I included this photograph in color. I can't think of a more distinctive paint scheme— on a Staggerwing, or any other airplane. (William T. Larkins)

Don Quinn's D17S over the Bay of Panama in July, 1965. Shot taken from Lt. Col. Donald E. Payne's D17S, s/n 4886, N51745. Both Quinn's N9113H and Payne's N51745 are hangared at Albrook AFB, Canal Zone. (Robert A. Maiden)

Pioneer aviatrix Peggy Kelman's Beechcraft C17L, s/n 107, in repose at "Bonnie Doon," her cattle station near Yamala in Queensland, Australia. Mrs. Kelman found the C17L an excellent airplane for covering Australia's long distances. She especially liked the C17L's speed and load carrying ability. In late 1962 she sold the airplane, now lives in Brisbane, and son John runs "Bonnie Doon." (Peggy Kelman)

D17S s/n 6688 on takeoff. The pilot has just actuated the landing gear for retraction. This paint trim design was used on some very early models of the Beechcraft 17. (Emil Strasser)

Three Navy Staggerwings in formation. Some Navy Staggerwings were all silver, some were camouflaged with the greenish-gray paint on top, pale blue on the underside.

(*Beech Photo*)

F17D s/n 258. Notice the "modernized" bird stripe and unique engine cowl trim, and bird on fin and rudder.

(*Ralph Nankey*)

This drawing was made by James M. Triggs. I suggested the general layout, Jim snorted, "Everybody thinks he's an artist", and turned out this excellent piece of work.

(James M. Triggs)

THE FIRST STAGGERWING
BEECHCRAFT MODEL 17R
NC499N
WICHITA, KANSAS — 1932

106

(W. C. Yarbrough)

William C. "Dub" Yarbrough flying "Big Red", G17S, s/n B-3.

Dub Yarbrough and Mrs. Olive Ann Beech in an informal pose at the 1966 Staggerwing Convention in Wichita. Mrs. Beech took over management of the Beech factory after Walter's death in 1950, and is still its head. She is also still very fond of the Staggerwing, and the Beechcraft production era it represents. *(W. C. Yarbrough)*

Frank Thera at the controls of his D17S during the 1965 Wichita Convention. *(W. C. Yarbrough)*

World famous aviator, author, Staggerwing pilot, last of the big spenders, R. T. Smith at Saffold Field, Savannah, Georgia in 1957 with C17L-130. *(Robert P. Hofer)*

Staggerwing owners at the 1966 Convention stand in front of a Travel Air 4000. The airplanes in this photograph, from the Travel Air 4000, to the Staggerwings, to the current production Beech airplanes in the background, represent over 40 years of Walter H. Beech's influence on civil aviation in this country. *(W. C. Yarbrough)*

Staggerwing completing final turn at Beech factory draws crowd of Beech employees at the 1965 National Staggerwing Club convention in Wichita. Though sleek, new models are impressive airplanes, the Staggerwings always had a crowd around them during their visit to the factory. *(W. C. Yarbrough)*

William C. "Dub" Yarbrough, president of the National Staggerwing Club with his G17S at the 1965 Wichita Convention. *(W. C. Yarbrough)*

Photographed recently over Cleveland, Ohio, ex-Navy D17S s/n 6703 sports non-standard, but attractive paint trim. Streamlined ADF loop housing under lower wing centersection was standard on many military airplanes; some also carried it atop fuselage just aft of upper wing. *(William P. Reefe)*

Colorful lineup of Staggerwings at the 1964 Antique Airplane Association annual meet at Ottumwa, Iowa. Prop spinner was not standard on production Staggerwings except the G17S, but most have them installed today. *(Emil Strasser)*

G17S s/n B-3 on takeoff with landing gear coming up. Shiny objects on underside of lower wing are retractable landing lights. *(Emil Strasser)*

Jack Raines' D17S s/n 1020 is an early Navy model. Rear fuselage lines are clearly evident in this unusual aerial shot. This shot also shows, to good advantage, the lower wing to fuselage fillets. *(Emil Strasser)*

Cockpit shot of C17L s/n 130. Crank on right sidewall is side window crank which could be rolled down in flight, but was very noisy. Windshield and all windows on Staggerwings are glass, not plexiglass. *(Robert T. Smith)*

C17B s/n 112 with 300 hp R-680-E3B Lycoming engine. This is a recent photograph made after many years of hard work rebuilding the airframe from the basic structure outward. Note entrance door—left side was standard location, but optional righthand door was available. *(Leslie Steen)*

Noel Goursolle's D17S, s/n 4888, on its back on a mountain airfield in the Rockies. *(Noel Goursolle)*

Towing Goursolle's Beechcraft home for repairs. *(Noel Goursolle)*

D17S on takeoff. *(Noel Goursolle)*

Photo of Noel Goursolle's D17S shot from entrance door looking aft shows intricate wood framework of a Staggerwing fuselage. Basic structure, hidden in this view was, of course, steel tubing. *(Noel Goursolle)*

C17R, s/n 81, during its rebuilding in California a couple of years ago. The box-like steel tubing structure of the Beechcraft 17 was covered by an elaborate and complex secondary structure of wooden formers, stringers, and plywood fairings making a rebuilding job a far more complicated task than most people want to undertake. *(William C. Yarbrough)*

Rebuilt and in the air again, s/n 81 is shown here on takeoff. Shortly after this photo was made the airplane was sold to National Staggerwing Club president William C. Yarbrough who sold the airplane to Lt. Col. James T. Winkler. *(Emil Strasser)*

Robert C. Ellis en route to Paipa in the Andes Mountains. Instruments show his D17S (s/n 3093) is indicating 144 mph at 10,300 feet. In South America's tropical heat this would probably be a true airspeed of around 190 mph. Bob uses his Staggerwing extensively for personal travel, says it is an excellent mountain airplane, even at Paipa's 8,400 foot elevation! *(Robert C. Ellis)*

D17S s/n 4891 in flight. Protrusion under lower wing center-section is a set of two venturi tubes for gyro driven instruments. Close examination of aft edge of engine cowling will reveal an extension which smooths engine cowling into fuse-lage—this was done by the owner, is not standard. *(M. E. Park)*

W. C. Yarbrough running up "Big Red"—G17S s/n B-3. He's in there—just leaning down looking at something on the lower edge of the instrument panel. *(Floyd Jillson)*

Rebuilt from 1956 to 1960, this D17S (s/n 263) is owned by Anderson, Indiana businessman William P. Thompson who fell in love with Staggerwings as a boy during the 1930's. He learned to fly in 1950, purchased this Staggerwing, in dismantled pieces, in 1956 and rebuilt it himself. Today he uses it for business transportation. *(William P. Thompson)*

114

POSTSCRIPT TO PART I

Just as I mailed the completed, final manuscript of Part I to the printer, C. R. "Scotty" Burmood returned from an extended trip to South America, and called me on the phone from Houston, Texas.

In the late 1930's Scotty was Generalissimo Chiang Kai-shek's personal pilot. Fighting the communists on one side, and the Japanese on the other, the Generalissimo had to maintain a high degree of mobility—he had to be able to move fast if both enemies should attempt to surround him. A fast, long-range airplane had to be selected, and it had to be one that could get out of a pea-patch.

The Generalissimo feared that, if he were ever hemmed in, he would not have time to gather his party, drive by automobile to the airport, and make good his escape in an airplane. He had to have an airplane that could takeoff from some small field, or perhaps a city street, close to his headquarters. Scotty Burmood picked a Staggerwing for this purpose, and the first one we have a record of, was D17R s/n 181, although I do not know if this was Chiang's personal airplane. He purchased a large number of Staggerwings, and his personal airplane could have been any one of them, but it was probably the first one delivered.

Scotty told me the airplane was equipped with seven fuel tanks, and could fly for 1600 miles, nonstop. With this range, he could take the Generalissimo out of harm's way in event the enemy (or enemies) began to surround their headquarters.

The Staggerwing was hidden in a building near the headquarters, and a nearby street was covered with cinders to make a suitable surface for takeoff and landing. Thus, when the battle neared, the Generalissimo could quickly assemble his staff, rush to the airplane, and take off on the cinder covered street.

Scotty said he flew the Staggerwing many times into and out of, streets, and tiny fields. The theme in his flying was to avoid the ordinary, to keep Chiang off the regular airfields where the enemy could easily get to him. It made for an interesting, and sometimes hairy, life. He said only a Staggerwing could have done the things he had to do. Today Scotty lives in Houston, Texas and pursues a more sedate life than he lived in the 1930's when he flew for Generalissimo Chiang Kai-shek.

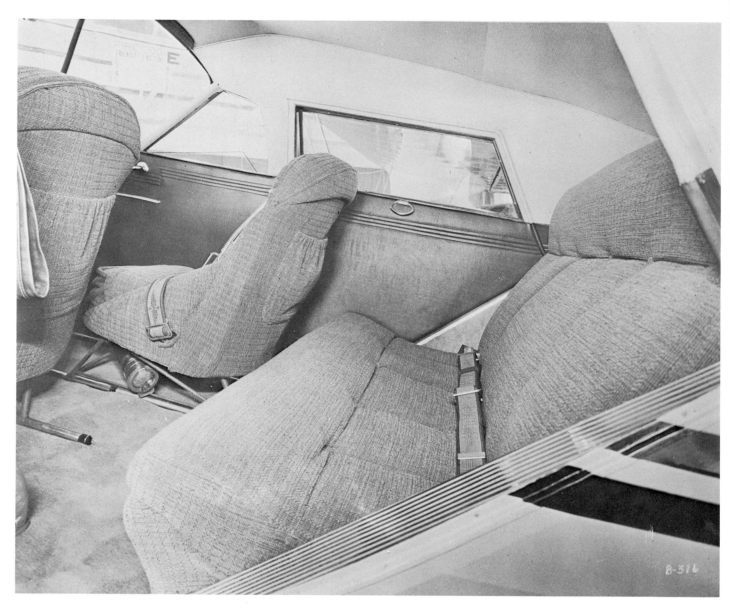

Staggerwing interior showing cloth upholstery. This airplane has the optional righthand door, and chairchutes in the front seats—notice the "D" ring in the right, front seat.
(C. L. Elwell)

G17S s/n B-10 at an east Indian tea plantation. Owned by Associated Airworks in Calcutta, it is used extensively for charter. *(D. Ghosh)*

Corpus Christi, Tex. — Jan. 1937

In the photo at left we have George J. Pearson on the right, Ben Miller on left. Miller was killed in World War Two flying a DC-3 for American Airlines. In the photo at the right we see George Pearson's Staggerwing demonstrator, B17L-8, NC12590. After giving up his Beech dealership, George went to Corpus Christi, Texas, flew air charter in the Waco YKC in lefthand photo.

(Both photos George J. Pearson)

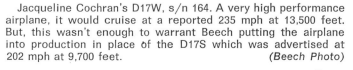

Jacqueline Cochran's D17W, s/n 164. A very high performance airplane, it would cruise at a reported 235 mph at 13,500 feet. But, this wasn't enough to warrant Beech putting the airplane into production in place of the D17S which was advertised at 202 mph at 9,700 feet.

(Beech Photo)

Close-up of the Pratt and Whitney R-985-SC-G engine installation in D17W, s/n 164. Although a little more crowded than the standard Model 17 engine compartment, this is nevertheless typical of the engine installations on the Model 17 series.

(Harvey Lippincott and the Connecticut Aeronautical Historical Association)

Vern Carstens, famed Beech test pilot, strikes thoughtful pose by the 8000th Bonanza built as he prepares to retire. Vern retired in February of this year, 1966. *(Beech Photo)*

PART TWO

TECHNICAL DATA AND INDIVIDUAL
SERIAL NUMBER LIST

Certain items of technical data, and the individual list of Beechcraft Model 17's by serial number, is presented in this section to avoid cluttering the main story with a constant recitation of numbers and figures.

The data presented here was compiled from old records, personal accounts, and the U.S. Civil Register. Where possible, data was crosschecked with several sources, and not included unless all sources agreed. The data and information in this section is the result of six years of research on my part, and several more years research on the part of at least two dozen individual aviation historians who contributed heavily to this part, and without whose help it could not have been done.

TECHNICAL DATA

Beechcraft Model 17 Series

Series	Years Produced	Variants	Remarks
17	1932-33	17R	Prototype and one production airplane; both 17R.
A17	1934	A17F, A17FS	A17F had Wright Cyclone of 690 hp; A17FS had Wright Cyclone of 710 hp.
B17	1934-36	B17L, B17B, B17E, B17R, SB17L	First real production series; first with fully retractable landing gear.
C17	1936-37	C17L, C17B, C17E, C17R, SC17L, SC17B, SC17R	Replaced B17 Series.
D17	1937-44	D17A, D17R, D17S, D17W, SD17S	Larger, more improved over C17 Series; not a replacement for entire C17 Series.
E17	1937-41[1]	E17L, E17B, SE17B	Replaced lower powered models in C17 Series.
F17	1938-41[1]	F17D, SF17D	Similar to E17 Series.
G17	1946[2]	G17S	D17S with improved engine cowling, wheel fairings, vertical fin outline.

NOTES: "S" in front of model indicates floatplane variant, i.e. SD17S would be a D17S on floats.

[1] Some sources claim E17 and F17 series were produced during World War Two for the military, but I have not been able to identify an E17 or F17 serial number manufactured after 1941. The U.S. Army in WWII did use the E17 and F17, but these were impressed from civilian owners.

[2] All twenty G17S models were built in 1946, but not all were assembled and sold that year. The prototype G17S was D17S serial number 424 modified to G17S configuration.

Engine Suffixes Used On Beechcraft 17 Airplanes

	Engine	Horse-power	Remarks
A	Wright R-760-E2	350	Seven Cylinder Radial
B	Jacobs L-5	285	Seven Cylinder Radial
D	Jacobs L-6	330	Seven Cylinder Radial
E	Wright R-760-E1	285	Seven Cylinder Radial
F	Wright R-1820	690	"Cyclone" Nine Cylinder Radial installed in A17F serial number 5. A17FS serial number 11 had Wright R-1820-F3 of 710 horsepower.
L	Jacobs L-4	225	Seven Cylinder Radial
R	Wright R-975-E3	420	"Whirlwind". Nine Cylinder Radial.
S	Pratt & Whitney R-985	450	Nine Cylinder Radial. Many variants, "Wasp Jr." civil model to R-985 military models used.
W	Pratt & Whitney R-985-SC-G	600	Experimental engine installed in D17W. Never type certificated.

Military Models

Army Model	Navy Model	Civil Model	Remarks
	JB-1	C17R	One 1936 model C17R procured by Navy directly from Beech.
YC-43		D17S	Three procured in 1939 for use by U.S. Air Attaché Office. These were procured from Beech directly.
	GB-1	D17S	Production order of 7 airplanes in 1939, 3 in 1940, and 8 from civil impressments in 1942-43.
UC-43	GB-2	D17S	Production order totaling 207 airplanes.
UC-43A		D17R	Thirteen airplanes.
UC-43B	GB-2	D17S	Thirteen Army aircraft, 138 Navy aircraft, including production orders and civil impressments.
UC-43C		F17D	Thirty-eight airplanes.
UC-43D		E17B	Thirty-one airplanes.
UC-43E		C17R	Five airplanes.
UC-43F		D17A	One airplane.
UC-43G		C17B	Ten airplanes.
UC-43H		B17R	Three airplanes.
UC-43J		C17L	Three airplanes.
UC-43K		D17W	One airplane. This was Jacqueline Cochran's airplane.

NOTES: Due to its possible confusion with the number "1," the Army did not use the letter "I", so there was no UC-43I.

Because of the number of UC-43C (F17D), and UC-43D (E17B) airplanes procured by the Army, it is possible that they were produced in 1942-43, but it has not been possible to identify serial numbers. "Fahey's U.S. Army Aircraft, 1908-1946" lists 1942 as the production year for the UC-43C and UC-43D, but does not give either Beech nor Army serial numbers. The Army serial numbers for these aircraft do not run consecutively in groups of more than two (except in one case of five UC-43C airplanes). I have concluded that all of the UC-43C and UC-43D airplanes are civil impressments.

Army and Navy models of the Beechcraft 17 series were identical in construction details to their civil counterparts. For example, the Army UC-43 and UC-43B are identical to the civil D17S.

Description of Beechcraft 17 Series

I have selected ten parameters to describe the many Beechcraft 17 variants. In describing the airplanes, I followed these ground rules . . .

General: Just what it says—general comments.

Dimensions: Dimensions are given for the landplane versions only. They are not repeated from model to model except to point out differences.

Weights: Empty weights are the factory advertised weights where known. Seaplane empty weights were obtained by adding weight of the floatplane installation to the landplane empty weight. Maximum weights were taken from CAA/FAA Specs, when available. Seaplane weights are shown in parentheses.

Engine: The basic engine series is listed. In many cases, later models of the same basic engine have been installed such as the Jacobs R-755-9 and L-4MB in models specifying the basic Jacobs L-4 engine. The propeller noted is generally the standard propeller installed at the factory.

Wing: Parameters on the wing are Airfoil, Area, Construction notes, Aileron location, and location and type flap installed.

Fuselage: General construction notes. All Beechcraft 17 fuselages are basically the same steel tube, fabric construction with wooden and metal formers, and wood stringers.

Empennage: The parameters here are trim tabs, aerodynamic balance horns, and type of bracing used.

Landing Gear: Whether retractable or fixed, type retraction, and long or short main landing gear legs were the main parameters used for the landing gear notes.

Fuel System: The basic fuel system offered in a standard production airplane is described followed by a brief description of approved optional tankage. No attempt was made to describe the details of fuel plumbing.

Performance: Speeds listed here are those attainable as advertised by the factory, where known from old Beech advertising literature. CAA/FAA "redline" and other limit airspeeds are not shown. They will be shown in a short tabulation at the end of the list of descriptions. Speeds shown are for landplanes.

Model 17R — ATC 496

General: Prototype Beechcraft 17. Only two built.

Dimensions:
Wingspan—34' 4"
Length—24' 2½"
Height—8' 7½"

Weights:
Empty—2700 Lbs.
Gross Weight—4500 Lbs.
Wing Loading—13.9 Lbs./Sq. Ft.[1]

Engine:
Wright R-760-E2 "Whirlwind" of 420 hp.
Power Loading—10.7 Lbs./H.P.
Propeller—Smith Controllable

Wing:
Airfoil—Navy N-9
Area—323 Sq. Ft. (Includes half area of fuselage)[1]
Construction—Steel tube truss spars, 6" rib spacing, fabric covering, streamlined "I" strut and flying and landing wires.
Ailerons—Conventional, mounted on lower wing.
Flaps—None (Serial number one later modified to drag flaps on underside of upper wing.)

Fuselage: Conventional steel tubing with wood and metal formers, wood stringers. Forward sections metal covered, aft sections fabric covered. Steel truss in lower wing center-section area carries landing gear loads.

Empennage: Built as a unit with wire braced, conventional horizontal and vertical surfaces. No balance horns on rudder or elevators. Empennage attached to fuselage with hinges and electric jackscrew to give pitch trim.

Landing Gear: Conventional tailwheel type. Main wheels faired and panted, retract electrically into pants leaving about six inches of tire exposed. Tail wheel faired, non-swivelling, non-steerable. (Landing gear on serial number one modified to A17 configuration before delivery).

Fuel System: Two fuselage tanks located under cabin, fore and aft. Engine driven fuel pump and manually operated hand pump. Sump drains in rear of main wheel pants. Capacity totals 145 gallons.

Performance:
Maximum Speed—201 mph
Cruising Speed—170 mph
Landing Speed—60-65 mph

[1] One source gives 300 Sq. Ft. wing area with wing loading of 15 Lbs./Sq. Ft.

Model A17F — ATC 548
Model A17FS — ATC 577

General: Model A17F and A17FS identical except for engine. Both were equipped with Wright "Cyclone", but one had slightly different "Cyclone" model than the other.

Dimensions:
Wingspan—(See scale drawings)
Length—(See scale drawings)
Height—(See scale drawings)

Weights
Empty—Unknown
Gross Weight—5200 Lbs. (A17F), 6000 Lbs. (A17FS)
Wing Loading—16 Lbs./Sq. Ft. (A17F), 18.6 Lbs./Sq. Ft. (A17FS)

Engine:
Wright R-1820 "Cyclone" of 690 hp (A17F)
Wright R-1820-F3 "Cyclone" of 710 hp (A17FS)
Power Loading—7.5 Lbs./H.P. (A17F), 8.5 Lbs./H.P. (A17FS)
Propeller—Hamilton Standard Controllable.

Wing:
Airfoil—Navy N-9
Area—Approximately 323 Sq. Ft. (Includes half area of fuselage)
Construction—Steel tube spars with ribs spaced 6" apart. Fabric covering.
Ailerons—Conventional, mounted on lower wing.
Flaps—Drag flap underside of upper wing (forward of trailing edge)

Fuselage: Conventional steel tubing with wood and metal formers, wood stringers. Forward sections metal covered, aft sections fabric covered. Steel truss in lower wing center-section area carries landing gear loads.

Empennage: Conventional unit with fabric covering. Balance horns on rudder and elevators. Cockpit adjustable trim tabs installed on rudder and elevators. Empennage strut braced to fuselage.

Landing Gear: Conventional tailwheel type. Main wheels faired and panted, retract electrically into pants leaving about six inches of tire exposed. Tread considerably wider than 17R. Tail wheel full swivelling, non-steerable.
Fuel System: Same as 17R, but capacity unknown.

Performance:
Maximum Speed—250 mph
Cruising Speed—212 mph
Landing Speed—Estimated 65-70 mph

Model B17L — ATC 560

General: Lightweight, lower horsepower development of 17R.

Dimensions:
Wingspan—32'
Length—24' 5"
Height—8' 6"

Weights:
Empty—1600 Lbs. (Approximately 2052 Lbs., SB17L)
Gross Weight—3165 Lbs. (3525 Lbs., SB17L)
Wing Loading—11.6 Lbs./Sq. Ft. (12.9 Lbs./Sq. Ft., SB17L)

Engine:
Jacobs L-4 of 225 hp.
Power Loading—14 Lbs./H.P. (15.8 Lbs./H.P., SB17L)
Propeller—Hartzell #707 Wood, Fixed Pitch (Curtiss 55501 and Lycoming Smith controllable metal also approved).

Wing:
Airfoil—Modified Clark Y
Area—273 Sq. Ft.
Construction—Spruce spars with wooden truss ribs. Rib spacing approximately 7½" apart. Fabric cover.
Ailerons—Conventional, mounted on lower wing.
Flaps—Drag type mounted on lower surface of lower wings immediately forward of aileron.

Fuselage: Conventional steel tubing with wood and metal formers, wood stringers. Fabric covering. Same basic construction as 17R and A17F, but lighter in weight.

Empennage: Strut braced with balance horns on rudder and elevators. Cockpit adjustable elevator trim tabs standard; rudder trim tab available as optional equipment.

Landing Gear: Fully retractable with long main landing gear legs. Early models had Heywood air starters on the engine, and used air for gear retraction. This was changed to electric retraction when electric engine starters were installed. Landing gear fully faired when retracted. (Edo 38-3430 floats installed on SB17L.)

Fuel System: Gravity feed from two, 25 gallon tanks, one in each upper wing. Optional equipment included 20, 23, or 25 gallon fuel tanks in lower wings, and one 20 gallon fuselage tank.

Performance:
Maximum Speed—175 mph
Cruising Speed—150 mph
Landing Speed—45 mph

Model B17B—ATC 560

General: Identical to B17L model except for engine. Only data that differs from B17L is presented.

Engine:
Jacobs L-5 of 285 hp.
Power Loading—11.1 Lbs./H.P.
Propeller—Curtiss fixed pitch metal.

Performance:
Maximum Speed—185 mph
Cruising Speed—165 mph
Landing Speed—50-55 mph

Model B17E — ATC 566

General: Basically identical to the B17L series, only those items that were different will be noted.

Dimensions:
Wingspan—32'
Length—24' 5"
Height—8' 2"

Weights:
Empty—Unknown (Approximately 2150 Lbs.)
Gross Weight—3615 Lbs.
Wing Loading—13.5 Lbs./Sq. Ft.

Engine:
Wright R-760-E1 of 285 hp.
Power Loading—12.7 Lbs./H.P.
Propeller—Curtiss 55501 fixed pitch metal.

Wing:
Airfoil—Modified Clark Y
Area—267 Sq. Ft.
Construction—Same as B17L, but slightly different wingtip planform, hence the slight reduction in wing area.
Ailerons—On lower wing.
Flaps—Drag flap mounted on under side of upper wing forward of trailing edge.

Landing Gear: Same as B17L, but a shorter landing gear leg.

Fuel System: Standard tankage consisted of a forward and aft fuselage fuel tank. The forward tank carried 28 gallons; the aft tank 42 gallons. Optional wing tanks for the upper and lower wings could be carried. The buyer could select either a 23 or 25 gallon capacity wing tank.

Performance:
Maximum Speed—185 mph
Cruising Speed—165 mph
Landing Speed—55 mph

Model B17R — ATC 579

General: The B17R is identical to the B17E in every respect except for the engine installed. Power loading in the B17R is reduced to 8.6 Lbs./H.P.

Engine:
Wright R-975-E2/E3 of 420 hp.
Power Loading—8.6 Lbs./H.P.
Propeller—Hamilton Standard 2D30 or 5406 Hub.

Performance:
Maximum Speed—211 mph
Cruising Speed—202 mph at 9700 Ft.
Landing Speed—55-60 mph

Model C17L — ATC 602

General: The C17 series replaced the B17 series in production. Except for minor improvements, they are identical to their B17 counterparts.

Dimensions:
Wingspan—32'
Length—24' 5"
Height—8' 6"

Weights:
Empty—1825 Lbs. (Approximately 2315 Lbs., SC17L)
Gross Weight—3165 Lbs. (3525 Lbs., SC17L)
Wing Loading—11.6 Lbs./Sq. Ft. (12.9 Lbs./Sq. Ft., SC17L)

Engine:
Jacobs L-4 series of 225 hp.
Power Loading—14 Lbs./H.P. (15.7 Lbs./H.P., SC17L)
Propeller—Hartzell #707 fixed pitch wood.

Wing:
Airfoil—Modified Clark Y
Area—273 Sq. Ft.
Construction—Wood spars with wooden truss ribs spaced 8½ inches apart, fabric covered.
Ailerons—Lower wing.
Flaps—Drag flap mounted on lower surface of lower wing immediately forward of aileron.

Fuselage: Same as B17 series.

Empennage: Same as B17 series.

Landing Gear: Same as B17 series with short main landing gear legs. (Edo 38-3430 floats installed on SC17L)

Fuel System: Standard tanks included two upper wing tanks of 23 gallons each plus one 28 gallon forward fuselage tank for a total of 74 gallons. Optional tankage included installing 25 gallon wing tanks in all wings plus a 42 gallon rear fuselage tank in addition to the standard 28 gallon forward fuselage tank for a possible total fuel capacity of 170 gallons.

Performance:
Maximum Speed—175 mph
Cruising Speed—166 mph at 7200 Ft.
Landing Speed—45 mph

Model D17S — ATC 649

General: Without a doubt the most popular of the Beechcraft 17 series, the D17S differs from the D17R only in the engine installed.

Dimensions:
Wingspan—32′
Length—25′ $\frac{11}{16}$″
Height—8′

Weights:
Empty—2570 Lbs. (Approximately 3100 Lbs., SD17S)
Gross Weight—4250 Lbs. (4650 Lbs., SD17S)
Wing Loading—14.2 Lbs./Sq. Ft. (15.6 Lbs./Sq. Ft., SD17S)

Engine:
Pratt and Whitney SB Wasp Jr. (R-985) of 450 hp.
Power Loading—9.5 Lbs./H.P. (10.3 Lbs./H.P., SD17S)
Propeller—Hamilton Standard 2D30 Constant Speed

Landing Gear: Same as D17R. (SD17S used Edo model WA-4665 floats)

Model D17A — ATC 713

General: Except for the engine, the D17A is identical to the D17R and D17S.

Dimensions:
Wingspan—32′
Length—26′ 7⅞″
Height—8′

Weights:
Empty—2465 Lbs.
Gross Weight—4250 Lbs.
Wing Loading—14.2 Lbs./Sq. Ft.

Engine:
Wright R-760-E2 of 350 hp.
Power Loading—12.1 Lbs./H.P.
Propeller—Hamilton Standard 2D30 Constant Speed

Performance:
Maximum Speed—Approximately 185 mph
Cruising Speed—170 mph at 9600 Ft.
Landing Speed—60 mph

Model D17W—No ATC-Experimental Model

General: Except for the engine, the D17W was identical to the D17R and D17S. Built as an experimental airplane with an experimental Pratt and Whitney engine, the D17W was never type certificated by the CAA.

Dimensions:
Wingspan—32′
Length—26′ 11¾″
Height—8′

Weights:
Empty—2800 Lbs.
Gross Weight—4250 Lbs.
Wing Loading—14.2 Lbs./Sq. Ft.

Engine:
Pratt and Whitney R-985-SC-G of 600 hp.
Power Loading—7.1 Lbs./H.P.
Propeller—Large Diameter Hamilton Standard Constant Speed

Performance:
Maximum Speed—Approximately 235 mph at 14,500 Ft.
Cruising Speed—225 mph at 14,500 Ft.
Landing Speed—60 mph

Model E17B — ATC 641

General: Introduced in 1937, the E17 series has the upper wing ailerons and lower wing flaps, and long fuselage of the D17 series, but uses the strut braced empennage similar to the C17 series.

Dimensions:
Wingspan—32′
Length—25′ 11¼″
Height—8′

Weights:
Empty—2120 Lbs. (Approximately 2600 Lbs., SE17B)
Gross Weight—3390 Lbs. (3740 Lbs., SE17B)
Wing Loading—11.4 Lbs./Sq. Ft. (12.6 Lbs./Sq. Ft., SE17B)

Engine:
Jacobs L-5 of 285 hp.
Power Loading—11.9 Lbs./H.P. (13.1 Lbs./H.P., SE17B)
Propeller—Curtiss-Reed Fixed Pitch Metal

Wing: Identical to D17 series except 8″ rib spacing, less plywood on wing tips.
Empennage: Similar to C17B, i.e. strut braced. Wood fixed surfaces, metal moveable surfaces, fabric covering on all. Rudder and elevators have balance horns.

Fuel System: A 29 gallon forward fuselage tank, and two 24 gallon lower wing tanks made up the standard fuel system, but optional 23 or 24 gallon fuel tanks could be installed in the remaining wings.

Performance:
Maximum Speed—188 mph
Cruising Speed—177 mph at 7200 Ft.
Landing Speed—50 mph

Model C17B — ATC 602

General: Identical in all respects to C17L and SC17L except for engine installed. Also, one C17B was built with amphibian floats, described under **Landing Gear.** Other aspects of C17B landing gear are identical to C17L.

Engine:
Jacobs L-5 of 285 hp.
Power Loading—11.1 Lbs./Sq. Ft. (12.4 Lbs./Sq. Ft., SC17B)
Propeller—Hamilton Standard 2B20.

Landing Gear: C17B serial number 99 had Edo amphibian floats model 49-3875 installed. They used conventional tailwheel type landing gear with 7.50-10 Hayes 750A wheels and 7.50-10 six ply tires. There was no actual tailwheel, the airplane set back on the rear end of the floats.

Performance:
Maximum Speed—Approximately 185 mph
Cruising Speed—177 mph at 7200 Ft.
Landing Speed—50-55 mph.

Model C17E — ATC 615

General: The C17E replaced the B17E, and was very much identical to it, especially with regard to dimensions, weights, engine and propeller, performance, etc.

Fuel System: Standard production airplane had three tanks— one 23 gallon tank in a lower wing, front fuselage of 28 gallons, and rear fuselage of 47 gallons. Optional tanks included 23 or 25 gallon tanks in upper and lower wings.

Model C17R — ATC 604

General: Basically identical to C17E except for engine, and maximum gross weight. Performance same as B17R.

Weights:
Empty—2225 Lbs. (Approximately 2750 Lbs., SC17R)
Gross Weight—3915 Lbs. (4105 Lbs., SC17R)
Wing Loading—14.6 Lbs./Sq. Ft. (15.4 Lbs./Sq. Ft., SC17R)

Engine:
Wright R-975-E2/E3 of 420 hp.
Power Loading—9.3 Lbs./H.P. (9.8 Lbs./H.P., SC17R)
Propeller—Curtiss Fixed Pitch Metal (Hamilton Standard 2D30, SC17R)

Landing Gear: Same as C17E. (SC17R used Edo model 39-4000 floats.)

Model D17R — ATC 638

General: The D17 series marked the first major change in general model 17 design since the B17L of 1934. The B17 and C17 series had a "short" fuselage. With the D17, the fuselage was lengthened 13⁵⁄₁₆ inches to provide better elevator power for improved landing characteristics. All subsequent model 17's (E17, F17, and G17) used the "long" fuselage. A second change (D17 and G17 only) was the use of a fully cantilever empennage, and location of the ailerons on the upper wing with a plain flap on the lower wing.

Dimensions:
Wingspan—32'
Length—26' 10¹¹⁄₁₆"
Height—8'

Weights:
Empty—2570 Lbs.
Gross Weight—4250 Lbs.
Wing Loading—14.2 Lbs./Sq. Ft.

Engine:
Wright R-975-E3 of 420 hp.
Power Loading—10.1 Lbs./H.P.
Propeller—Hamilton Standard 2D30 Constant Speed

Wing:
Airfoil—NACA 23012
Area—296.5 Sq. Ft.
Construction—Basically similar to former models, but with more plywood covering on wing tip, and 6½" rib spacing. Fabric covered.
Ailerons—Located on upper wings.
Flaps—Plain flap mounted on lower wing trailing edge.

Fuselage: Same as former models but 13⁵⁄₁₆ inches longer.

Empennage: Fully cantilever horizontal and vertical stabilizers of all wood construction with plywood and fabric cover. Rudder and elevators are constructed of steel tubing with fabric covering, and have balance horns. The elevators have metal balance weights. Cockpit adjustable trim tabs are installed on elevator and rudder.

Landing Gear: Fully retractable. Electric actuation same as C17 series.

Fuel System: Standard tanks were a 29 gallon forward fuselage tank, 49 gallon rear fuselage tank, and a 24 gallon tank installed in the right, lower wing. Additional optional tanks were a 23 or 24 gallon tank in each of the other three wings. Ordered with four 24 gallon wing tanks plus the standard fuselage tanks, maximum capacity could be as high as 174 gallons.

Performance:
Maximum Speed—212 mph
Cruising Speed—202 mph at 9700 Ft.
Landing Speed—60 mph

Model E17L — ATC 641

General: E17L same as E17B except for engine.

Weights:
Empty—2055 Lbs.
Gross Weight—3390 Lbs.
Wing Loading—11.4 Lbs./Sq. Ft.

Engine:
Jacobs L-4 of 225 hp
Power Loading—15 Lbs./H.P.
Propeller—Curtiss-Reed Fixed Pitch Metal

Fuel System: Standard capacity is 53 gallons contained in 29 gallon forward fuselage tank, and one 24 gallon lower wing tank. Optional tanks same as E17B.

Performance:
Maximum Speed—Approximately 175 mph
Cruising Speed—166 mph at 7200 Ft.
Landing Speed—50 mph

Model F17D — ATC 689

General: The F17D has the long fuselage, upper wing ailerons, and lower wing flaps of the D17 series, but uses the strut braced empennage of the E17 series.

Dimensions:
Wingspan—32'
Length—25' 11½"
Height—8'

Weights:
Empty—2155 Lbs. (Approximately 2650 Lbs., SF17D)
Gross Weight—3590 Lbs. (3940 Lbs., SF17D)
Wing Loading—12.1 Lbs./Sq. Ft. (13.3 Lbs./Sq. Ft., SF17D)

Engine:
Jacobs L-6 of 330 hp
Power Loading—10.9 Lbs./H.P. (11.9 Lbs./H.P., SF17D)
Propeller—Curtiss-Reed Fixed Pitch Metal

Wing: Identical to D17 and E17 except rib spacing is 8".

Fuel System: One 29 gallon forward fuselage tank plus two 24 gallon lower wing tanks totalled 77 gallons in the standard F17D, but 23 or 24 gallon fuel tanks could be ordered as optional equipment for installation in the wings.

Performance:
Maximum Speed—Approximately 185 mph
Cruising Speed—182 mph at 10,000 Ft.
Landing Speed—45-50 mph

Model G17S — ATC 779

General: The G17S was a post-World War Two development of the D17S. Identical to the D17S, the major differences were in engine cowling, windshield, and landing gear fairing doors. Built in 1946, these airplanes were assembled and sold on customer demand, hence they were, for all practical purposes, custom built. The first G17S was D17S serial number 424 converted and modified to G17S configuration as the G17S prototype.

Dimensions:
Wingspan—32'
Length—26' 9¼"
Height—8'

Weights: Same as D17S

Engine:
Pratt and Whitney R-985-AN-4 (with one 4½N and one 9N damper) of 450 hp.
Power Loading—9.5 Lbs./H.P.
Propeller—Hamilton Standard 2D30 Constant Speed

Wing: Same as D17S

Fuselage: Same as D17S except engine cowling and windshield. Engine cowling similar to D18S engine cowl.

Empennage: Same as D17S except slightly different vertical fin and rudder shape.

Landing Gear: Same as D17S except different main landing gear fairing doors.

Fuel System: A fuel capacity of 124 gallons is listed in the CAA/FAA Specifications as standard. This was carried in a forward fuselage tank of 29 gallons, rear fuselage tank of 49 gallons, and two lower wing tanks of 23 gallons each. Optional tanks were two upper wing tanks of 23 gallons each which make the potential fuel capacity some 170 gallons.

Performance: (Same as D17S)
Maximum Speed—212 mph
Cruising Speed—202 mph at 9700 Ft.
Landing Speed—60 mph

Beechcraft 17 Maximum Allowable Airspeeds

Model	Glide or Dive	Level Flight or Climb	Flaps Extended
17R	Unknown	Unknown	Unknown
A17F, A17FS	Unknown	Unknown	Unknown
B17L, B17B	225 mph	170 mph	115 mph
SB17L	223 mph	150 mph	100 mph
B17R, B17E	225 mph	206 mph	100 mph
C17L, C17B	225 mph	183 mph	100 mph
SC17L, SC17B	223 mph	150 mph	100 mph
SC17B Amphibian	223 mph	160 mph	100 mph
C17E, C17R	225 mph	206 mph	100 mph
SC17R	216 mph	178 mph	100 mph
D17R, D17S, D17A	240 mph	211 mph	115 mph
SD17S	209 mph	172 mph	115 mph
D17W	Unknown	Unknown	Unknown
E17L, E17B	222 mph	183 mph	115 mph
SE17B	202 mph	167 mph	115 mph
F17D	222 mph	189 mph	117 mph
SF17D	169 mph	140 mph	117 mph
G17S	240 mph	211 mph	175 mph

Airspeeds given above are True Indicated Airspeed which is the same as Calibrated Airspeed, the airspeed read on the airspeed indicator corrected for installation error.

"Glide or Dive" maximum airspeed is the maximum airspeed in smooth air with no abrupt maneuvering.

"Level Flight or Climb" maximum airspeed is the maximum airspeed for moderately turbulent air with moderate aircraft maneuvering.

The Beechcraft Model 17 Series is stressed for roughly 6 G's (six times the force of gravity, i.e. the weight of the airplane) positive and 4 G's negative. Whether these are the ultimate limits, or the design limits was not specified by the correspondent who supplied them, but in either case, a prudent pilot would not today (1966) perform abrupt maneuvers in a Beechcraft 17.

BEECHCRAFT MODEL 17

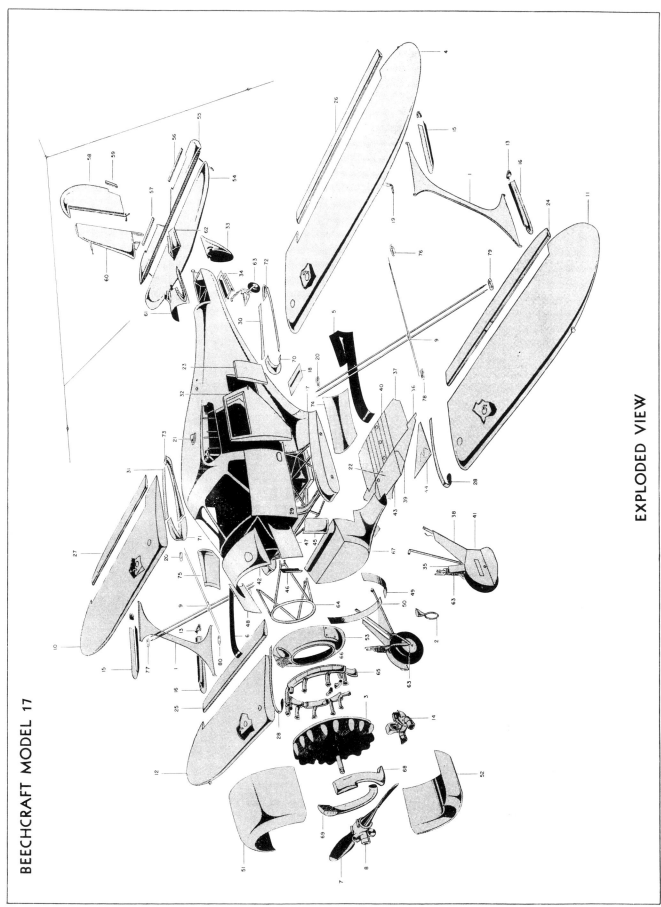

EXPLODED VIEW

1. D17530 — STRUT ASSEMBLY — 1
2. MN20C — LOOP — ANTENNAE
3. R985 AN-1 OR AN-2 ENGINE
4. D171006 — WING ASSEMBLY — UPPER LEFT
5. D170890 — MAT. — LEFT WING WALK
6. D170891 — MAT. — RIGHT WING WALK
7. 6167A-15 — BLADE — PROPELLER
8. 2D-30 — HUB — PROPELLER
9. D17096 — SPREADER — INTERPLANE WIRE
10. D171001 — WING ASSEMBLY — UPPER RIGHT
11. D171004 L.H. — WING ASSEMBLY — LOWER LEFT
12. D171004 R.H. — WING ASSEMBLY — LOWER RIGHT
13. D175295 — FAIRING — 1 STRUT LOWER REAR
14. D1759150 — SCOOP ASSEMBLY — CARBURETOR AIR
15. D175309 — FAIRING ASSEMBLY — 1 STRUT UPPER
16. D175310 — FAIRING ASSEMBLY — 1 STRUT LOWER
17. D175434-1 & -2 — FILLET — LOWER WING REAR
18. D171711 — PLATE — BELLY INSPECTION
19. D171742 — TUBE ASSEMBLY — HEATED PITOT
20. D17175-1 — PLATE — EXTERNAL TIE ROD UPPER ROOT
21. D173931 — COVER — CABIN VENT
22. D175047 — BULKHEAD ASSEMBLY — FRONT
23. D175250 — DOOR ASSEMBLY — BAGGAGE
24. D17160 L.H. — FLAP ASSEMBLY — L.H.
25. D17160 R.H. — FLAP ASSEMBLY — R.H.
26. D17130 L.H. — AILERON ASSEMBLY — L.H.
27. D17130 R.H. — AILERON ASSEMBLY — R.H.
28. D175441 — STRIP — WING WALK FAIRING L.H.
29. D175450 — SHEET — SIDE
30. D175597 — STRIP — WING ROOT FAIRING UPPER L.H.
31. D175597-1 — STRIP — WING ROOT FAIRING UPPER R.H.
32. D17560 — DOOR ASSEMBLY — CABIN
33. D175710 — COWLING ASSEMBLY — TAIL
34. D175720 — DOOR ASSEMBLY — TAIL WHEEL
35. D175780 — FAIRING ASSEMBLY — SHOCK ABSORBER
36. D175793 — FAIRING ASSEMBLY — REAR SIDE BELLY
37. D175794 — COWLING ASSEMBLY — REAR BELLY SIDE
38. D175796 — FAIRING ASSEMBLY — REAR LEG
39. D175797 — DOOR ASSEMBLY — BELLY FAIRING BULKHEAD
40. D175799 — COWL ASSEMBLY — REAR CENTER BELLY

41. D175800 — FAIRING ASSEMBLY — WHEEL
42. D175864 — SHEET — TOP WRAPPER
43. D175868 — COWL ASSEMBLY — BULKHEAD POINT
44. D175869 — FAIRING ASSEMBLY — FRONT SIDE BELLY
45. D175870 L.H. — GILL — ENGINE COMPARTMENT L.H.
46. D175870 R.H. — GILL — ENGINE COMPARTMENT R.H.
47. D175880 -2 L.H. — DOOR ASSEMBLY — ENGINE COMPARTMENT LOUVRE L.H.
48. D175880 -2 R.H. — DOOR ASSEMBLY — ENGINE COMPARTMENT LOUVRE R.H.
49. D175904 — WRAPPER ASSEMBLY — SIDE COWL LEFT
50. D175905 — WRAPPER ASSEMBLY — SIDE COWL RIGHT
51. D175911 — COWLING ASSEMBLY — ENGINE UPPER
52. D175912 — COWLING ASSEMBLY — ENGINE LOWER
53. D175950 — COWLING ASSEMBLY — ENGINE INNER
54. D176050 — STABILIZER ASSEMBLY
55. D17610 — ELEVATOR ASSEMBLY
56. D176111 L.H. — TAB ASSEMBLY — ELEVATOR L.H.
57. D176111 R.H. — TAB ASSEMBLY — ELEVATOR R.H.
58. D17620 — RUDDER ASSEMBLY
59. D176210 — TAB ASSEMBLY — RUDDER
60. D176300 — FIN ASSEMBLY
61. D176400 — FAIRING ASSEMBLY — FIN AND STABILIZER
62. D176406 — DOOR ASSEMBLY — TAIL FAIRING
63. D17800 — GEAR ASSEMBLY — LANDING
64. D1759100 — MOUNT ASSEMBLY — ENGINE
65. D175920 — STACK ASSEMBLY — EXHAUST
66. D17925 — HEATER — CABIN AND CARBURETOR
67. D179545 — COWLING ASSEMBLY — REAR FIREWALL
68. 189123 — DUCT ASSEMBLY — CARB. AIR FILTER L.H.
69. 189124 — DUCT ASSEMBLY — CARB. AIR FILTER R.H.
70. D175431 L.H. — FILLET — UPPER WING NOSE L.H.
71. D175431 R.H. — FILLET — UPPER WING NOSE R.H.
72. D175432 L.H. — FILLET — UPPER WING REAR
73. D175432 R.H. — FILLET — UPPER WING REAR
74. D175433 L.H. — FILLET — LOWER WING FRONT
75. 1175469 — RADIO ACCESS DOOR
76. D17175-2 L.H. — PLATE — EXTERNAL TIE ROD UPPER STRUT L.H.
77. D17175-2 R.H. — PLATE — EXTERNAL TIE ROD UPPER STRUT R.H.
78. D17175-3 L.H. — PLATE — EXTERNAL TIE ROD LOWER ROOT L.H.
79. D17175-4 L.H. — PLATE — EXTERNAL TIE ROD LOWER STRUT L.H.
80. D17175-4 R.H. — PLATE — EXTERNAL TIE ROD LOWER STRUT R.H.

BEECHCRAFT MODEL 17

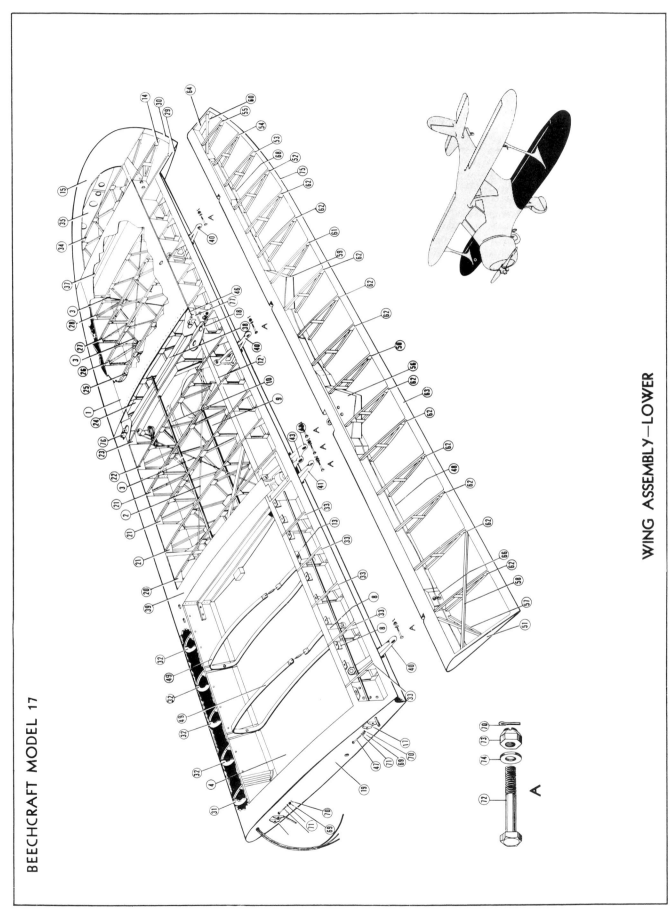

WING ASSEMBLY—LOWER

142

REF. NO.	PART NO.	PART NAME
1	D171004-3	PANEL — WING TIP REINFORCING BOTTOM
1	D171004-31	PANEL — WING TIP REINFORCING UPPER
2	D17090-2	ROD ASSEMBLY — LOWER WING TIE
3	D17090-4	ROD ASSEMBLY — LOWER WING TIE
4	D171012	BOTTOM ASSEMBLY — LOWER WING TANK COMPARTMENT
5	D171032-4	EDGE ASSEMBLY — LOWER WING LEADING LH
6	D171032-3	EDGE ASSEMBLY — LOWER WING LEADING RH
7	D171043	BRACKET ASSEMBLY — WING TANK COVER
8	D171045 LH	BRACKET ASSEMBLY — METAL WING TANK COVER LH
9	D171077	STRIP ASSEMBLY — LOWER WING RIB STRAIGHTENER
10	D171078	STRIP ASSEMBLY — LOWER WING RIB STRAIGHTENER
11	D17142-1 LH & RH	SPAR ASSEMBLY — LOWER WING FRONT
12	D17142-15 LH & RH	SPAR ASSEMBLY — LOWER WING LOWER REAR
13	D171444 LH & RH	BLOCK ASSEMBLY — LOWER TANK COVER SPAR
14	D171105 LH & RH	STRIP ASSEMBLY — WING TIP FORMER
15	D171115 LH & RH	COVER ASSEMBLY — WING TIP
16	D171718 LH & RH	FRAME ASSEMBLY — INSPECTION
17	D17210-1 LH & RH	FITTING — WING ROOT LH
18	D171721-2	SUPPORT — EXTERNAL TIE ROD FABRIC
19	D17185 LH & RH	RIB ASSEMBLY — LOWER WING ROOT
20	D171857 LH & RH	RIB ASSEMBLY — NO. 7 LOWER WING
21	D171858	RIB ASSEMBLY — NO. 8, 9, 10, LOWER WING
22	D171861 LH & RH	RIB ASSEMBLY — NO. 11 LOWER WING
23	D171862	RIB ASSEMBLY — NO. 12 LOWER WING
24	D171863 LH & RH	RIB ASSEMBLY — NO. 13 LOWER WING
25	D171864	RIB ASSEMBLY — NO. 14 LOWER WING
26	D171865 LH & RH	RIB ASSEMBLY — NO. 15 LOWER WING
27	D171866	RIB ASSEMBLY — NO. 16 LOWER WING
28	D171867	RIB ASSEMBLY — NO. 17 LOWER WING
29	D171868 LH & RH	RIB ASSEMBLY — NO. 18 LOWER WING
30	D171869 LH & RH	RIB ASSEMBLY — NO. 19 LOWER WING
31	D171881 LH & RH	RIB ASSEMBLY — LOWER WING NO. 1 NOSE
32	D171882	RIB ASSEMBLY — LOWER WING NO. 2, 3, 4, 5, 6, NOSE
33	D171891	RIB ASSEMBLY — LOWER NO. 1, 2, 3, 4, 5, TAIL
34	D171823	RIB ASSEMBLY — NO. 20 LOWER
35	D171824	RIB ASSEMBLY — NO. 21 LOWER
36	D171896 LH & RH	RIB — NO. 6 LOWER WING TAIL
37	D172133	MEMBER ASSEMBLY — LOWER WING COMPRESSION
38	D172134 LH & RH	MEMBER ASSEMBLY — LOWER WING COMPRESSION
39	D172140 LH & RH	MEMBER ASSEMBLY — LOWER WING COMPRESSION
40	D17264-1	HINGE ASSEMBLY — FLAP
41	D17264-2	HINGE ASSEMBLY — FLAP
42	D172641	HINGE ASSEMBLY — FLAP
43	D172660	MECHANISM ASSEMBLY — FLAP OPERATING WING
44	D172668	HOUSING ASSEMBLY — FLEXIBLE SHAFT IN WING
45	D171004-30	BRACE — LOWER WING
46	D171004-32	BLOCK — LOWER WING
47	AN5-21	BOLT (THIS IS NOT ON PARTS LIST)
49	D17965	STRAP ASSEMBLY — WING FUEL TANK
76	D17210-8	FITTING — STRUT LOWER FRONT
77	D17210-4	FITTING — REAR STRUT
		FLAP D17160
48	D17160-1	SPAR ASSEMBLY — FLAP
50	D17160-9	RIB ASSEMBLY — FLAP
51	D17160-11	RIB ASSEMBLY — FLAP INBOARD
52	D17160-12	RIB ASSEMBLY — FLAP
53	D17160-13	RIB ASSEMBLY — FLAP
54	D17160-14	RIB ASSEMBLY — FLAP
55	D17160-15	RIB ASSEMBLY — FLAP
56	D17160-18	GUSSET ASSEMBLY — FLAP REINFORCING
57	D17160-27	BRACE — FLAP REINFORCEMENT
58	D17160-28	BRACE — FLAP REINFORCEMENT
59	D17160-34	GUSSET ASSEMBLY — FLAP REINFORCING
60	D17160-41	BRACE — FLAP REINFORCEMENT
61	D17160-47	RIB ASSEMBLY — FLAP
62	D17160-8	RIB ASSEMBLY — FLAP
63	D17160-71	EDGE — FLAP TRAILING
64	D17160-89	RIB ASSEMBLY — FLAP OUTBOARD
65	D17131-1	FITTING ASSEMBLY — FLAP HINGE
66	D17160-3	BLOCK — SPAR REINFORCEMENT
67	D17160-4	BLOCK — SPAR REINFORCEMENT
68	D17160-6	BLOCK — SPAR REINFORCEMENT
69	AN310-5	NUT
70	AN380-2-2	PIN
71	AN960-516	WASHER
72	AN4-11	BOLT
73	AN310-4	NUT
74	AN960-416	WASHER
75	D17132-5	TUBE — FLAP TRAILING EDGE

BEECHCRAFT MODEL 17

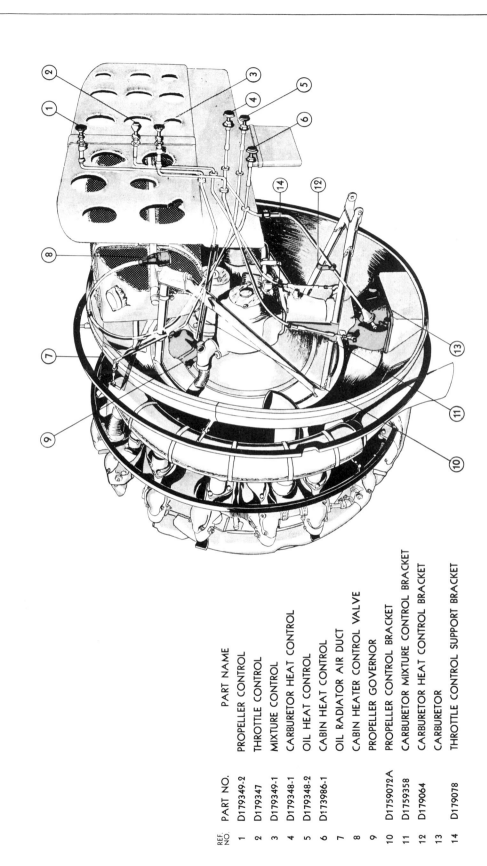

REF. NO.	PART NO.	PART NAME
1	D179349-2	PROPELLER CONTROL
2	D179347	THROTTLE CONTROL
3	D179349-1	MIXTURE CONTROL
4	D179348-1	CARBURETOR HEAT CONTROL
5	D179348-2	OIL HEAT CONTROL
6	D173986-1	CABIN HEAT CONTROL
7		OIL RADIATOR AIR DUCT
8		CABIN HEATER CONTROL VALVE
9		PROPELLER GOVERNOR
10	D1759072A	PROPELLER CONTROL BRACKET
11	D1759358	CARBURETOR MIXTURE CONTROL BRACKET
12	D179064	CARBURETOR HEAT CONTROL BRACKET
13		CARBURETOR
14	D179078	THROTTLE CONTROL SUPPORT BRACKET

ENGINE CONTROL SYSTEM

BEECHCRAFT MODEL 17

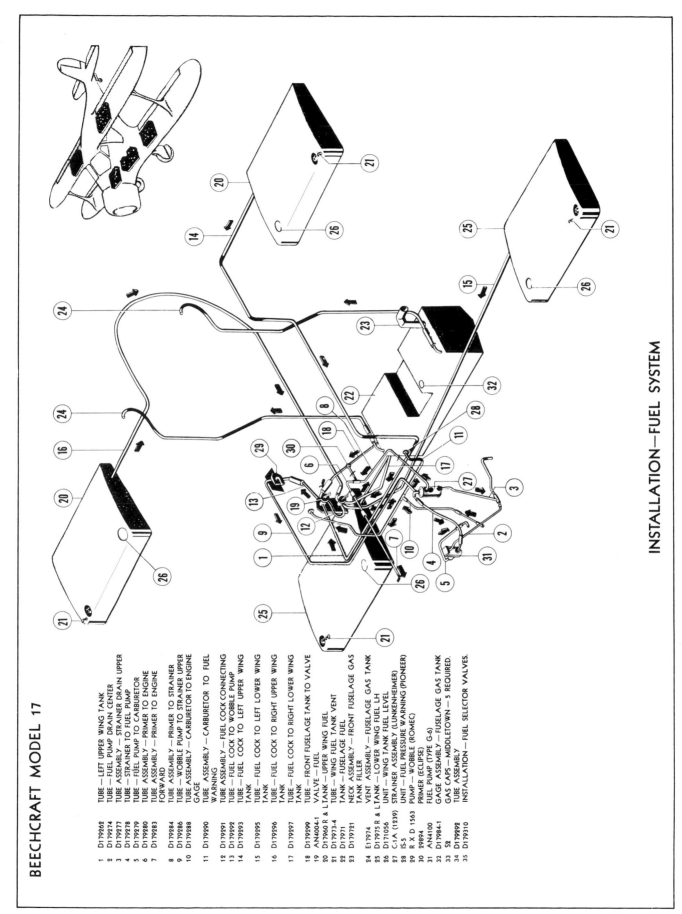

1	D179262	TUBE — LEFT UPPER WING TANK
2	D179274	TUBE — FUEL PUMP DRAIN CENTER
3	D179277	TUBE ASSEMBLY — STRAINER DRAIN UPPER
4	D179278	TUBE — STRAINER TO FUEL PUMP
5	D179279	TUBE — FUEL PUMP TO CARBURETOR
6	D179280	TUBE ASSEMBLY — PRIMER TO ENGINE
7	D179283	TUBE ASSEMBLY — PRIMER TO ENGINE FORWARD
8	D179284	TUBE ASSEMBLY — PRIMER TO STRAINER
9	D179286	TUBE — WOBBLE PUMP TO STRAINER UPPER
10	D179288	TUBE ASSEMBLY — CARBURETOR TO ENGINE GAGE
11	D179990	TUBE ASSEMBLY — CARBURETOR TO FUEL WARNING
12	D179991	TUBE ASSEMBLY — FUEL COCK CONNECTING
13	D179992	TUBE — FUEL COCK TO WOBBLE PUMP
14	D179993	TUBE — FUEL COCK TO LEFT UPPER WING TANK
15	D179995	TUBE — FUEL COCK TO LEFT LOWER WING TANK
16	D179996	TUBE — FUEL COCK TO RIGHT UPPER WING TANK
17	D179997	TUBE — FUEL COCK TO RIGHT LOWER WING TANK
18	D179999	TUBE — FRONT FUSELAGE TANK TO VALVE
19	AN404-1	VALVE — FUEL
20	D179960 R & L	TANK — UPPER WING FUEL
21	D17973-4	TUBE — WING FUEL TANK VENT
22	D17971	TANK — FUSELAGE FUEL
23	D179791	NECK ASSEMBLY — FRONT FUSELAGE GAS TANK FILLER
24	E17974	VENT ASSEMBLY — FUSELAGE GAS TANK
25	D17975 R & L	TANK — LOWER WING FUEL LH
26	D171056	UNIT — WING TANK FUEL LEVEL
27	C-1A (1239)	STRAINER ASSEMBLY (LUNKENHEIMER)
28	IS-5	UNIT — FUEL PRESSURE WARNING (PIONEER)
29	R X D 1563	PUMP — WOBBLE (ROMEC)
30	29894	PRIMER (ECLIPSE)
31	AN4100	FUEL PUMP (TYPE G-6)
32	D17984-1	GAGE ASSEMBLY — FUSELAGE GAS TANK
33	S2	GAS CAPS — MIDDLETOWN — 5 REQUIRED.
34	D179992	TUBE ASSEMBLY
35	D179310	INSTALLATION — FUEL SELECTOR VALVES.

INSTALLATION—FUEL SYSTEM

BEECHCRAFT MODEL 17

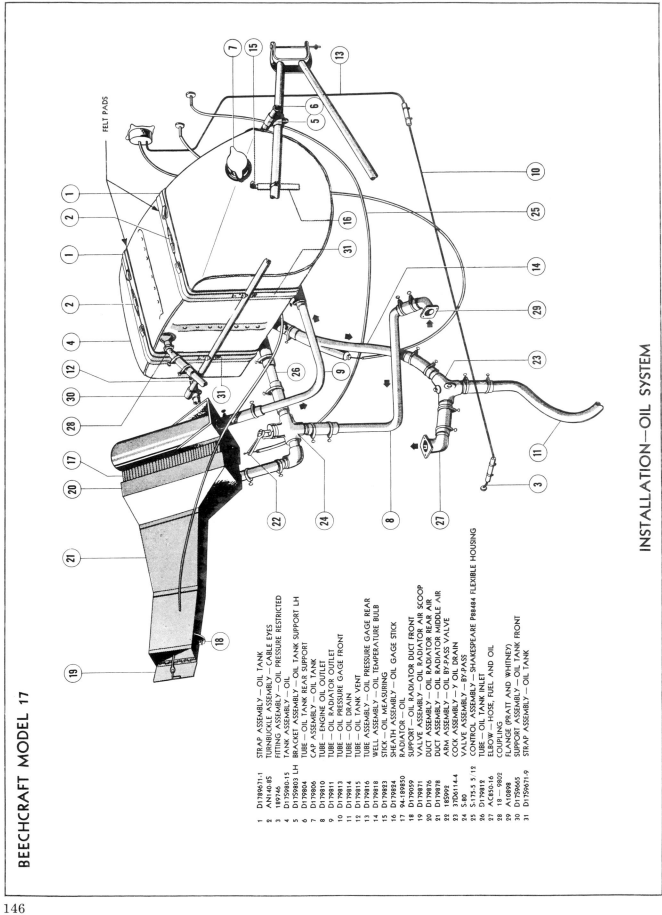

FELT PADS

1	D1789671-1	STRAP ASSEMBLY — OIL TANK
2	AN140-8S	TURNBUCKLE ASSEMBLY — CABLE EYES
3	189746	FITTING ASSEMBLY — OIL PRESSURE RESTRICTED
4	D175980-15	TANK ASSEMBLY — OIL
5	D175980B LH	BRACKET ASSEMBLY — OIL TANK SUPPORT LH
6	D179804	TUBE — OIL TANK REAR SUPPORT
7	D179806	CAP ASSEMBLY — OIL TANK
8	D179810	TUBE — ENGINE OIL OUTLET
9	D179811	TUBE — OIL RADIATOR OUTLET
10	D179813	TUBE — OIL PRESSURE GAGE FRONT
11	D179814	TUBE — OIL DRAIN
12	D179815	TUBE — OIL TANK VENT
13	D179816	TUBE ASSEMBLY — OIL PRESSURE GAGE REAR
14	D179818	WELL ASSEMBLY — OIL TEMPERATURE BULB
15	D179823	STICK — OIL MEASURING
16	D179824	SHEATH ASSEMBLY — OIL GAGE STICK
17	94-189850	RADIATOR — OIL
18	D179059	SUPPORT — OIL RADIATOR DUCT FRONT
19	D179871	VALVE ASSEMBLY — OIL RADIATOR AIR SCOOP
20	D179876	DUCT ASSEMBLY — OIL RADIATOR REAR AIR
21	D179878	DUCT ASSEMBLY — OIL RADIATOR MIDDLE AIR
22	18S992	ARM ASSEMBLY — OIL BY-PASS VALVE
23	37D6114-4	COCK ASSEMBLY — Y OIL DRAIN
24	S-80	VALVE ASSEMBLY — BY-PASS
25	S-175-5 5/12	CONTROL ASSEMBLY — SHAKESPEARE P88484 FLEXIBLE HOUSING
26	D179812	TUBE — OIL TANK INLET
27	AC850-16	ELBOW — HOSE, FUEL AND OIL
28	18 — 9802	COUPLING
29	A10898	FLANGE (PRATT AND WHITNEY)
30	D1759665	SUPPORT ASSEMBLY — OIL TANK FRONT
31	D1759671-9	STRAP ASSEMBLY — OIL TANK

146

BEECHCRAFT MODEL 17

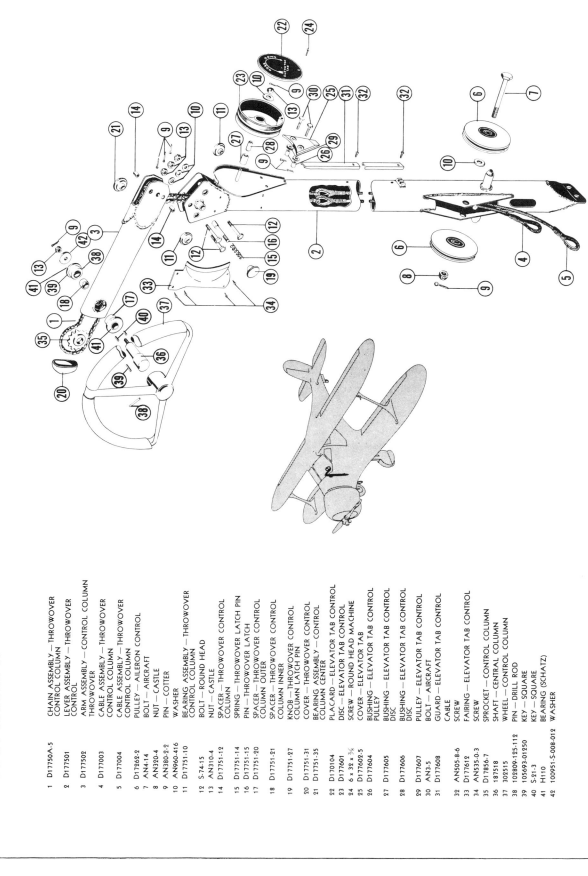

1	D17750A-5	CHAIN ASSEMBLY — THROWOVER CONTROL COLUMN
2	D177501	LEVER ASSEMBLY — THROWOVER CONTROL
3	D177502	ARM ASSEMBLY — CONTROL COLUMN THROWOVER
4	D177003	CABLE ASSEMBLY — THROWOVER CONTROL COLUMN
5	D177004	CABLE ASSEMBLY — THROWOVER CONTROL COLUMN
6	D17262-2	PULLEY — AILERON CONTROL
7	AN4-14	BOLT — AIRCRAFT
8	AN320.4	NUT — CASTLE
9	AN380-2-2	PIN — COTTER
10	AN960-416	WASHER
11	D17751-10	BEARING ASSEMBLY — THROWOVER CONTROL COLUMN
12	S-74-15	BOLT — ROUND HEAD
13	AN310-4	NUT — CASTLE
14	D17751-12	SPACER — THROWOVER CONTROL COLUMN
15	D17751-14	SPRING — THROWOVER LATCH PIN
16	D17751-15	PIN — THROWOVER LATCH
17	D17751-20	SPACER — THROWOVER CONTROL COLUMN OUTER
18	D17751-21	SPACER — THROWOVER CONTROL COLUMN INNER
19	D17751-27	KNOB — THROWOVER CONTROL COLUMN LATCH PIN
20	D17751-31	COVER — THROWOVER CONTROL
21	D17751-35	BEARING ASSEMBLY — CONTROL COLUMN CENTER
22	D170104	PLACARD — ELEVATOR TAB CONTROL
23	D177601	DISC — ELEVATOR TAB CONTROL
24	6 x 32 x ⅜	SCREW — ROUND HEAD MACHINE
25	D177602-5	COVER — ELEVATOR TAB
26	D177604	BUSHING — ELEVATOR TAB CONTROL PULLEY
27	D177605	BUSHING — ELEVATOR TAB CONTROL DISC
28	D177606	BUSHING — ELEVATOR TAB CONTROL DISC
29	D177607	PULLEY — ELEVATOR TAB CONTROL
30	AN3-5	BOLT — AIRCRAFT
31	D177608	GUARD — ELEVATOR TAB CONTROL CABLE
32	AN505-8-6	SCREW
33	D177612	FAIRING — ELEVATOR TAB CONTROL
34	AN535-0-3	SCREW
35	D17856-7	SPROCKET — CONTROL COLUMN
36	187518	SHAFT — CENTRAL COLUMN
37	302515	WHEEL — CONTROL COLUMN
38	102809-125-112	PIN — DRILL ROD
39	105693-01950	KEY — SQUARE
40	S-21-3	KEY — SQUARE
41	H110	BEARING (SCHATZ)
42	100951-S-008-012	WASHER

CONTROL COLUMN ASSEMBLY

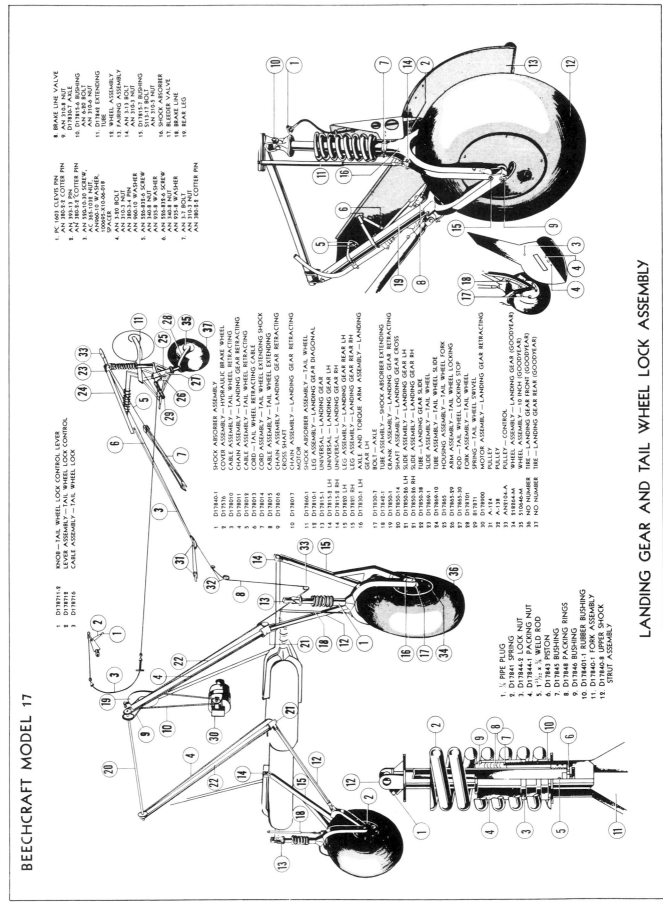

BEECHCRAFT MODEL 17

LANDING GEAR AND TAIL WHEEL LOCK ASSEMBLY

1. PC 1603 CLEVIS PIN
   AN 380-2-2 COTTER PIN
2. AN 393-13 PIN
   AN 380-2-2 COTTER PIN
3. AN 590-10-30 SCREW,
   AC 365-1032 NUT,
   AN960-10 WASHER,
   100695-X10-06-018 SPACER
4. AN 3-20 BOLT
   AN 310-3 NUT
   AN 380-3-4 PIN
   AN 960-10 WASHER
5. 526-832-6 SCREW
   340-8 NUT
   935-8 WASHER
6. 595-832-6 SCREW
   340-8 NUT
   935-8 WASHER
7. AN 3-7 BOLT
   AN 310-3 NUT
   AN 380-2-2 COTTER PIN

8. BRAKE LINE VALVE
9. AN 310-8 NUT
   D17830-7 AXLE
10. D17815-6 BUSHING
    AN 6-30 BOLT
    AN 310-6 NUT
11. D17842 EXTENDING TUBE
12. WHEEL ASSEMBLY
13. FAIRING ASSEMBLY
14. AN 3-13 BOLT
    AN 310-3 NUT
15. D17815-7 BUSHING
    S113-17 BOLT
    AN 310-5 NUT
16. SHOCK ABSORBER
17. BLEEDER VALVE
18. BRAKE LINE
19. REAR LEG

1	D17871-2	KNOB — TAIL WHEEL LOCK CONTROL LEVER
2	D178712	LEVER ASSEMBLY — TAIL WHEEL LOCK CONTROL
3	D178716	CABLE ASSEMBLY — TAIL WHEEL LOCK

1	D17840-1	SHOCK ABSORBER ASSEMBLY
2	D17576	COVER ASSEMBLY — HYDRAULIC BRAKE WHEEL
3	D178010	CABLE ASSEMBLY — TAIL WHEEL RETRACTING
4	D178011	CHAIN ASSEMBLY — LANDING GEAR RETRACTING
5	D178012	CABLE ASSEMBLY — TAIL WHEEL RETRACTING
6	D178013	CORD — TAIL WHEEL RETRACTING CABLE
7	D178014	CORD ASSEMBLY — TAIL WHEEL EXTENDING SHOCK
8	D178015	CABLE ASSEMBLY — TAIL WHEEL EXTENDING
9	D178016	CHAIN ASSEMBLY — LANDING GEAR RETRACTING CROSS SHAFT
10	D178017	CHAIN ASSEMBLY — LANDING GEAR RETRACTING MOTOR
11	D17860-1	SHOCK ABSORBER ASSEMBLY — TAIL WHEEL
12	D17810-1	LEG ASSEMBLY — LANDING GEAR DIAGONAL
13	D17815-1	UNIVERSAL — LANDING GEAR LH
14	D17815-2 LH	UNIVERSAL — LANDING GEAR LH
15	D17890 LH	LEG ASSEMBLY — LANDING GEAR REAR LH
15	D17815-2 RH	UNIVERSAL — LANDING GEAR RH
16	D17890 RH	LEG ASSEMBLY — LANDING GEAR REAR RH
		AXLE AND TORQUE ARM ASSEMBLY — LANDING GEAR LH
17	D17830-7	BOLT — AXLE
18	D17849-1	TUBE ASSEMBLY — SHOCK ABSORBER EXTENDING
19	D17850-1	CRANK ASSEMBLY — LANDING GEAR RETRACTING
20	D17850-14	SHAFT ASSEMBLY — LANDING GEAR CROSS
21	D17850-26 LH	SLIDE ASSEMBLY — LANDING GEAR LH
21	D17850-26 RH	SLIDE ASSEMBLY — LANDING GEAR RH
22	D17850-38	TUBE — LANDING GEAR SLIDE
23	D17869-1	SLIDE ASSEMBLY — TAIL WHEEL
24	D17869-10	TUBE ASSEMBLY — TAIL WHEEL SLIDE
25	D17865	HOUSING ASSEMBLY — TAIL WHEEL LOCKING
26	D17865-29	ARM ASSEMBLY — TAIL WHEEL LOCKING
27	D17865-30	ROD — TAIL WHEEL LOCKING STOP
28	D17870-1	FORK ASSEMBLY — TAIL WHEEL
29	B17871	SPRING — TAIL WHEEL SWIVEL
30	D178900	MOTOR ASSEMBLY — LANDING GEAR RETRACTING
31	A-194	PULLEY
32	A-138	PULLEY
33	AN9104-A	PULLEY — CONTROL
34	919864-M	WHEEL ASSEMBLY — LANDING GEAR (GOODYEAR)
35	510646-M	WHEEL ASSEMBLY — 10 INCH (GOODYEAR)
36	NO NUMBER	TIRE — LANDING GEAR FRONT (GOODYEAR)
37	NO NUMBER	TIRE — LANDING GEAR REAR (GOODYEAR)

1. ⅛ PIPE PLUG
2. D17841 SPRING
3. D17844-2 LOCK NUT
4. D17844-1 PACKING NUT
5. 1-13/32 x ⅛ WELD ROD
6. D17843 PISTON
7. D17845 BUSHING
8. D17848 PACKING RINGS
9. D17846 BUSHING
10. D178401-1 RUBBER BUSHING
11. D17840-1 FORK ASSEMBLY
12. D17840-8 UPPER SHOCK STRUT ASSEMBLY

BEECHCRAFT MODEL 17

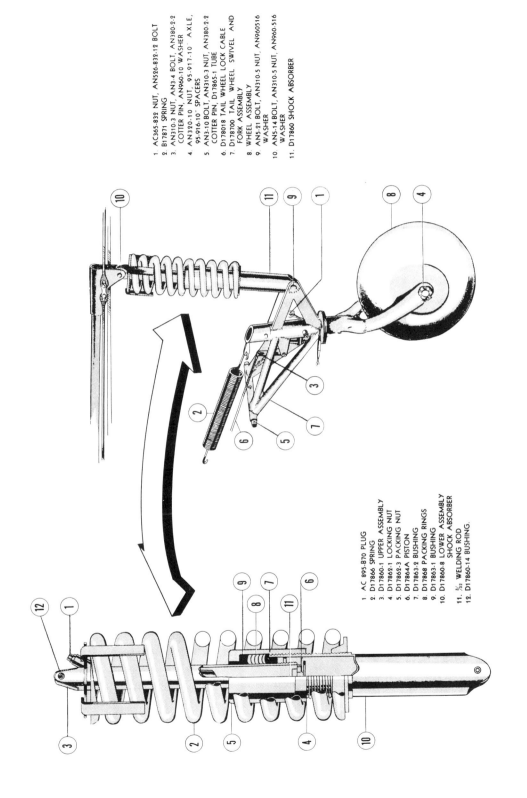

1. AC365-832 NUT, AN526-832-12 BOLT
2. B17871 SPRING
3. AN310-3 NUT, AN3-4 BOLT, AN380-2-2 COTTER PIN, AN960-10 WASHER
4. AN320-10 NUT, 95-917-10 AXLE, 95-916-10' SPACERS
5. AN3-10 BOLT, AN310-3 NUT, AN380-2-2 COTTER PIN, D17865-1 TUBE
6. D178018 TAIL WHEEL LOCK CABLE
7. D178700 TAIL WHEEL SWIVEL AND FORK ASSEMBLY
8. WHEEL ASSEMBLY
9. AN5-21 BOLT, AN310-5 NUT, AN960516 WASHER
10. AN5-14 BOLT, AN310-5 NUT, AN960-516 WASHER
11. D17860 SHOCK ABSORBER

1. AC 895-870 PLUG
2. D17860 SPRING
3. D17860-1 UPPER ASSEMBLY
4. D17869-1 LOCKING NUT
5. D17862-3 PACKING NUT
6. D17864A PISTON
7. D17863-2 BUSHING
8. D17868 PACKING RINGS
9. D17863-1 BUSHING
10. D17860-8 LOWER ASSEMBLY SHOCK ABSORBER
11. ³⁄₃₂ WELDING ROD
12. D17860-14 BUSHING.

EXPLODED TAILWHEEL ASSEMBLY

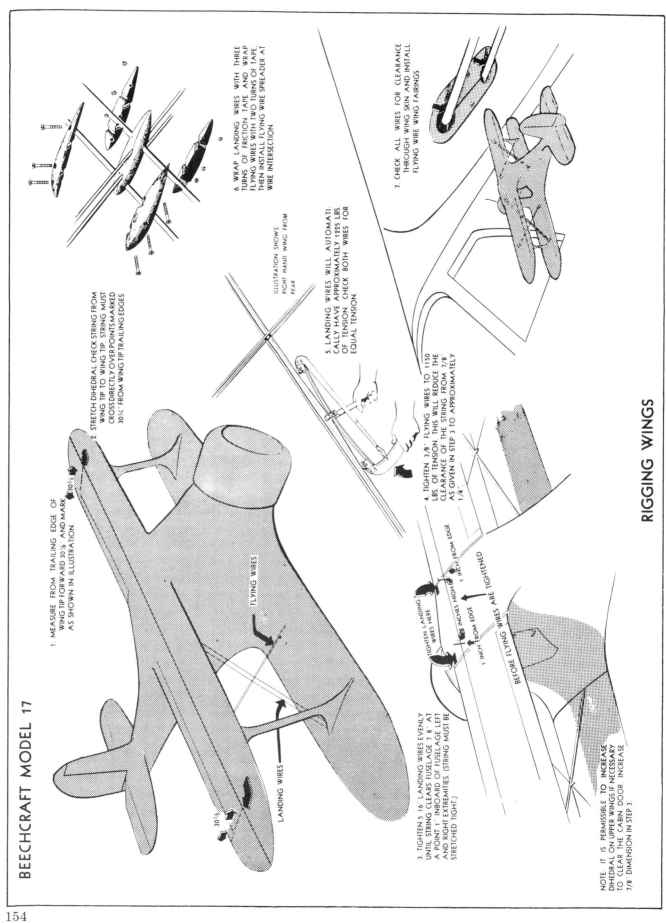

BEECHCRAFT MODEL 17

1. MEASURE FROM TRAILING EDGE OF WING TIP FORWARD 30½ AND MARK AS SHOWN IN ILLUSTRATION.

2. STRETCH DIHEDRAL CHECK STRING FROM WING TIP TO WING TIP. STRING MUST CROSS DIRECTLY OVER POINTS MARKED 30½" FROM WING TIP TRAILING EDGES.

3. TIGHTEN S 16' LANDING WIRES EVENLY UNTIL STRING CLEARS FUSELAGE 7 8 AT A POINT 1' INBOARD OF FUSELAGE LEFT AND RIGHT EXTREMITIES (STRING MUST BE STRETCHED TIGHT.)

FLYING WIRES

LANDING WIRES

ILLUSTRATION SHOWS RIGHT HAND WING FROM REAR

4. TIGHTEN 3/8" FLYING WIRES TO 1150 LBS. OF TENSION. THIS WILL REDUCE THE CLEARANCE OF THE STRING FROM 7/8" AS GIVEN IN STEP 3 TO APPROXIMATELY 1/4.

5. LANDING WIRES WILL AUTOMATICALLY HAVE APPROXIMATELY 1225 LBS. OF TENSION. CHECK BOTH WIRES FOR EQUAL TENSION.

6. WRAP LANDING WIRES WITH THREE TURNS OF FRICTION TAPE AND WRAP FLYING WIRES WITH TWO TURNS OF TAPE, THEN INSTALL FLYING WIRE SPREADER AT WIRE INTERSECTION.

7. CHECK ALL WIRES FOR CLEARANCE THROUGH WING SKIN AND INSTALL FLYING WIRE WING FAIRINGS.

TIGHTEN LANDING WIRES HERE

1 INCH FROM EDGE

8 INCHES HIGH

BEFORE FLYING WIRES ARE TIGHTENED

1 INCH FROM EDGE

NOTE. IT IS PERMISSIBLE TO INCREASE DIHEDRAL ON UPPER WINGS IF NECESSARY TO CLEAR THE CABIN DOOR. INCREASE 7/8 DIMENSION IN STEP 3.

RIGGING WINGS

154

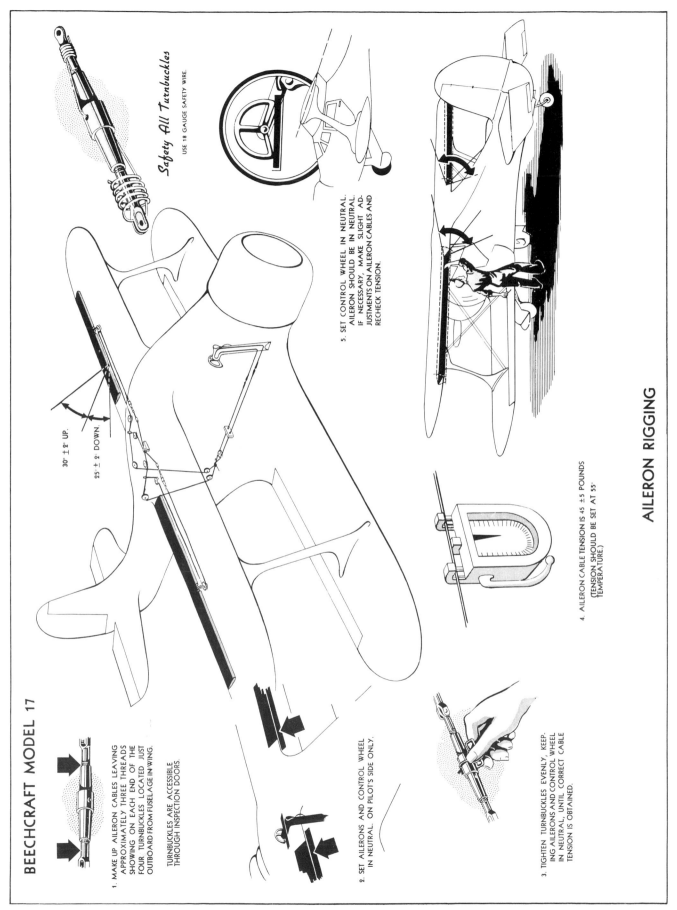

BEECHCRAFT MODEL 17

Safety All Turnbuckles

USE 18 GAUGE SAFETY WIRE.

30° ± 2° UP.

25° ± 2° DOWN.

1. MAKE UP AILERON CABLES LEAVING APPROXIMATELY THREE THREADS SHOWING ON EACH END OF THE FOUR TURNBUCKLES LOCATED JUST OUTBOARD FROM FUSELAGE IN WING.

TURNBUCKLES ARE ACCESSIBLE THROUGH INSPECTION DOORS.

2. SET AILERONS AND CONTROL WHEEL IN NEUTRAL, ON PILOT'S SIDE ONLY.

3. TIGHTEN TURNBUCKLES EVENLY, KEEPING AILERONS AND CONTROL WHEEL IN NEUTRAL, UNTIL CORRECT CABLE TENSION IS OBTAINED.

4. AILERON CABLE TENSION IS 45 ±5 POUNDS (TENSION SHOULD BE SET AT 55° TEMPERATURE.)

5. SET CONTROL WHEEL IN NEUTRAL. AILERON SHOULD BE IN NEUTRAL. IF NECESSARY, MAKE SLIGHT ADJUSTMENTS ON AILERON CABLES AND RECHECK TENSION.

AILERON RIGGING

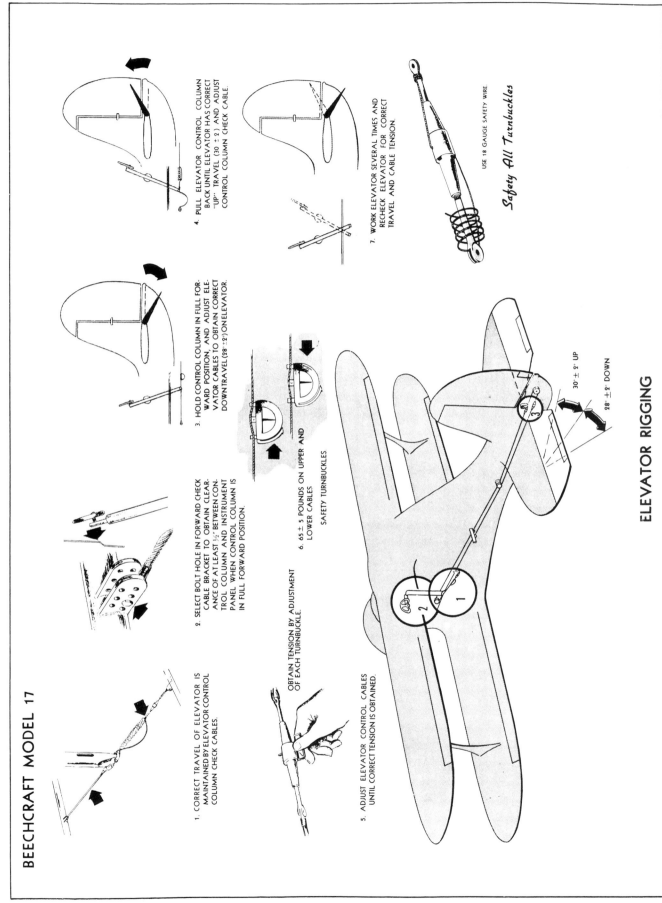

BEECHCRAFT MODEL 17

1. CORRECT TRAVEL OF ELEVATOR IS MAINTAINED BY ELEVATOR CONTROL COLUMN CHECK CABLES.

2. SELECT BOLT HOLE IN FORWARD CHECK CABLE BRACKET TO OBTAIN CLEARANCE OF AT LEAST ½" BETWEEN CONTROL COLUMN AND INSTRUMENT PANEL WHEN CONTROL COLUMN IS IN FULL FORWARD POSITION.

3. HOLD CONTROL COLUMN IN FULL FORWARD POSITION, AND ADJUST ELEVATOR CABLES TO OBTAIN CORRECT DOWN TRAVEL (28° ± 2°) ON ELEVATOR.

4. PULL ELEVATOR CONTROL COLUMN BACK UNTIL ELEVATOR HAS CORRECT "UP" TRAVEL (30 ± 2) AND ADJUST CONTROL COLUMN CHECK CABLE.

5. ADJUST ELEVATOR CONTROL CABLES UNTIL CORRECT TENSION IS OBTAINED.

OBTAIN TENSION BY ADJUSTMENT OF EACH TURNBUCKLE.

6. 65 ± 5 POUNDS ON UPPER AND LOWER CABLES

SAFETY TURNBUCKLES

7. WORK ELEVATOR SEVERAL TIMES AND RECHECK ELEVATOR FOR CORRECT TRAVEL AND CABLE TENSION.

USE 18 GAUGE SAFETY WIRE.

Safety All Turnbuckles

30° ± 2° UP

28° ± 2° DOWN

ELEVATOR RIGGING

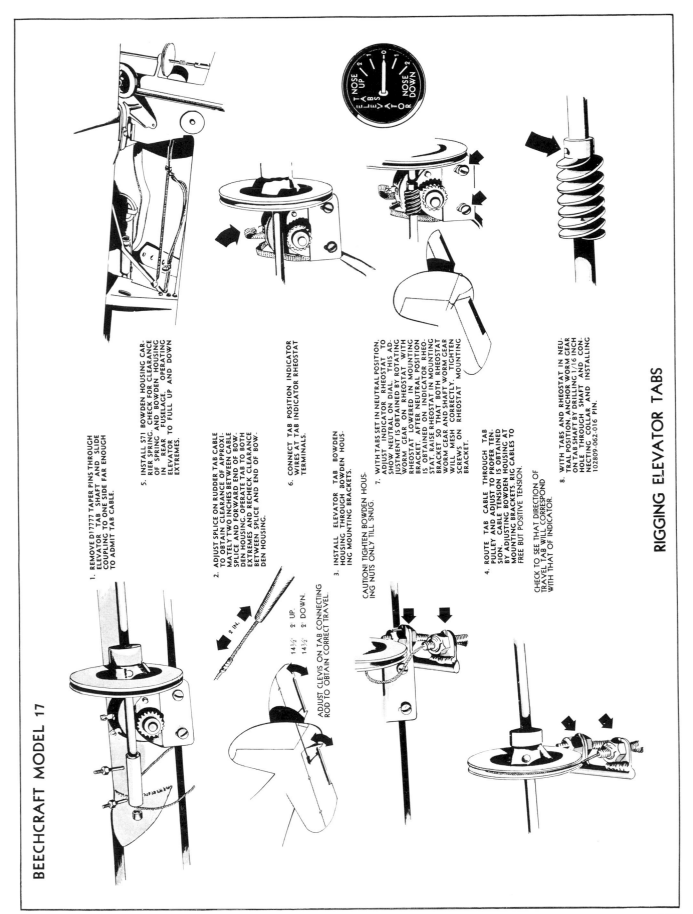

BEECHCRAFT MODEL 17

1. REMOVE D17777 TAPER PINS THROUGH ELEVATOR TAB SHAFT AND SLIDE COUPLING TO ONE SIDE FAR ENOUGH TO ADMIT TAB CABLE.

2. ADJUST SPLICE ON RUDDER TAB CABLE TO OBTAIN CLEARANCE OF APPROXIMATELY TWO INCHES BETWEEN CABLE SPLICE AND FORWARD END OF BOWDEN HOUSING. OPERATE TAB TO BOTH EXTREMES AND RECHECK CLEARANCE BETWEEN SPLICE AND END OF BOWDEN HOUSING.

3. INSTALL ELEVATOR TAB BOWDEN HOUSING THROUGH BOWDEN HOUSING MOUNTING BRACKETS.

CAUTION! TIGHTEN BOWDEN HOUSING NUTS ONLY TILL SNUG.

4. ROUTE TAB CABLE THROUGH TAB PULLEY AND ADJUST TO PROPER TENSION. CABLE TENSION IS OBTAINED BY ADJUSTING BOWDEN HOUSING AT MOUNTING BRACKETS. RIG CABLES TO FREE BUT POSITIVE TENSION.

CHECK TO SEE THAT DIRECTION OF TRAVEL TAB WILL CORRESPOND WITH THAT OF INDICATOR.

5. INSTALL 571 BOWDEN HOUSING CARRIER SPRING. CHECK FOR CLEARANCE OF SPRING AND BOWDEN HOUSING IN REAR FUSELAGE. OPERATING ELEVATOR TO FULL UP AND DOWN EXTREMES.

6. CONNECT TAB POSITION INDICATOR WIRES AT TAB INDICATOR RHEOSTAT TERMINALS.

7. WITH TABS SET IN NEUTRAL POSITION, ADJUST INDICATOR RHEOSTAT TO SHOW NEUTRAL ON DIAL. THIS ADJUSTMENT IS OBTAINED BY ROTATING WORM GEAR ON RHEOSTAT WITH RHEOSTAT LOWERED IN MOUNTING BRACKET. AFTER NEUTRAL POSITION IS OBTAINED ON INDICATOR RHEOSTAT, RAISE RHEOSTAT IN MOUNTING BRACKET SO THAT BOTH RHEOSTAT WORM GEAR AND SHAFT WORM GEAR WILL MESH CORRECTLY. TIGHTEN SCREWS ON RHEOSTAT MOUNTING BRACKET.

8. WITH TABS AND RHEOSTAT IN NEUTRAL POSITION, ANCHOR WORM GEAR ON TAB SHAFT BY DRILLING 1/16 INCH HOLE THROUGH SHAFT AND CONNECTING COLLAR AND INSTALLING 102809-062-016 PIN.

ADJUST CLEVIS ON TAB CONNECTING ROD TO OBTAIN CORRECT TRAVEL.

9 IN.

14½ 2° UP.
14½ 2° DOWN.

NOSE UP ELEVATOR NOSE DOWN

RIGGING ELEVATOR TABS

159

BEECHCRAFT MODEL 17

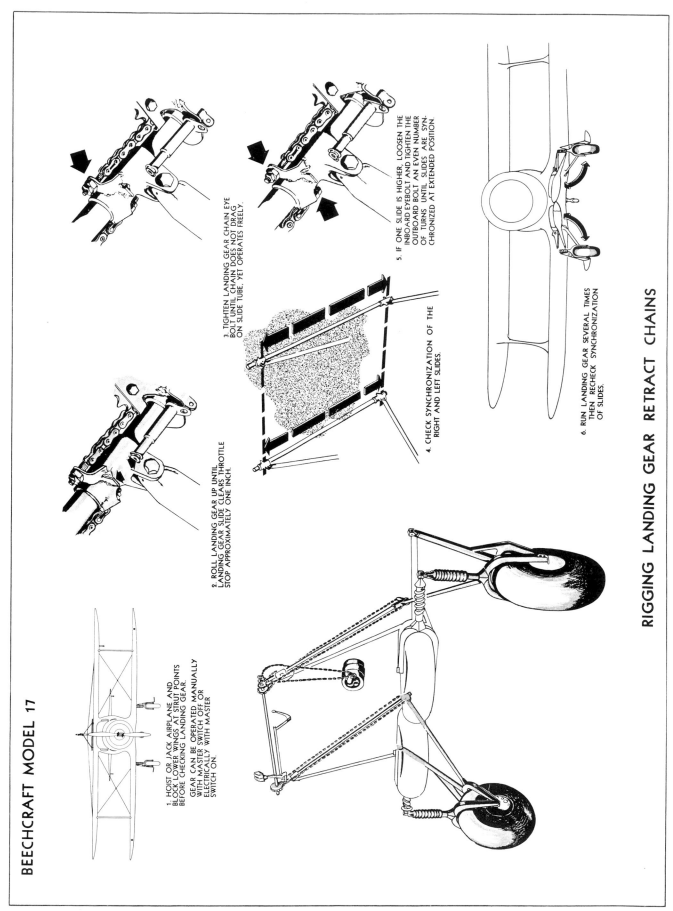

1. HOIST OR JACK AIRPLANE AND BLOCK LOWER WINGS AT STRUT POINTS BEFORE CHECKING LANDING GEAR.

GEAR CAN BE OPERATED MANUALLY WITH MASTER SWITCH OFF OR ELECTRICALLY WITH MASTER SWITCH ON.

2. ROLL LANDING GEAR UP UNTIL LANDING GEAR SLIDE CLEARS THROTTLE STOP APPROXIMATELY ONE INCH.

3. TIGHTEN LANDING GEAR CHAIN EYE BOLT UNTIL CHAIN DOES NOT DRAG ON SLIDE TUBE, YET OPERATES FREELY.

4. CHECK SYNCHRONIZATION OF THE RIGHT AND LEFT SLIDES.

5. IF ONE SLIDE IS HIGHER, LOOSEN THE INBOARD EYEBOLT AND TIGHTEN THE OUTBOARD BOLT AN EVEN NUMBER OF TURNS UNTIL SLIDES ARE SYNCHRONIZED AT EXTENDED POSITION.

6. RUN LANDING GEAR SEVERAL TIMES THEN RECHECK SYNCHRONIZATION OF SLIDES.

RIGGING LANDING GEAR RETRACT CHAINS

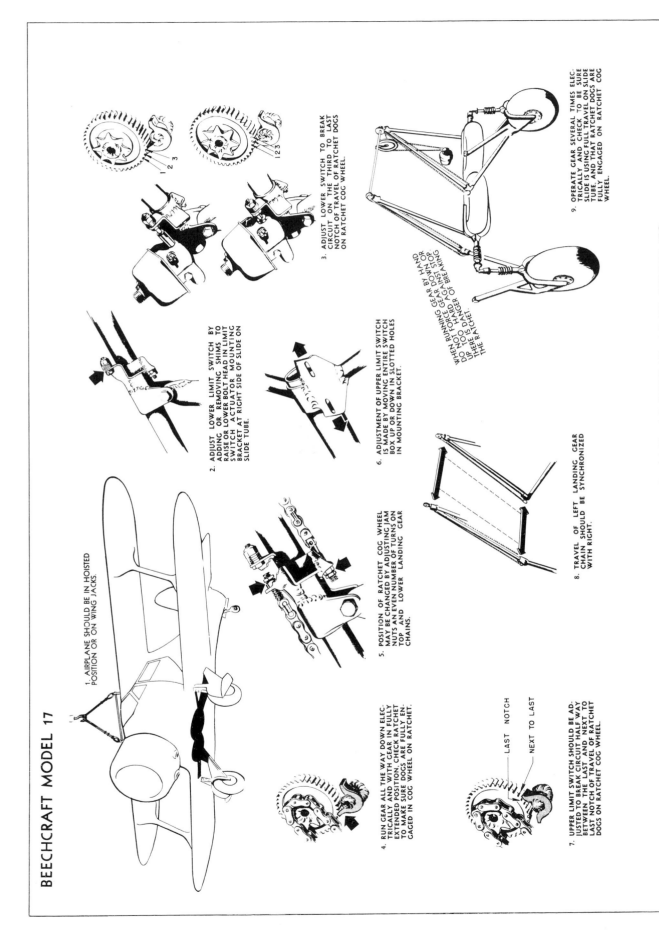

BEECHCRAFT MODEL 17

1. AIRPLANE SHOULD BE IN HOISTED POSITION OR ON WING JACKS.

2. ADJUST LOWER LIMIT SWITCH BY ADDING OR REMOVING SHIMS TO RAISE OR LOWER BOLT HEAD IN LIMIT SWITCH ACTUATOR MOUNTING BRACKET AT RIGHT SIDE OF SLIDE ON SLIDE TUBE.

3. ADJUST LOWER SWITCH TO BREAK CIRCUIT ON THE THIRD TO LAST NOTCH OF TRAVEL OF RATCHET DOGS ON RATCHET COG WHEEL.

4. RUN GEAR ALL THE WAY DOWN ELECTRICALLY AND WITH GEAR IN FULLY EXTENDED POSITION, CHECK RATCHET TO MAKE SURE DOGS ARE FULLY ENGAGED IN COG WHEEL ON RATCHET.

5. POSITION OF RATCHET COG WHEEL MAY BE CHANGED BY ADJUSTING JAM NUTS AN EVEN NUMBER OF TURNS ON TOP AND LOWER LANDING GEAR CHAINS.

6. ADJUSTMENT OF UPPER LIMIT SWITCH IS MADE BY MOVING ENTIRE SWITCH BOX UP OR DOWN IN SLOTTED HOLES IN MOUNTING BRACKET.

7. UPPER LIMIT SWITCH SHOULD BE ADJUSTED TO BREAK CIRCUIT HALF WAY BETWEEN THE LAST AND NEXT TO LAST NOTCH OF TRAVEL OF RATCHET DOGS ON RATCHET COG WHEEL.

LAST NOTCH

NEXT TO LAST

WHEN RUNNING GEAR DOWN OR UP DO NOT FORCE GEAR AGAINST STOP. IF TOO HARD THERE IS DANGER OF BREAKING THE RATCHET.

8. TRAVEL OF LEFT LANDING GEAR CHAIN SHOULD BE SYNCHRONIZED WITH RIGHT.

9. OPERATE GEAR SEVERAL TIMES ELECTRICALLY AND CHECK TO BE SURE SLIDE IS USING FULL TRAVEL ON SLIDE TUBE, AND THAT RATCHET DOGS ARE FULLY ENGAGED ON RATCHET COG WHEEL.

RIGGING MAIN LANDING GEAR AND ADJUSTING LIMIT SWITCHES

163

BEECHCRAFT MODEL 17

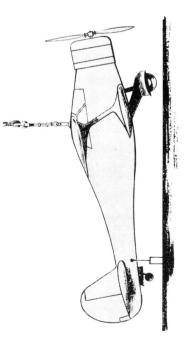

1. HOIST AIRPLANE.

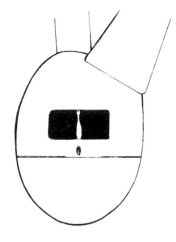

2. RETRACT LANDING GEAR TO FULL "UP" POSITION AND CHECK CABLE TENSION ON HINGED DOOR.

3. ADJUST DOOR BY TIGHTENING TURN-BUCKLE TO INCREASE TENSION ON DOOR OR BY LOOSENING TURN-BUCKLE TO RELIEVE TENSION.

4. EXTEND GEAR TO FULL DOWN POSITION. PLACE DOOR AT A 90 ANGLE WITH MAIN WHEEL FAIRING.

90°

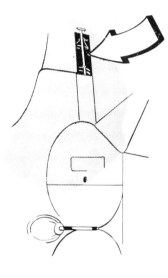

5. HOLDING DOOR AT 90 ANGLE WITH MAIN WHEEL FAIRING, PULL CABLE TIGHT AT INBOARD END.

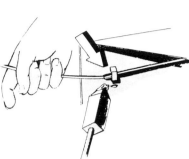

6. PLACE WASHER AND FERRULE SNUG AGAINST INBOARD CABLE FAIRLEAD AND SOLDER IN PLACE.

ALL FAIRING SHOULD HAVE ⅛ TO ¼ CLEARANCE BETWEEN BELLY OPENINGS.

RIGGING MAIN LANDING GEAR FAIRING

BEECHCRAFT MODEL 17

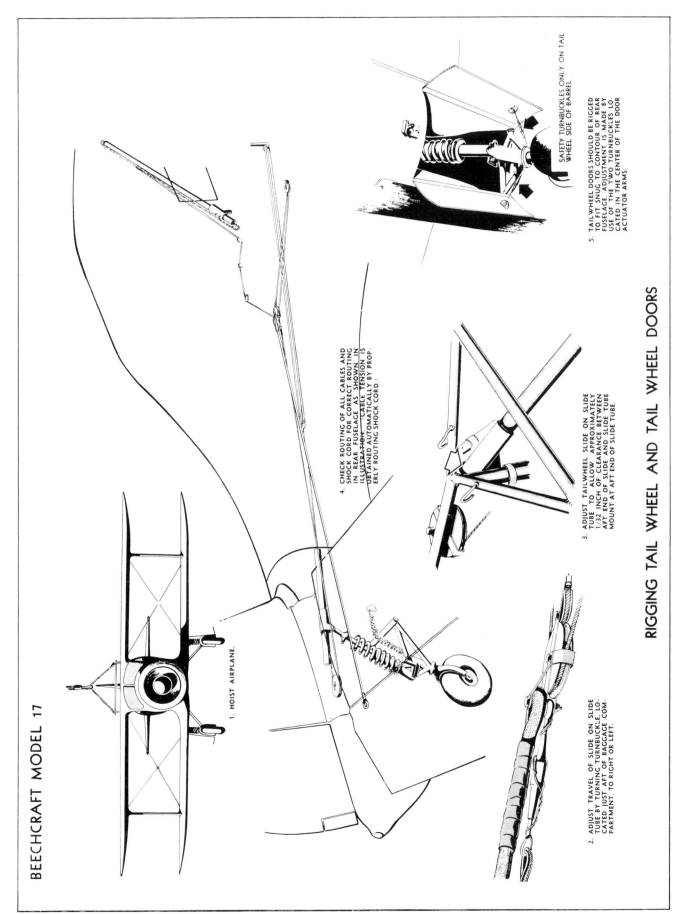

1. HOIST AIRPLANE.

2. ADJUST TRAVEL OF SLIDE ON SLIDE TUBE BY TURNING TURNBUCKLE. LOCATED JUST AFT OF BAGGAGE COMPARTMENT. TO RIGHT OR LEFT.

3. ADJUST TAILWHEEL SLIDE ON SLIDE TUBE TO ALLOW APPROXIMATELY 1/32 INCH OF CLEARANCE BETWEEN AFT END OF SLIDE AND SLIDE TUBE MOUNT AT AFT END OF SLIDE TUBE.

4. CHECK ROUTING OF ALL CABLES AND SHOCK CORD FOR CORRECT ROUTING IN REAR FUSELAGE AS SHOWN IN ILLUSTRATION. (CABLE TENSION IS OBTAINED AUTOMATICALLY BY PROPERLY ROUTING SHOCK CORD.)

5. TAILWHEEL DOORS SHOULD BE RIGGED TO FIT SNUG, TO CONTOUR OF REAR FUSELAGE. ADJUSTMENT IS MADE BY USE OF THE TWO TURNBUCKLES LOCATED IN THE CENTER OF THE DOOR ACTUATOR ARMS.

SAFETY TURNBUCKLES ONLY ON TAIL WHEEL SIDE OF BARREL.

RIGGING TAIL WHEEL AND TAIL WHEEL DOORS

165

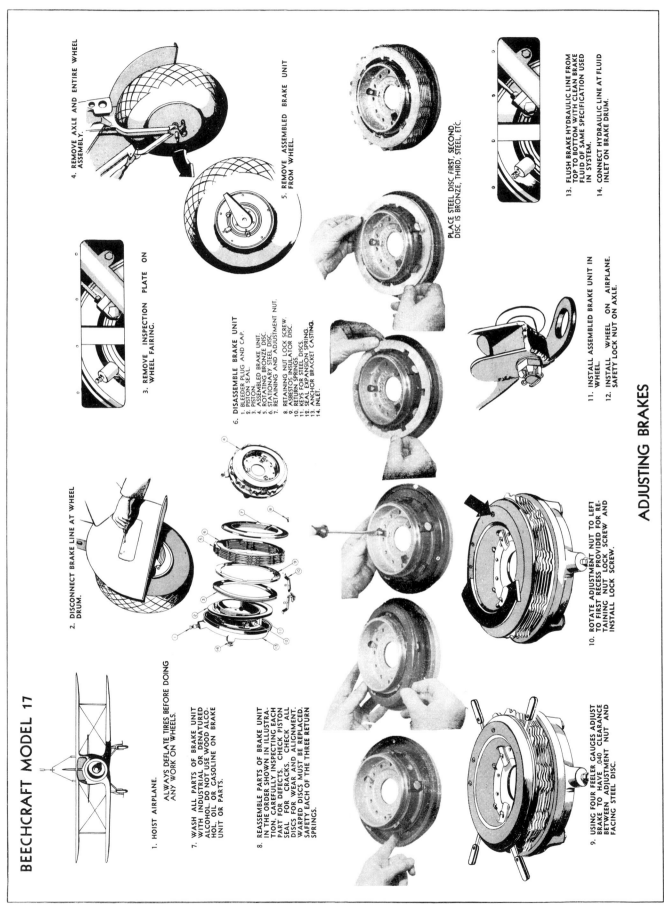

BEECHCRAFT MODEL 17

1. HOIST AIRPLANE.

ALWAYS DEFLATE TIRES BEFORE DOING ANY WORK ON WHEELS.

7. WASH ALL PARTS OF BRAKE UNIT WITH INDUSTRIAL OR DENATURED ALCOHOL. DO NOT USE WOOD ALCOHOL, OIL OR GASOLINE ON BRAKE UNIT OR PARTS.

8. REASSEMBLE PARTS OF BRAKE UNIT IN THE ORDER SHOWN IN ILLUSTRATION. CAREFULLY INSPECTING EACH PART FOR DEFECTS. CHECK PISTON SEAL FOR CRACKS. CHECK ALL DISCS FOR WEAR AND ALIGNMENT. WARPED DISCS MUST BE REPLACED. SAFETY EACH OF THE THREE RETURN SPRINGS.

2. DISCONNECT BRAKE LINE AT WHEEL DRUM.

3. REMOVE INSPECTION PLATE ON WHEEL FAIRING.

4. REMOVE AXLE AND ENTIRE WHEEL ASSEMBLY.

5. REMOVE ASSEMBLED BRAKE UNIT FROM WHEEL.

6. DISASSEMBLE BRAKE UNIT
   1. BLEEDER PLUG AND CAP.
   2. PISTON SEAL.
   3. PISTON.
   4. ASSEMBLED BRONZE DISC.
   5. ROTATING BRONZE DISC.
   6. STATIONARY STEEL DISC.
   7. RETAINING AND ADJUSTMENT NUT.
   8. RETAINING NUT LOCK SCREW.
   9. ASBESTOS INSULATOR DISC.
   10. RETURN SPRINGS.
   11. KEYS FOR STEEL DISCS.
   12. SEAL EXPANSION SPRING.
   13. ANCHOR BRACKET CASTING.
   14. INLET.

9. USING FOUR FEELER GAUGES ADJUST BRAKE TO HAVE .040 CLEARANCE BETWEEN ADJUSTMENT NUT AND FACING STEEL DISC.

10. ROTATE ADJUSTMENT NUT TO LEFT TO FIRST RECESS PROVIDED FOR RETAINING NUT LOCK SCREW AND INSTALL LOCK SCREW.

PLACE STEEL DISC FIRST, SECOND, DISC IS BRONZE, THIRD, STEEL, ETC.

11. INSTALL ASSEMBLED BRAKE UNIT IN WHEEL.

12. INSTALL WHEEL ON AIRPLANE. SAFETY LOCK NUT ON AXLE.

13. FLUSH BRAKE HYDRAULIC LINE FROM TOP TO BOTTOM WITH CLEAN BRAKE FLUID OF SAME SPECIFICATION USED IN SYSTEM.

14. CONNECT HYDRAULIC LINE AT FLUID INLET ON BRAKE DRUM.

ADJUSTING BRAKES

BEECHCRAFT MODEL 17

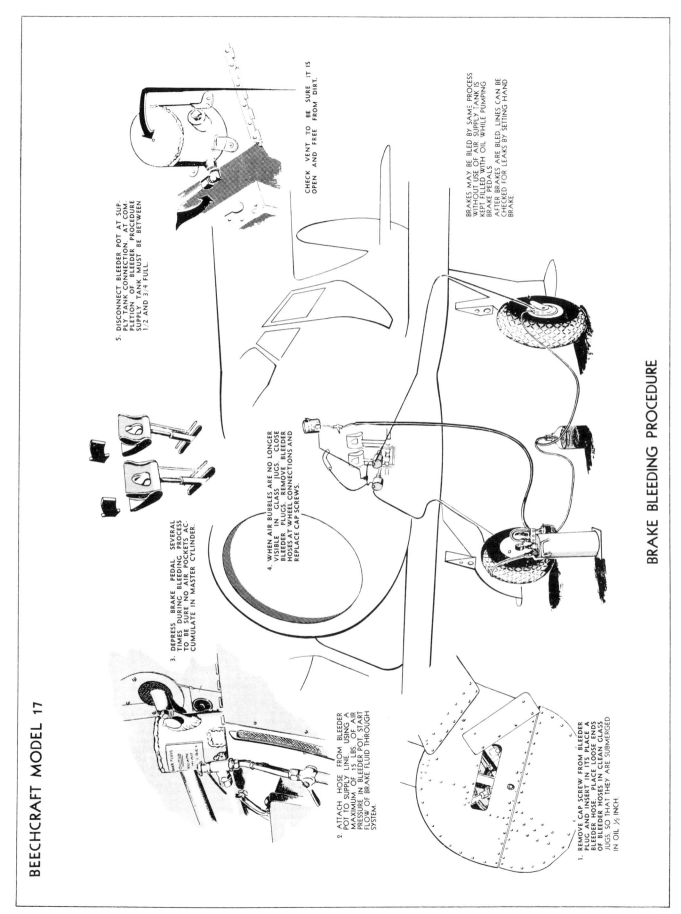

BRAKE BLEEDING PROCEDURE

1. REMOVE CAP SCREW FROM BLEEDER PLUG AND INSERT IN ITS PLACE A BLEEDER HOSE. PLACE LOOSE ENDS OF BLEEDER HOSES IN CLEAN GLASS JUGS, SO THAT THEY ARE SUBMERGED IN OIL 1/2 INCH.

2. ATTACH HOSE FROM BLEEDER POT TO SUPPLY LINE. USING A MAXIMUM OF 15 LBS. OF AIR PRESSURE IN BLEEDER POT, START FLOW OF BRAKE FLUID THROUGH SYSTEM.

3. DEPRESS BRAKE PEDAL SEVERAL TIMES DURING BLEEDING PROCESS TO BE SURE NO AIR POCKETS ACCUMULATE IN MASTER CYLINDER.

4. WHEN AIR BUBBLES ARE NO LONGER VISIBLE IN GLASS JUGS, CLOSE BLEEDER PLUGS. REMOVE BLEEDER HOSES AT WHEEL CONNECTIONS AND REPLACE CAP SCREWS.

5. DISCONNECT BLEEDER POT AT SUPPLY TANK CONNECTION. AT COMPLETION OF BLEEDER PROCEDURE SUPPLY TANK MUST BE BETWEEN 1/2 AND 3/4 FULL.

CHECK VENT TO BE SURE IT IS OPEN AND FREE FROM DIRT.

BRAKES MAY BE BLED BY SAME PROCESS WITHOUT USE OF AIR. SUPPLY TANK IS KEPT FILLED WITH OIL WHILE PUMPING BRAKE PEDALS.

AFTER BRAKES ARE BLED, LINES CAN BE CHECKED FOR LEAKS BY SETTING HAND BRAKE.

167

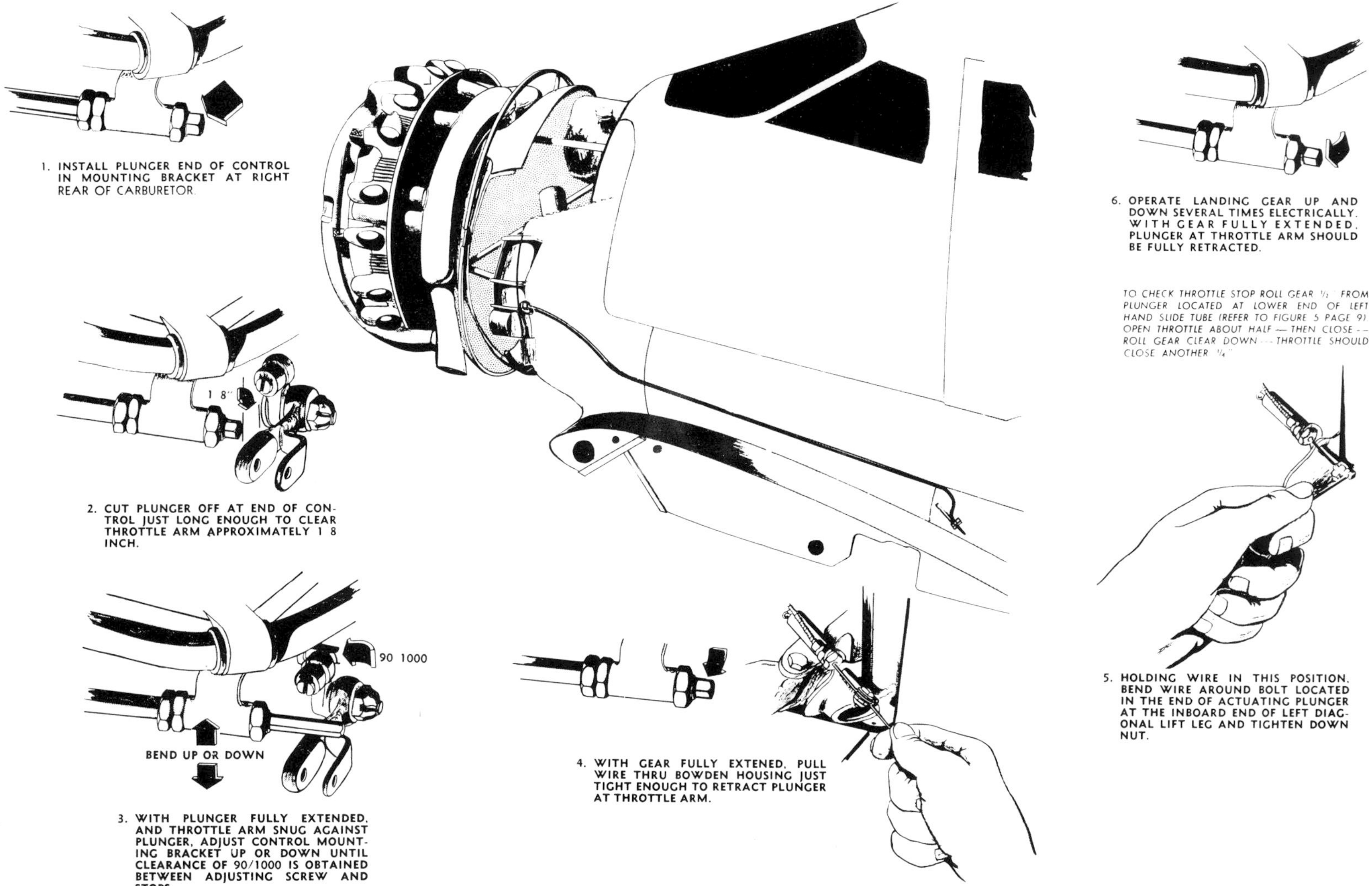

BEECHCRAFT MODEL 17

1. INSTALL PLUNGER END OF CONTROL IN MOUNTING BRACKET AT RIGHT REAR OF CARBURETOR.

2. CUT PLUNGER OFF AT END OF CONTROL JUST LONG ENOUGH TO CLEAR THROTTLE ARM APPROXIMATELY 1 8 INCH.

90 1000

BEND UP OR DOWN

3. WITH PLUNGER FULLY EXTENDED, AND THROTTLE ARM SNUG AGAINST PLUNGER, ADJUST CONTROL MOUNTING BRACKET UP OR DOWN UNTIL CLEARANCE OF 90/1000 IS OBTAINED BETWEEN ADJUSTING SCREW AND STOPS.

4. WITH GEAR FULLY EXTENDED, PULL WIRE THRU BOWDEN HOUSING JUST TIGHT ENOUGH TO RETRACT PLUNGER AT THROTTLE ARM.

5. HOLDING WIRE IN THIS POSITION, BEND WIRE AROUND BOLT LOCATED IN THE END OF ACTUATING PLUNGER AT THE INBOARD END OF LEFT DIAGONAL LIFT LEG AND TIGHTEN DOWN NUT.

TO CHECK THROTTLE STOP ROLL GEAR ½ FROM PLUNGER LOCATED AT LOWER END OF LEFT HAND SLIDE TUBE (REFER TO FIGURE 5 PAGE 9) OPEN THROTTLE ABOUT HALF — THEN CLOSE — ROLL GEAR CLEAR DOWN — THROTTLE SHOULD CLOSE ANOTHER ½.

6. OPERATE LANDING GEAR UP AND DOWN SEVERAL TIMES ELECTRICALLY. WITH GEAR FULLY EXTENDED, PLUNGER AT THROTTLE ARM SHOULD BE FULLY RETRACTED.

RIGGING THROTTLE STOPS

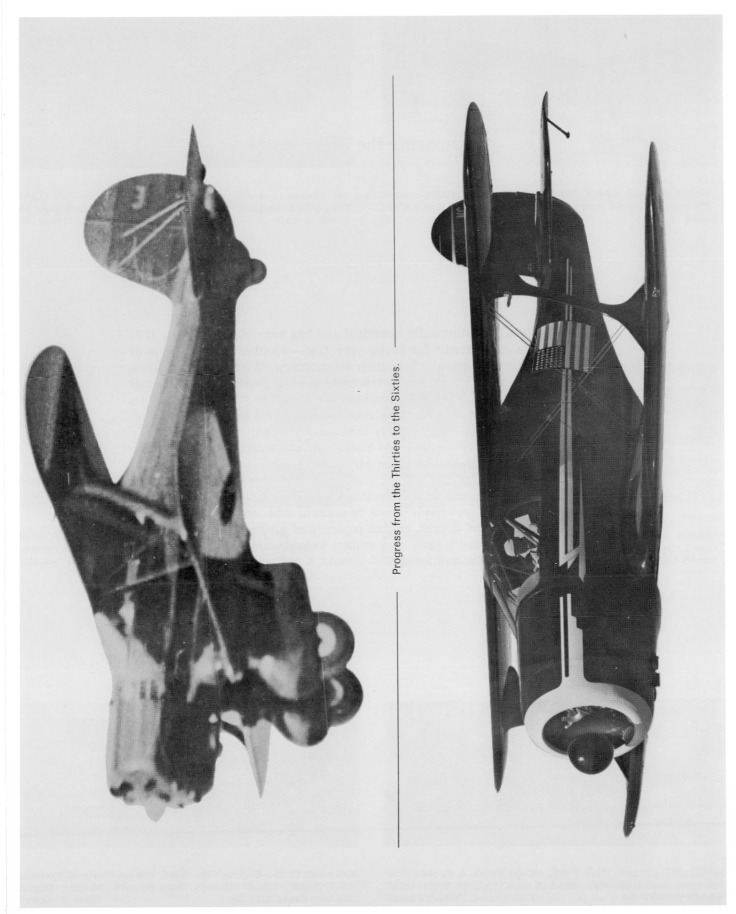

Progress from the Thirties to the Sixties.

INDIVIDUAL SERIAL NUMBER LIST

This is a listing, chronologically by serial number, of all of the Beechcraft Model 17's—both civil and military airplanes. The Beech Aircraft Corporation did not supply this list—it was gleaned from old records, individuals, magazines, books, and the U.S. Civil Aircraft Register. Larry Smalley and William T. Larkins started this list several years before I thought of doing this book. When they learned I was working on it, they gladly gave me all of the information they had.

Many other individuals helped me complete this list, notably John Hopton of Australia, Peter Berry of England, and John E. H. Pitt, Gary G. Kuhn, and Leo J. Kohn of the United States.

Now, I don't claim this list is 100% complete. As Bill Larkins once said, "It is almost impossible to say that *any* given list is *absolutely* 100% complete." I may have missed one or two Model 17's. But, if an individual serial number of a Beechcraft Model 17 is *not* in this list, it is not the fault of the best aviation historians in the business—myself not necessarily included.

A project I took entirely upon myself was to include a photograph of every individual Beechcraft 17 built in this listing. My project was just slightly less than half successful. Just under half of the Beechcraft 17's in the list are illustrated with a photograph. These photos came, in large number, from aviation photo collectors. Many more came painfully from individual Beechcraft 17 owners, former owners, enthusiasts, companies, corporations, and many from Beech Aircraft Corporation. Surprisingly enough, I have obtained as many photographs of Beechcraft 17's no longer in existence as I have of those still flying. In fact, and though I have written current owners many times, there will be Beechcraft 17's in this listing that are currently flying, and are not illustrated in this book. C'est la vie.

Registration — Serial Number Cross Reference List

The purpose of this list is to enable the reader to find the serial number of an airplane if he knows its registration mark. Registrations are in numerical or alphabetical order depending on the country of registration. There are some registrations for which I have no serial number, and no way to find out the serial number. The N or NC is not shown on United States registrations, but NL, NR, and NX will be.

UNITED STATES REGISTRATIONS

Registration	Serial Number	Registration	Serial Number	Registration	Serial Number	Registration	Serial Number
2	80	35E	167	69H	4896	156	6691
16	6765	36E	264	70E	B-11	161K	4821
16M	6765	40E	6685	71	146	162	6672
16V	299	40Y	209	91	219	163	1015
18	6869	42	285	91H	219	163E	1015
18V	6869	44G	B-3	113Q	4815	164E	6933
22	6750	47D	289	114	411	171M	6919
25	6881	50A	271	114H	327	192H	6723
25K	6881	50E	6759	115LK	7	213	423
27E	6883	58	6762	124D	257	230	4835
28A	6760	58E	6762	126	199	236E	3179
30E	6888	58Y	2	127J	272	238Y	272
33	6698	66	26	129M	396	239E	4916
33H	6698	NS66	36	133	415	239Y	355
34R	424	NS68	11	133E	414	240Y	406

Registration	Serial Number	Registration	Serial Number	Registration	Serial Number	Registration	Serial Number
241	287	1180V	6904	5734N	4836	14418	31
241K	287	1181V	6706	6402N	4921	14453	32
248E	6871	1182V	6753	7769	146	14454	33
249E	287	1183V	6704	7778B	4870	14455	34
262C	B-15	1184V	6748	8464A	B-16	14456	35
264	4888	1185V	6746	8589A	B-18	14457	36
264E	4888	1189V	299	8590A	B-19	14458	49
265E	4940	1190V	398	9000C	4837	15021	4880
270Y	3	1192V	6884	9113H	4823	15400	37
278V	60	1193V	6701	9115H	1014	15401	39
281Y	68	1195V	6749	9169H	6879	15402	40
282Y	75	1196V	6703	9290H	6726	15403	41
284Y	206	1213V	1016	9370H	4846	15404	42
285D	256	1254N	1029	9376H	2685	15405	43
285Y	225	1255N	4829	9405H	4803	15406	44
289Y	259	1256N	4858	9450H	6764	15407	45
290Y	258	1324	187	9451H	6669	15408	46
291Y	261	1333V	6894	9454H	6705	15409	47
291Y	B-9	1334V	6890	9455H	6687	15410	55
292Y	273	1335V	6752	9456H	6745	15411	54
293Y	388	1336V	6897	9458H	6870	15412	51
322H	3184	1341V	6728	9459H	6700	15413	52
333	B-5	1359V	6920	9461H	6760	15414	53
333E	4878	1367M	6926	9463H	6900	15483	56
334E	355	1422T	413	9464H	301	15484	57
368	4883	1502	4880	9465H	6898	15485	58
385	335	1503M	4794	9466H	6688	15486	59
397	3102	1532M	3108	9470H	6670	15487	73
397	3108	1591V	4885	9595H	3098	15488	61
400	166	1600	79	9597H	4840	15489	65
420E	6671	1609	4865	9724H	4807	15496	64
477FT	4906	2000	116	9873H	4839	15810	62
480	4810	2099	226	9885H	3091	15811	66
499N	1	2388	163	9886H	6910	15812	67
663	4903	2422	304	9936H	4808	15813	83
700N	B-19	2595	250	12569	10	15814	69
722MD	6750	2623	6912	NR12569	11	15815	70
787MD	4815	2625	4801	12570	6	15816	71
787MD	6751	2626	283	12583	5	15817	72
800K	25	2627	281	12584	4	15833	74
838	6731	2663	330	12589	7	15834	76
839	4831	2801	392	12590	8	15835	77
900	362	2832D	1025	12591	9	15835	81
903	205	3104G	16	12592	12	15836	109
911	B-12	3775C	6672	12593	22	15837	79
962W	100	3776C	6691	12594	13	15838	110
996	74	4008B	6926	12597	14	15839	121
1015M	3114	4512N	6737	12598	15	15840	93
1020M	4813	4574N	6727	14403	16	15841	84
1027M	4870	4607N	6927	14404	17	15842	85
1030	409	4612N	6874	14405	24	15843	86
1038	1017	4626N	6919	14406	19	15844	87
1038M	1017	4688N	6682	14408	20	15845	88
1054M	6918	4710V	B-13	14409	21	15846	89
1112M	6684	4926V	6738	14412	25	15847	90
1120V	6734	5074N	6680	14413	38	15848	91
1172V	6893	5099N	6750	14414	27	15849	92
1174V	6892	5400N	6767	14415	28	16434	82
1175V	6747	5447N	4875	14416	29	16435	94
1178V	6917	5653N	6766	14417	30	16436	95

Registration	Serial Number	Registration	Serial Number	Registration	Serial Number	Registration	Serial Number
16437	96	18568	255	20772	310	48413	156
16438	97	18570	228	20773	311	48968	335
16439	98	18573	256	20774	312	48973	405
16440	99	18574	257	20776	313	48974	191
16441	100	18575	179	20777	314	49301	250
16442	101	18576	180	20778	357	49704	261
16443	102	18577	195	20779	398	49788	4850
16444	103	18579	183	20780	339	50256	258
16445	122	18580	184	20785	271	50587	310
16446	105	18581	185	20786	1674	50650	143
16447	106	18582	186	20787	270	50959	305
16449	141	18584	188	20788	358	51120	4902
17060	111	18585	189	20789	275	51121	4914
17061	112	18587	196	20790	276	51152	137
17062	127	18588	197	20791	277	51444	4874
17063	125	18775	198	20792	278	51745	4886
17064	128	18776	199	20793	279	51746	4890
17065	126	18777	200	20795	397	51969	4898
17066	154	18778	280	20798	333	52414	6886
17068	119	18779	202	20799	286	52686	4882
17069	155	18781	204	21904	327	52832	4837
17071	156	18782	240	21905	363	52931	4833
17072	130	18783	241	21906	356	52941	4815
17073	131	18784	207	21917	401	52950	3109
17074	132	18785	208	21918	402	52962	6880
17078	133	18786	211	21919	405	52996	4825
17079	134	18787	212	21920	407	53298	4900
17080	135	18788	213	21921	391	53754	275
17081	136	18789	214	21922	393	54657	4906
17082	137	18790	215	21926	418	57827	197
17083	138	18791	216	21930	419	57828	242
17084	139	18792	282	21931	414	57829	198
17085	140	18793	218	21932	412	57831	207
17091	142	19451	331	21933	421	57839	138
17092	143	19453	305	21934	424	59700	413
17643	4827	19454	242	21935	413	59701	272
17679	6911	19466	230	21936	424	59719	4876
18025	144	19467	231	38937	120	60148	4872
18026	145	19468	284	39392	6875	60149	4867
18027	146	19470	285	41663	196	61208	4798
18028	147	19471	243	41852	160	61278	4859
18029	148	19472	244	44561	6922	61862	4877
18038	149	19473	245	44562	6923	63476	4818
18039	150	19474	246	44564	6925	63477	6720
18040	151	19475	247	46291	98	63549	6729
18041	152	19477	249	46292	167	63599	6929
18042	153	19479	251	46293	142	65044	4824
18043	190	19480	252	46296	332	65297	199
18044	191	19482	254	46431	4893	65590	6741
18555	157	19492	262	46492	394	65594	3097
18556	158	19493	263	46493	205	65596	4811
18557	159	19494	264	46810	4891	66282	407
18558	192	20750	287	47024	102	66300	4804
18559	193	20752	289	47458	190	66426	6718
18560	162	20753	395	47571	389	67197	3110
18561	210	20755	400	47833	72	67198	6913
18562	164	20768	306	47834	134	67426	6916
18563	165	20769	307	47939	289	67430	4822
18565	167	20770	308	47950	256	67445	1024
18566	168	20771	337	48401	151	67487	6735

Registration	Serial Number	Registration	Serial Number
67494	6878	75606	6907
67543	6908	75614	4806
67550	6717	75620	6712
67555	6876	75728	3086
67677	6724	75729	3181
67714	4817	75922	6915
67716	6733	79091	1020
67717	4841	79484	4917
67734	3093	79996	6751
67735	6935	80024	4915
67736	4848	80302	B-1
67737	6914	80303	B-2
67747	4847	80304	B-3
67769	146	80305	B-4
67783	4816	80306	B-5
68104	6732	80307	B-6
68113	6723	80308	B-7
68916	6715	80309	B-8
69217	3100	80312	B-11
69267	3100	80313	B-12
74584	1013	80315	B-14
75499	3107	80316	B-15
75512	6714	80317	B-16
75544	3088	80321	B-20
75554	1019	91397	295

AUSTRALIA

Registration	Serial Number	Registration	Serial Number
VH-ACU	248	VH-MLC	6763
VH-AFP	357	VH-PMG	107
VH-BBL	6763	VH-UXP	108
VH-BOU	107	VH-UYI	129
VH-MJE	4922		

BELGIUM

Registration	Serial Number
OO-TAX	3119
OO-VIT	4920

BOLIVIA

Registration
CP-613

BRAZIL

Registration	Serial Number	Registration	Serial Number
PP-DDH	2718	PP-TCQ	123
PP-FAA	229	PP-TGE	354
PP-FER	4879	PT-ADT	3081
PP-NAC	314	PT-BDL	314

CANADA

Registration	Serial Number	Registration	Serial Number
CF-BBB	113	CF-ESU	B-13
CF-BIF	120	CF-FEQ	3098
CF-BJD	201	CF-GCJ	6915
CF-BKQ	227	CF-GKW	120
CF-BLU	238	CF-GKY	4874
CF-CCA	203	CF-GLL	6914
CF-DTE	403	CF-GPO	1013
CF-DTF	404	CF-HSK	3186
CF-EKA	4813		

CANAL ZONE (PANAMA)

Registration	Serial Number
CZ-116	48

CHILE

Registration	Serial Number
CC-CAA	—

CUBA

Registration	Serial Number	Registration	Serial Number
CU-N217	—	CU-398	—
CU-N298	—	CU-463	—

EL SALVADOR

Registration	Serial Number
YS-83	6926

ENGLAND

Registration	Serial Number	Registration	Serial Number
G-ADDH	23	G-AIHZ	6905
G-ADLD	4921	G-AJJE	4925
G-ADLE	50	G-AJJJ	4922
G-AENY	114	G-AJLA	4935
G-AESJ	118	G-ALNN	6699
G-AHXJ	6686	G-AMBY	295

FINLAND

Registration	Serial Number
OH-PKA	124
OH-VKN	6885

FRANCE

Registration	Serial Number	Registration	Serial Number
F-APFB	83	F-BEXJ	6681
F-APFD	66	F-BEXK	4812
F-BATL	6699	F-BDRX	3121
F-BCJY	4923	F-DADL	4935
F-BEEK	3119	F-OABR	4937
F-BEXA	4793	F-OACT	6699

HONG KONG

Registration	Serial Number
VR-HEE	4937

INDIA

Registration	Serial Number	Registration	Serial Number
VT-AKJ	232	VT-ALV	336
VT-AKK	233	VT-ALY	399
VT-AKL	234	VT-CIT	B-10

ITALY

Registration	Serial Number
I-IBIS	71

LUXEMBOURG

Registration	Serial Number
LX-TAX	3119

MEXICO

Registration	Serial Number	Registration	Serial Number
XA-BKO	75	XB-LEQ	6738
XB-AGO	334	XB-LIF	4838
XB-AIZ	10	XB-PAN	6904
XB-HAY	6890	XB-YOE	6735
XB-JUI	6748		

NETHERLANDS EAST INDIES

Registration	Serial Number
PK-SAM	280

NEW ZEALAND

Registration	Serial Number
ZK-AEU	107
ZK-AJS	107

NORWAY

Registration	Serial Number	Registration	Serial Number
LN-HAG	6885	LN-HAI	6758
LN-HAH	6763	LN-HAK	6699

PORTUGUESE COLONIES

Registration	Serial Number
CR-LBF	6768

SOUTHERN RHODESIA

Registration	Serial Number
VP-YIT	4925
VP-YIV	295

SWEDEN

Registration	Serial Number
SE-BRY	4920

SWITZERLAND

Registration	Serial Number
HB-UIH	4920
HB-KID	4935

UNION OF SOUTH AFRICA

Registration	Serial Number
ZS-BBC	18
ZS-BBC	124
ZS-BBZ	6768
ZS-CLM	4885

URUGUAY

Registration	Serial Number
CX-ABE	—
CX-AQG	6915

Format For Individual Listing

③ ② 299   GB-1 (D17S)   BuNo 1590, N1189V, N16V. ④
Built 1939   P&W R-985, 450 hp. ⑥

⑤ NOTES: To U.S. Navy originally. Survived the war (World War Two), and existed until early 1960's, but not currently listed.
(Richard C. Seeley) ①
⑦

(1) Photo credit. The name listed is the name of the person who supplied the photograph, not necessarily the name of the actual photographer. Every effort was made to credit the proper person, but photos are traded frequently, and the individual who originally snapped the camera shutter is often lost to history. For that reason, the person who sent the photo to the author is named in almost all cases where the original photographer is not known, or where any doubt exists as to who actually made the picture.

(2) The Beech serial number. This is the c/n (constructor's number) in British historian parlance, but is shown as s/n (serial number) in this book. Beech serial numbers were assigned consecutively, without regard to model, from the origin of the company in 1932 to about the end of World War Two. At that time, serial numbers were assigned to individual Beech models. In this listing, only model 17 s/n are shown. In the pre-war years an effort is made to denote other model serial numbers, but in the World War Two production listing, only airplanes that can be identified are shown. And, other models are not noted. In the World War Two production listing (the four-digit serials), only those airplanes for which a photo exists, or for which a civil registration is known, will be shown.

(3) Model Designation. This is shown for the pre-war, three-digit serial numbers only. The model is shown as originally produced, not as modified in service. For example, many B17B, and C17B airplanes were later modified to B17L and C17L airplanes by having their original 285 hp Jacobs L-5 engines removed, and the 225 hp Jacobs or Military R-755-9 engines installed. This change is not shown. Only the original configuration is shown. For the few three-digit models procured by the military services, the military model is shown with the civil counterpart shown in parentheses. In the four-digit serial, war production listing, no model designations are shown as all war production is assumed to be the D17S.

(4)   Registrations. They will be listed in the order assigned to the airplane. Military serials will be shown for three-digit serial numbers, but for four-digit war production airplanes, the military serials will be shown in a listed tabulation, and not with individual airplanes. Foreign registrations that will appear in this list are;

Country	Registration Letters
Australia	VH
Belgium	OO
Bolivia	CP
Brazil	PT or PP
Canada	CF
Canal Zone	CZ*
Chile	CC
El Salvador	YS
England	G
Finland	OH
France	F
Hong Kong	VR
India	VT
Italy	I
Luxembourg	LX
Mexico	XA or XB
Netherlands East Indies	PK
New Zealand	ZK
Norway	LN
Portuguese Colonies	CR
Southern Rhodesia	VP
Sweden	SE
Switzerland	HB
Union of South Africa	ZS
Uruguay	CX

*(No longer used)

(5)   The date built is given for all three-digit, pre-war airplanes, but not for war production aircraft. For many airplanes it was possible to obtain the month-day-year of production, but for many only the year built is shown. By careful examination of the list, the reader can determine approximately when any specific airplane was built.

(6)   Engine installed. This is always the production engine. For early airplanes, an attempt was made to show the specific engine installed, but for later airplanes, only the basic engine model is shown. The engine shown is the model installed at production. Jacobs engines were generally interchangeable on the B17B, B17L, C17B and C17L models, and most airplanes of this series today carry the Jacobs military R-755-9 of 245 hp, but on this list the original Jacobs L-4 of 225 hp and L-5 of 285 hp is shown. On models using the Wright and Pratt and Whitney engines, only the basic engine is indicated, such as P&W R-985 for all models equipped with the Pratt and Whitney, and Wright R-975 or Wright R-760 for the Wright engine models. Some F17D airplanes have been equipped with the P&W R-985 in place of the original Jacobs L-6 of 330 hp, and these are noted in the NOTES. Any other non-production engines installed will be noted in the NOTES section of each individual listing.

(7)   NOTES can include anything. In all cases, it will be noted whether or not the airplane has a current airworthiness (annual) inspection. In this way, the reader can identify which airplanes are still in existence, or likely still in existence. This book is being written in 1966 so any reference to "today" or "now," or "currently" will mean the year 1966. Any airplane currently registered is assumed to have a current airworthiness (annual) inspection unless otherwise noted. In the preparation of this serial number listing, I obtained lists of the U.S. Civil Register for the years 1955, 1961, 1964, and 1966. The 1955 list was given to me by William T. Larkins who obtained it from the late Paul Mantz. The 1955 list is as of May, 1955. The 1961 list is dated September, 1961. The 1964 list is as of February, 1964, and the 1966 list was obtained in February, 1966. When it is noted that an airplane appeared on a certain list, and the notation "no further listing" is used, it means the airplane does not appear on any subsequent list. The phrase "not currently listed" means the airplane does not appear on the 1955, 1961, 1964, or 1966 list, but its existence prior to 1955 has been verified.

1   17R   NC499N
Built Nov. 4, 1932   Wright R-760-E2, 420 hp

NOTES: The first Staggerwing! First flown on November 4, 1932, the airplane was not sold to Ethyl Corporation of New York until 1934. Photo shows the original configuration and paint scheme. Colors were deep maroon and red with white pin striping. Before delivery to Ethyl Corp., the landing gear was modified to A17F configuration, the airplane was repainted. Piloted for Ethyl Corp. by Dewey Noyes, it crashed near Nunda, New York on December 10, 1935 in an ice storm, and pilot Dewey Noyes was killed.   *(Peter M. Bowers)*

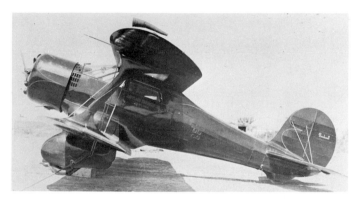

2   17R   NC58Y
Built July 1, 1933   Wright R-760-E2, 420 hp

NOTES: Identical to serial number 1. Ordered by Tom Loffland early in 1933 after he had a demonstration ride in NC499N. Piloted by E. F. Ross for Loffland Brothers Company of Tulsa, Oklahoma, the airplane was traded in to Beech in the summer of 1935. Evidently it was dismantled by the factory.   *(E. F. Ross Collection)*

3   B17L   NC270Y
Built May, 1934   Jacobs L-4, 225 hp

NOTES: First B17L, and first retractable gear Model 17. It was used initially as a demonstrator, later sold to Charlotte Frye of Griffin, Georgia. Afterwards Stephens College in Missouri owned it for years. Its remains now belong to Lt./Col. James T. Winkler of the USAF who plans to rebuild it.   *(Robert Esposito)*

4   B17L   NC12584
Built 1934   Jacobs L-4, 225 hp

NOTES: Sold to Aero Mobiloil, and shown on one list as belonging to John P. Gaty of Wichita, Kansas. Not currently listed.   *(R. T. O'Dell)*

5   A17F   NX12583, NC12583, NR12583
Built Feb., 1934   Wright R-1820, 690 hp

NOTES: Purchased by Sanford Mills, Sanford, Maine, and piloted by Robert Fogg, Sr. Flown by him until November, 1934. Sold shortly thereafter to Howard Hughes, Hollywood, California. Bob Perlick started it in both the 1937 and 1938 Bendix races, but it did not complete either race. Last registered January 1, 1937 to Hughes Tool Company, Hollywood, California, but rumored to still be in existence.
(Warren D. Shipp)

6   B17L   NC12570
Built 1934   Jacobs L-4, 225 hp

NOTES: First registered to Beechcraft dealer O. J. Whitney in New York, later sold to New Jersey Air Service, Inc. in Atlantic City, New Jersey. Not currently listed.

7   B17L   NC12589, N115LK
Built 1934   Jacobs L-4, 225 hp

NOTES: Loaned to Loffland Brothers Company, Tulsa, Oklahoma while they waited on delivery of another model. They reportedly purchased it. Later it was sold to Boston-Maine Airways in Boston, Massachusetts. Norbert Dybowski in New York owned it in mid-1950's, belly landed it around 1957. Now owned by Leo Kelly, Hyannis, Massachusetts.
(George Johnson)

8   B17L   NC12590
Built 1934   Jacob L-4, 225 hp

NOTES: Sold to Ward-Pearson, Inc. at Roosevelt Field, New York. Pilot/salesman George Pearson remembers this airplane well, used it as a demonstrator in making several early Beechcraft sales. It later went to Howard E. Behr, Anderson, South Carolina. After World War Two it changed hands many times, finally ending up with Carl Petersen of Napier Field, Alabama who is rebuilding it.   *(Frank Hartman)*

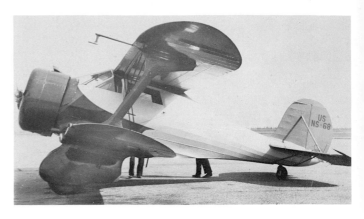

11   A17FS   NR12569, NS68
Built Nov., 1934   Wright R-1820-F3, 710 hp

NOTES: Built for Louise Thaden and Robert Fogg Sr. to fly in the MacRobertson race. They withdrew, and the airplane was sold to the Bureau of Air Commerce who flew it for several years. It was reportedly dismantled by them. Last registered Jan. 1, 1937.   *(Warren D. Shipp)*

9   B17L   NC12591
Built 1934   Jacobs L-4 engine, 225 hp

NOTES: Sold as a demonstrator to "Strick" Strickland of Newark Air Service, Inc., Newark Airport. Above photo was taken in September, 1934.   *(Emil Strasser)*

12   B17L   NC12592
Built 1934   Jacobs L-4, 225 hp

NOTES: Originally purchased by the Standard Oil Company of New Jersey, this airplane saw many owners, finally ended up in Oregon. Currently owned by David L. Seiler, Vancouver, Washington.   *(Warren D. Shipp)*

10   B17L   XB-AIZ, NC12569
Built 1934   Jacobs L-4 engine, 225 hp

NOTES: Sir Harold Farquhar's first Beechcraft. He later traded it in on the B17R he flew around the world (serial number 50).   *(Ing. José Villela, Jr.)*

13   B17L   NC12594
Built Aug., 1934   Jacobs L-4, 225 hp

NOTES: Registered to James W. Combs of Petaluma, California in 1955. No record in 1961.   *(Warren D. Shipp)*

14   B17L   NC12597
Built 1934   Jacobs L-4, 225 hp

NOTES: Owned by Richard M. Wilhoit for years, it last had an annual inspection in 1949 but is still registered to Mr. Wilhoit. He wrote me in 1963 that he had sold the airplane, but did not say to whom. Possibly it still exists.   *(Peter M. Bowers)*

15   B17L   NC12598
Built Aug., 1934   Jacobs L-4, 225 hp

NOTES: Sold to Beech Air Sales Co., New York, but no current record.   *(Beech Photo)*

16   B17L   NC14403, N3104G
Built 1934   Jacobs L-4, 225 hp

NOTES: Sold to Beech Air Sales Co. in New York. Registered to Margaret MacRae Wiberg of Avalon, California in 1964. No further listing.   *(Warren D. Shipp)*

17   B17L   NC14404
Built 1934   Jacobs L-4, 225 hp

NOTES: Sold to Beech Air Sales Co. in New York. No further history.   *(Emil Strasser)*

18   B17L   ZS-BBC
Built 1934   Jacobs L-4, 225 hp

NOTES: Sold to Captain O. Thaning of Johannesburg, South Africa. It crashed in September of 1936, and Capt. Thaning purchased serial number 124.

19   B17L   NC14406
Built 1934   Jacobs L-4, 225 hp

NOTES: Sold to Gilpin Airlines, Ltd., Municipal Airport, Tucson, Arizona in late 1930's. Not currently listed.

20   B17B   NC14408
Built Nov., 1934   Jacobs L-5, 285 hp

NOTES: First B17B. Registered in 1955 to W. B. Mean, West Orange, New Jersey with a date of last annual inspection of August, 1949. Assumed destroyed or dismantled.

21   B17L   NC14409
Built 1934   Jacobs L-4, 225 hp

NOTES: Owned by James Reese in Freewater, Oregon in 1955; L. T. Jagiello of China Lake, California in 1961; currently registered (1966) to Herbert L. Thomas of Hayward, California. Photo taken about 1956 with B17R serial number 38 in the background. Note engine cowl on s/n 21, and see s/n 28.   *(Merle Olmsted)*

22   B17E   NC12593
Built 1935   Wright R-760, 285 hp

NOTES: First B17E. To H. G. Harper, Harper Aircraft Company, Joplin, Missouri in late 1930's. Not currently listed.   *(Beech Photo)*

23　　B17L　　G-ADDH
Built Mar., 1935　　Jacobs L-4, 225 hp

NOTES: Purchased in March, 1935 by Mrs. Amy Mollison, it was registered in England on June 4, 1935. Forced landing at Orpington, Kent on October 21, 1936. Sold out of England in July, 1937 as spares. To Thor Solberg, Oslo, Norway, 1939. No current data.

24　　B17L　　NC14405
Built 1935　　Jacobs L-4, 225 hp

NOTES: Sold to the King of Ethiopia and destroyed during the war.

25　　B17L　　NC14412
Built 1935

NOTES: Photo shows airplane on March 26, 1938 at Mines Field, California. Currently registered to Gordon L. Kraft in Atlanta, Georgia, the airplane is being rebuilt.
(Peter M. Bowers)

26　　B17L　　NS66, NC66
Built 1935　　Jacobs L-4, 225 hp

NOTES: Purchased by the Bureau of Air Commerce. No current listing.
(Richard C. Seeley)

27　　B17L　　NC14414
Built 1935　　Jacobs L-4, 225 hp

NOTES: E. S. McCurdy of San Francisco, California owned it in 1939. Not currently listed.

28　　B17L　　NC14415
Built 1935　　Jacobs L-4, 225 hp

NOTES: Owned by Conrad E. Schroff of Boulder, Colorado in 1955, and Bernard W. Mugleston of Denver in 1961, the airplane is currently registered to Mugleston. Note the engine cowling and exhaust stack—they are not standard Beech cowling and stack. Are probably from Cessna UC-78.
(Larry Smalley)

29　　B17L　　NC14416
Built 1935　　Jacobs L-4, 225 hp

NOTES: Had short career—crashed October, 1935.

30　　B17L　　NC14417
Built June, 1935　　Jacobs L-4, 225 hp

NOTES: Production test flight on June 5, 1935 by Newman Wadlow, Beech test pilot. Purchased by R. M. Hardy, Yakima, Washington. To Capitol Air Lines, Boise, Idaho July 22, 1936. Empty weight 1834 lbs. as delivered to Mr. Hardy. Partially burned in 1953. Owned by Oliver Hill, Wichita, Kansas 1955, 1961, 1964. Owned by August F. Spies of Collinsville, Illinois who is rebuilding it from the 1953 fire.
(Peter M. Bowers)

31　　B17L　　NC14418
Built 1935　　Jacobs L-4, 225 hp

NOTES: Listed in 1939 as being owned by David Dows, Jr. of Glen Head, Long Island, New York. Not currently listed.

32　　B17L　　NC14453
Built 1935　　Jacobs L-4, 225 hp

NOTES: Owned by George Felt, Roseburg, Oregon, 1955, 1961. Sold to Ellis Hallman, and registered to him from 1964 on.
(William Steeneck)

33   B17L   NC14454
Built 1935   Jacobs L-4, 225 hp

NOTES: Sold to Automobiles Fernandez, S.A., Barcelona, Spain. No current information.

34   B17L   NC14455
Built 1935   Jacobs L-4, 225 hp

NOTES: Flown by R. W. Brown for Socony-Vacuum Oil Company (Aero Mobil). Registered to Carter Motor Company, Greensboro, North Carolina in 1955. No further listing.   (Roger Besecker)

35   B17L   NC14456
Built 1935   Jacobs L-4, 225 hp

NOTES: Listed to J. N. English, Houston, Texas in 1939. Photo taken July, 1935. Not currently listed.
(Emil Strasser)

36   B17L   NC14457, NS66
Built 1935   Jacobs L-4, 225 hp

NOTES: Sold to Bureau of Air Commerce. This is same photo shown with s/n (serial number) 26, and could be s/n 26 since both s/n 26 and s/n 36 were registered as NS66 at one time. Unfortunately, the photographer did not note s/n of the airplane at the time the photo was taken. The airplane is not listed on any current list.   (Richard C. Seeley)

37   B17L   NC15400
Built 1935   Jacobs L-4, 225 hp

NOTES: Listed to Mrs. Arlene Davis, 1939. Not currently listed.
(Truman C. Weaver)

38   B17R   NC14413
Built Mar., 1935   Wright R-975, 420 hp

NOTES: Originally a B17E, at request of Eddie Ross, pilot for Loffland Brothers Co., Tulsa, Okla. (first owner), it was modified to become first B17R. Engine changed in 1948 to P&W R 985. Currently owned by Richard Langford of Lewistown, Montana, and being rebuilt by him. Photo was taken May 30, 1936 when the airplane was owned by Loffland Brothers.   (Emil Strasser)

39   B17L   NC15401
Built 1935   Jacobs L-4, 225 hp

NOTES: Bessie Decker, Staten Island, New York in 1939. Not currently listed.

40   SB17L   NC15402
Built Sept. 7, 1935   Jacobs L-4, 225 hp

NOTES: First Beechcraft seaplane. Aero Trades Company, Mineola, Long Island, New York in 1939. Not currently listed.   (Warren D. Shipp)

41   B17L   NC15403
Built 1935   Jacobs L-4, 225 hp

NOTES: Not currently listed.

42   B17L   NC15404
Built 1935   Jacobs L-4, 225 hp

NOTES: West E. Moreau, Moreau Flying Service, Oakland, California in 1939. Not currently listed.

43   B17L   NC15405
Built 1935   Jacobs L-4, 225 hp

NOTES: George J. Pearson, salesman for Ward-Pearson, Inc. at Roosevelt Field, sold this airplane to William Lear of Lear Development, Inc. in New York. Lear was developing one of the first automatic direction finding (ADF) radio receivers, and had one installed on this airplane. Note large ADF loop antenna on top of fuselage.   *(Peter M. Bowers)*

44   B17L   NC15406
Built 1935   Jacobs L-4, 225 hp

NOTES: C. H. Carpenter, Superior Oil Co., 1939. Not currently listed.

45   B17L   NC15407
Built 1935   Jacobs L-4, 225 hp

NOTES: Owned by Donald Wonders 1955, Roger Vinck 1962, now the remains belong to Lt./Col. James T. Winkler. Photo taken at Gunnison, Colorado in 1962.   *(William Kupka)*

46   B17L   NC15408
Built 1935   Jacobs L-4, 225 hp

NOTES: Registered to Fenton Gingerich, Kokomo, Indiana in 1955, to George Howell, Denver, Colorado in 1961, and still registered to him.

47   B17L   NC15409
Built 1935   Jacobs L-4, 225 hp

NOTES: To O. J. Whitney, Beechcraft dealer in New York. Later to Dr. Samuel Bosch, Buenos Aires, Argentina. No current information.

48   B17L   CZ116
Built 1935   Jacobs L-4, 225 hp

NOTES: Delivered December 31, 1935 to Isthmian Airways, Ancon, Canal Zone. No current information.   *(Beech Photo)*

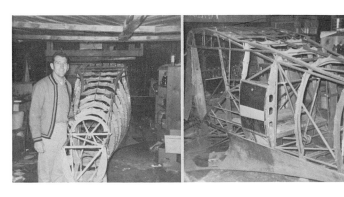

49   B17E   NC14458
Built May, 1935   Wright R-760, 285 hp

NOTES: Belly landed in the Los Angeles, California area in 1942. Purchased by James Hutton, it was stored in a barn pending rebuilding. Time passed, and in April, 1961 the late Dwight Addington heard about the airplane, and began an investigation to find it. He finally found it in a barn in a town of 60 people in the high Sierra Nevada Mountains of California. He brought the remains home, and began the difficult job of rebuilding the airplane. Dwight Addington was an enthusiastic and avid member of the aviation fraternity, and he gave me much help. He was killed on April 18, 1964 in a Fairchild 24 accident. The airplane now belongs to James Hudson of Hayward, California. The photo above is actually two photos sent to me by James, and shows s/n 49's fuselage. Photos by Dwight Addington appear elsewhere in this book.   *(James D. Hudson)*

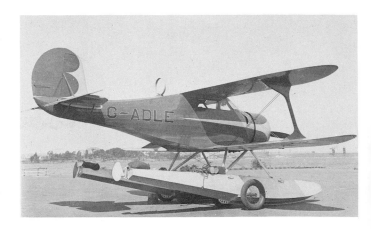

50   B17R   G-ADLE
Built July 18, 1935   Wright R-975, 420 hp

NOTES: G-ADLE was delivered to Sir Harold Farquhar on wheels, thus we show it as a B17R rather than an SB17R. The complete story appears elsewhere in this book. In 1939, the airplane was carried as being owned by Anthony George Anson Fisher, London, England, who may have been the one it belonged to when it crashed in January of that year.   *(Robert Esposito)*

51   B17E   NC15412
Built Aug. 23, 1935   Wright R-760, 285 hp

NOTES: To A. D. Knapp, Jackson, Michigan in 1939. No current listing.

52   B17R   NC15413
Built Oct. 1, 1935   Wright R-975, 420 hp

NOTES: Original owner, Continental Oil Company, Houston, Texas. No current listing.

53   B17R   NC15414
Built Oct. 15, 1935   Wright R-975, 420 hp

NOTES: Piloted by C. E. Cheney for Edgar Tobin Aerial Surveys in late thirties. They were based in San Antonio, Texas. No current listing.

54   B17R   NC15411
Built Nov. 7, 1935   Wright R-975, 420 hp

NOTES: To Aerial Explorations, Inc., of Long Island City, New York for aerial mapping. No current listing.   *(Robert Esposito)*

55   B17R   NC15410
Built Dec. 4, 1935   Wright R-975, 420 hp

NOTES: Listed to Dr. Samuel Bosch, Buenos Aires, Argentina in 1939. See s/n 47. No current information.

56   B17R   NC15483
Built Dec. 14, 1935   Wright R-975, 420 hp

NOTES: Crashed April, 1936. Not rebuilt.

57   B17L   NC15484
Built Dec. 28, 1935   Jacobs L-4, 225 hp

NOTES: Monarch Air Service, Inc., Chicago, Illinois with Harrison Bender as pilot in 1939. No current listing.

58   B17L   NC15485
Built Jan. 11, 1936   Jacobs L-4, 225 hp

NOTES: L. J. Perry, Kalamazoo, Michigan in 1939; Robert Laible, Salina, Kansas, 1955; Kenneth Toney, Wamego, Kansas, 1961, 1964; W. R. Beech (nephew of Walter Beech), Wichita, Kansas, 1966. Photo shows the airplane after a belly landing on September 3, 1939 at the National Air Races in Cleveland, Ohio. Note oil streaks on engine cowling. This is a good view of exhaust openings on the engine cowling.   *(Emil Strasser)*

59   B17L   NC15486
Built Jan. 27, 1936   Jacobs L-4, 225 hp

NOTES: No current listing.

60   B17L   NC278V
Built Feb. 28, 1936   Jacobs L-4, 225 hp

NOTES: Also carried by one authority as NC278U. Not currently listed.

61   B17L   NC15488
Built Mar. 14, 1936   Jacobs L-4, 225 hp

NOTES: Listed to James Pierce, Charleston, West Virginia in 1939. No current listing.

62   18A   NC15810
Built 1936   Two Wright R-760, 350 hp

NOTES: First Model 18 listed here for its historical significance. Future Model 18's will not be listed.   *(Beech Photo)*

63   B17R   NPC-28
Built 1936   Wright R-975, 420 hp

NOTES: To A. Soriano y Cia, Manila, Philippine Islands. Later sold to U. S. Government in Manila. Not currently listed.

64   B17R   NC15490
Built 1936   Wright R-975, 420 hp

NOTES: To George Hammond, Santa Barbara, California in 1939. Not currently listed.

65   B17R   NC15489
Built Feb. 8, 1936   Wright R-975, 420 hp

NOTES: Not currently listed.

66   B17R   NC15811, F-APFD
Built Feb. 8, 1936   Wright R-975, 420 hp

NOTES: Sold to Georges Lebeau, Paris, France, and registered in France on April 11, 1936. No current information.

67   C17B   NC15812
Built Mar., 1936   Jacobs L-5, 285 hp

NOTES: First C17B. To Edgar Tobin Aerial Surveys, San Antonio, Texas. Not currently listed.

68   B17R   NC281Y
Built Mar. 6, 1936   Wright R-975, 420 hp

NOTES: Not currently listed.

69   B17R   NC15814
Built Mar. 6, 1936   Wright R-975, 420 hp

NOTES: To Edgar Tobin Aerial Surveys, San Antonio, Texas. Not currently listed.

70   B17R   NC15815
Built Mar. 24, 1936   Wright R-975, 420 hp

NOTES: To Col. William Neblett, Los Angeles, California, 1939; Harry Falk, Boise, Idaho (see s/n 4818), 1955; Earl Snyder, Boise, Idaho, 1961, 1964, 1966. Last annual inspection is shown as 1955, so airplane may be dismantled.   *(Russell R. Hiatt)*

73   C17R   NC15487
Built May 1, 1936   Wright R-975, 420 hp

NOTES: First C17R. OCS Manufacturing Company, Coffeeville, Kansas in 1939; M. R. Jones, LaGrange, Illinois, 1955; Safari Coach Company, Joliet, Illinois, 1961; Chad Koppie, Elgin, Illinois, 1964, 1966. The airplane is being rebuilt by Koppie.   *(Leo J. Kohn)*

71   B17R   NC15816, I-IBIS
Built Apr. 1, 1936   Wright R-975, 420 hp

NOTES: Sold to James Haizlip, New York, then to Ala Littoria, Rome, Italy in 1938. Supposed to have been transported to Europe on the dirigible "Hindenburg". No current information.   *(Beech Photo)*

74   C17R   NC15833, N996
Built Apr. 30, 1936   Wright R-975, 420 hp

NOTES: To Harry Hammill, Austin, Texas, 1939; Stone-Wells Flying Service, Jacksonville, Florida, 1955; William Mack, St. Petersburg, Florida, 1961, 1964; John Falicki, Grand Rapids, Michigan, 1966. Formerly an aerial photo airplane, Falicki is changing it back to standard configuration. Photo taken at Davenport, Iowa in 1937.   *(Merle Olmsted)*

72   B17R   NC15817, NC47833
Built Apr. 2, 1936   Wright R-975, 420 hp

NOTES: To Richard Williams, San Francisco, California. Photo taken at Monterey, California in 1940. Compare paint trim to paint trim on G17S, s/n B-3.   *(William T. Larkins)*

75   C17R   NC282Y, XA-BKO, NC282Y
Built May, 1936   Wright R-975, 420 hp

NOTES: Owned by Manning and Martin Oil Company, Denver, Colorado in 1936. Their name is on airplane in photo above. Sold to Antonio Diaz Lombardo, Mexico City in 1939 with Aeronaves de Mexico, S.A. Sold back into the U. S. in 1942 to E. L. Erickson. Then to Mountain States Aviation, Denver, Colorado. To Sweetbriar Company, Denver, Colorado, 1944. Traded to Plains Airways, Cheyenne, Wyoming in April, 1946 for G17S, s/n B-2. Vest Aircraft in Denver had it in 1955; Robert Foster, Seattle, Washington, 1961; C. Biemond, San Jose, California, 1962; to W. G. Matthews, Williamina, Oregon, 1966. Airplane currently being rebuilt.   *(Leo J. Kohn)*

76   C17R   NC15834
Built 1936   Wright R-975, 420 hp

NOTES: Abrams Aerial Survey, Lansing, Michigan in 1939 with B. F. Hammond as pilot. Not currently listed.

77   C17R   NC15835
Built July 1, 1936   Wright R-975, 420 hp

NOTES: Started production as s/n 78, changed June 10, 1936 to s/n 77, and s/n 77 airframe changed to s/n 78. Originally built as a demonstrator, it was entered in the 1936 Bendix, and won. Before the Bendix it had been promised to Col. William C. Brooks in Honduras, and was sold to him. Actually, the airplane was owned by the government of Honduras, but Col. Brooks flew it. There is some speculation today (1966) that the airframe still exists. A number of photos exist of NC15835, but it is not easy to determine if any given photograph is s/n 77 or s/n 81. For this reason, and since both s/n 77 and s/n 81 were finished in identical paint trims, a photo of s/n 77 is not shown in this section of the book.

78   C17E   NC15836, J-BAOI
Built July, 1936   Wright R-760, 285 hp

NOTES: Started production as s/n 77, switched to s/n 78 on June 10, 1936. Sold to Japan Airways Co., Ltd., Tokyo, Japan.
(Richard M. Bueschel)

79   C17R   NC15837, NC1600
Built 1936   Wright R-975, 420 hp

NOTES: Listed to David McConnell, New York City in 1939. Not currently listed.

80   C17R   NC2
Built 1936   Wright R-975, 420 hp

NOTES: Sold to Dept. of Commerce. In 1939 was being used by the Civil Aeronautics Authority for air carrier inspection office at Meacham Field in Fort Worth, Texas. Not currently listed.

81   C17R   NC15835
Built Oct. 9, 1936   Wright R-975, 420 hp

NOTES: Built for Louise Thaden to replace s/n 77, the 1936 Bendix winner, s/n 81 was identical in every respect to the Bendix winner. Louise Thaden toured the country in this airplane, and it was held to be "the 1936 Bendix winner" although the record was very clear that s/n 77 was the airplane that won the 1936 Bendix race. Photo above was taken at Merced, California in 1963. Today the airplane is flying, and is in excellent condition. Current owner (1966) is W. C. Yarbrough, Atlanta, Georgia.
(Dustin Carter)

82   C17R   NC16434
Built 1936   Wright R-975, 420 hp

NOTES: Sold to Sucesion J. Serralles, Central Mercedita, Ponce, Puerto Rico with Dennis Pewelson listed as pilot. Not currently listed.

83   C17L   NC15813, F-APFB
Built Apr. 21, 1936   Jacobs L-4, 225 hp

NOTES: Although s/n 81 was built in October, 1936, and s/n 83 is two numbers afterwards, and was supposedly built back in April, 1936, there is no way I can reconcile the six month difference! But, official records support both production dates. Not currently listed. No notes on French registration, F-APFB.
(Tom Cuddy)

84   C17B   NC15841
Built 1936   Jacobs L-5, 285 hp

NOTES: Sold to Pacific Northwest Airways, Inc., Seattle, Washington. Last listing is to Holland Dusting Company, High Springs, Florida in 1955.

85   C17B   NC15842
Built 1936   Jacobs L-5, 285 hp

NOTES: Donald Provost, Newark, New Jersey shown as 1939 owner. Not currently listed.

86   C17B   NC15843
Built 1936   Jacobs L-5, 285 hp

NOTES: Sold to Colorado Aviation, Denver, Colorado. Later to Howard Arthur who operated a flying service in Pendleton, Oregon. Somewhere along the line the engine was changed to a Lycoming R-680-E3B of 300 hp. Perry Institute in Yakima, Washington had it in the late fifties; Wendle Ford, Spokane, Washington, 1961; Standford Leland, Spokane, Washington, 1964, 1966.
(Ralph Nortell)

87   C17B   NC15844
Built 1936   Jacobs L-5, 285 hp

NOTES: Sold to H. C. Mattes and Parnell S. Billings of the Belmont Radio Corporation, Chicago, Illinois. Not currently listed. *(B. B. Deatrick)*

88   C17B   NC15845
Built 1936   Jacobs L-5, 285 hp

NOTES: To Edgar Tobin Aerial Surveys, San Antonio, Texas. Not currently listed.

89   C17B   NC15846
Built 1936   Jacobs L-5, 285 hp

NOTES: Sold to Douglas-Ward Aviation, Mineola, Long Island, New York. Dorothy Guiling, Richmond, Indiana, 1955; James Stuart, Lancaster, California, 1961; Fred Comer, Los Angeles, California, 1964, 1966. Airplane dismantled, and parts reportedly used on another airplane. Photo taken March 23, 1957 after a wheels-up landing at Hayward Airport in California.   *(Larry Smalley)*

90   SC17B   NC15487
Built 1936   Jacobs L-5, 285 hp

NOTES: Sold to Thomas Rice, Meredity, New Hampshire, but it was evidently flown by his pilot, Floyd Miller, State Airport, Augusta, Maine. Not currently listed.   *(Tom Cuddy)*

91   C17B   NC15848
Built 1936   Jacobs L-5, 285 hp

NOTES: Sold to Loffland Brothers Company, Tulsa, Oklahoma. To Harry Heimple in Wichita, Kansas in 1939. Dr. Norman Wheeler, Globe, Arizona, 1955; no later listing.   *(Russell R. Hiatt)*

92   C17B   NC15849
Built 1936   Jacobs L-5, 285 hp

NOTES: Not currently listed.

93   C17B   NC15840
Built 1936   Jacobs L-5, 285 hp

NOTES: Mr. Louis M. Carle, Carle Petroleum Company, San Antonio, Texas, 1939; Clifford Adams, La Mesa, California, 1955; Harvey C. Dunbar, 1961, 1964, 1966. Currently out of commission, expected to be flying soon.   *(Harvey C. Dunbar)*

94   C17B   NC16435
Built 1936   Jacobs L-5, 285 hp

NOTES: Hartley Aviation Company, Duluth, Minnesota original owner. Not currently listed.

95   C17B   NC16436
Built 1936   Jacobs L-5, 285 hp

NOTES: Hartley Aviation Company, Duluth, Minnesota original owner. Not currently listed.   *(Leo J. Kohn)*

96   C17B   NC16437
Built 1936   Jacobs L-5, 285 hp

NOTES: John G. Anwiler, Oakland, California, 1939. Not currently listed.

97   C17B   NC16438
Built 1936   Jacobs L-5, 285 hp

NOTES: Joe Jenkins, Wyoming, Delaware, 1955; no further listing. Date photo was taken is not known. Note fuselage stripes—this is same paint trim used on s/n 77 and s/n 81.   *(Harold Andrews)*

98　C17B　　NC16439, NC46291
Built 1936　　Jacobs L-5, 285 hp

NOTES: Dan G. Best, Woodland, California, 1939; no further listing. Photo taken near San Francisco, California in August, 1939, and is a good side view of the typical Beech paint trim used in the 1935-36 period.　　　　　　　　　　　　*(William T. Larkins)*

99　SC17B　　NC16440
Built 1936　　Jacobs L-5, 285 hp

NOTES: The only Beechcraft 17 amphibian. Amphibious floats are used today on some airplanes (notably the Cessna 180), but they use two main wheels, and two nose wheels on the floats. This installation used main wheels with rear end of float as a "tail skid". Landing characteristics were not good, and the idea was abandoned. Airplane not currently listed.　　　　　　　　　　　　*(William T. Larkins)*

100　C17L　　NC16441, N962W
Built 1936　　Jacobs L-4, 225 hp

NOTES: Paul Mantz, Burbank, California, 1939. Photo was taken on August 18, 1939 in Burbank. Airplane eventually ended up on east coast. Overturned by a hurricane, it was purchased by Franklin A. Higgins who is presently (1966) rebuilding it.　　　　　*(B. B. Deatrick)*

101　C17B　　NC16442
Built 1936　　Jacobs L-5, 285 hp

NOTES: R. Z. Glass, Houston, Texas in 1939. Not currently listed.

102　C17B　　NC16443, NC47024
Built 1936　　Jacobs L-5, 285 hp

NOTES: Barney Cockburn, Arp, Texas, 1939; Harold Robinson, Baldwin Park, California, 1955; Roy Lufkin, San Fernando, California, 1961 to 1963; H. C. Hanwarren, Rubidoux, California 1964 to 1966.　　　　　　　　　　　　　　*(Roy Lufkin)*

103　C17B　　NC16444
Built 1936　　Jacobs L-5, 285 hp

NOTES: N. A. O'Mara, Papago Indian Trading Post. Sells, Arizona, 1939; George Brown, Lincoln, Illinois, 1955; John Burns, Canoga Park, California, 1961, 1964, 1966. Shows inspection date of 1955, so is either dismantled or destroyed.　　　　　　　　*(Leo J. Kohn)*

104　C17B　　Unknown
Built 1936　　Jacobs L-5, 285 hp

NOTES: Another Beechcraft to Dr. Samuel A. Bosch, Buenos Aires, Argentina. No current information.

105　C17L　　NC16446
Built 1936　　Jacobs L-5, 285 hp

NOTES: H. L. E. Meyer and Company, San Francisco, California in 1939. Ended up as a "live" project in a mechanics school. The late Dwight Addington attended the school in 1956. By this time the fuselage had been used up, but one of the school instructors had the wings and empennage. Dwight bought them from him, and still had the wings when he was killed in a Fairchild 24 accident in 1964.　　　　　　　　　　　　　*(Leo J. Kohn)*

106   C17B   NC16447
Built 1936   Jacobs L-5, 285 hp

NOTES: St. Louis Air Lines, Inc., St. Louis, Missouri, 1939. No further
listing.   (E. C. Haney)

107   C17L   ZK-AEU, NZ573, ZK-AJS, VH-BOU, VH-PMG
Built 1936   Jacobs L-4, 225 hp

NOTES: Auckland Aero Club, Auckland, New Zealand originally. Impressed into RNZAF military service during World War Two, and returned to the Auckland Aero Club after the war. In the early fifties it
was sold to J. M. Bonney of Cobar, New South Wales, Australia. In
March, 1955 it went to the late C. D. Kellman, Julia Creek, North
Queensland, Australia. It was later transferred to his wife, Peggy Kelman, a pioneer Australian aviatrix, at "Bonnie Doon", Yamala, C.Q.R.,
Queensland. Mrs. Kelman traded the airplane for a late model Cessna
in 1962. In March, 1963 the new owner registered the airplane as
VH-PMG.   (Beech Photo)

108   C17B   VH-UXP, A39-3, VH-UXP
Built 1936   Jacobs L-5, 285 hp

NOTES: Sold to James Loneragan (Mudgee) Co. Pty. Ltd., Mudgee, New
South Wales, Australia, and arrived in Australia in February, 1937.
Impressed by the RAAF on March 25, 1942 as A39-3 (It was earlier
impressed as A39-2, but was deferred). Returned to civilian life about
1948. It was still registered in 1964, hangared at Bankstown, New
South Wales, Australia. Compare engine cowling to s/n 107. The non-
standard cowling on s/n 108 was probably installed when the engine
was changed to a Jacobs L-4 which is the present engine in the
airplane.   (Peter Berry)

109   C17L   NC15836
Built 1936   Jacobs L-4, 225 hp

NOTES: To A. S. Swenson, Wichita, Kansas in 1939. Not currently listed.

110   C17B   NC15838
Built 1936   Jacobs L-5, 285 hp

NOTES: L. D. Thomas, Lubbock, Texas, 1939. No current listing. Compare paint trim on this airplane to paint trim on G17S, s/n B-3.
                                                                  (Beech Photo)

111   C17B   NC17060
Built 1936   Jacobs L-5, 285 hp

NOTES: Manning and Martin Oil Company until 1939. No current listing.

112   C17B   NC17061
Built Nov., 1936   Jacobs L-5, 285 hp

NOTES: Dr. William Dwyer, Hartford, Connecticut in 1939; to Dick
Hermann Associates, Detroit, Michigan, 1955; Leslie Steen, East Lansing,
Michigan, 1961, 1964, 1966. Converted to a Lycoming R-680-E3B of 300
hp in 1954.   (Leslie Steen)

113   SC17R   CF-BBB
Built 1936   Wright R-975, 420 hp

NOTES: Export certificate dated December 12, 1936 to Canada; Dec. 23,
1936 to Mackenzie Air Service, Edmonton, Alberta; May 9, 1942 to
Aircraft Repair, Edmonton, Alberta; sold to Northwest Industries, Edmonton, but not registered; May 22, 1946 Severn Enterprises, Toronto,
Ontario; June 19, 1946 L. J. Heit, Toronto (director of Severn Enterprises); July 16, 1946 registered to Severn Enterprises; November 6,
1950 Millard Auto-Aero-Marine, Toronto; February 26, 1951 P. S. Hoe-
berg, Algoma Mills, Ontario; June 25, 1952 East Coast Airways, St. John,
N. B.; June 9, 1955 LaTuque Air Services, LaTuque, P. Q. On October 21,
1955 pilot lost control after takeoff from the St. Maurice River at
Windigo, P. Q.—crashed and damaged beyond repair. (William T. Larkins)

114   C17R   G-AENY
Built Dec., 1936   Wright R-975, 420 hp

NOTES: Registered in England December 17, 1936 to C. E. Gardner, British racing pilot. Based at Croydon airport. Sold out of the British Isles December, 1937. No current listing.

115   C17R   BuNo 0801
Built 1937   Wright R-975, 420 hp

NOTES: A very rare airplane, this C17R was sold to the Navy as a model JB-1, the only one of its kind. Note the unique paint trim. Final disposition of the aircraft is not known. It is not currently listed.
(Beech Photo)

116   C17R   NC2000
Built 1937   Wright R-975, 420 hp

NOTES: Swiflite Aircraft Corporation, New York City, New York in 1939 with George Pomeroy as pilot. Not currently listed.

117   C17E   Unknown
Built 1937   Wright R-760, 285 hp

NOTES: Sold to Japan Airways Company, Ltd., Hikokan, Siba-Ku, Tokyo, Japan. No current information.

120   C17R   CF-BIF, NC38937, CF-GKW
Built 1937   Wright R-975, 420 hp

NOTES: Canadian Pacific Airlines, Hudson, Ontario, Canada. Sold to C. A. Martin, Fairbanks, Alaska May 4, 1944. Sold back into Canada December 15, 1951 to Uranium Corporation of British Columbia. R. Baker, Vancouver, B.C., August 10, 1953. Okanagan Broadcasters, Kelowna, B.C. on April 3, 1957, and operated by Pacific Western Airlines. Still listed as late as 1962.
(William T. Larkins)

121   C17B   NC15839
Built 1937   Jacobs L-5, 285 hp

NOTES: Not currently listed.

122   C17R   NC16445
Built 1937   Wright R-975, 420 hp

NOTES: Aero Trades, Inc., Roosevelt Field, Long Island, New York in 1939. No current listing.

123   C17B   PP-TCQ
Built 1937   Jacobs L-5, 285 hp

NOTES: Sold originally to Count Raul Crespi, San Paulo, Brazil. No current information.

124   C17L   ZS-BBC, BC-1, OH-PKA
Built 1937   Jacobs L-4, 225 hp

NOTES: Sold to Capt. O. Thaning of Johannesburg, South Africa to replace B17L, s/n 18 after it crashed. The same engine was used in both airplanes. Capt. Thaning presented the airplane to Finland for use during their Winter War, 1939-40. It was registered as OH-PKA in 1945, and crashed December 3, 1947 at Halli.

118   C17R   G-AESJ, DS180
Built 1937   Wright R-975, 420 hp

NOTES: To. Mr. C. E. Gardner in England, 1939. Registered in England first in April, 1937 as a demonstrator for Surrey Flying Services at Croydon airport. Impressed into war service as DS180. No current information.
(Emil Strasser)

119   C17R   NC17068
Built 1937   Wright R-975, 420 hp

NOTES: Harry A. Hammill, Austin, Texas in 1939. No current listing.

125   C17B   NC17063
Built 1937   Jacobs L-5, 285 hp

NOTES: Robert G. Payne, Hicksville, Long Island, New York in 1939. No current listing.
(Warren D. Shipp)

126   C17B   NC17065
Built 1937   Jacobs L-5, 285 hp

NOTES: Inter City Airlines, East Boston, Massachusetts in 1939. Not currently listed.

127   C17B   NC17062
Built 1937   Jacobs L-5, 285 hp

NOTES: Charles G. Grey, Paris, France in 1939. No current listing.

128   C17B   NC17064
Built 1937   Jacobs L-5, 285 hp

NOTES: At one time a State of New Jersey Forest Fire Service airplane, later an aerial photo ship in San Antonio, Texas, it is currently owned by James Halsted in Houston, Texas (1966 listing). While being flown as an aerial photo ship, it was powered by a Jacobs L6MB of 330 hp, and licensed in the restricted category. It now has a Jacobs L-4 of 225 hp.
(*Robert V. Williams*)

129   C17B   VH-UYI
Built 1937   Jacobs L-5, 285 hp

NOTES: No U. S. registration; sold originally in Australia. Crashed and destroyed at Archerfield, Queensland on 5/21/41.

132   C17B   NC17074
Built 1937   Jacobs L-5, 285 hp

NOTES: Flown by Mamer-Schreck Flying Service out of Felts Field, Spokane, Washington during the late 1930's. Emblem on fuselage is "Mamer-Schreck Air Transport". Photo was taken some years ago by Ed Carlson. Airplane registered 1966 to Bartram H. Dilkes, Jr., Latrobe, Pennsylvania.
(*Ralph Nortell*)

130   C17B   NC17072
Built Feb. 26, 1937   Jacobs L-5, 285 hp

NOTES: Author's old airplane. Flown extensively by Edna Whyte prior to World War Two, it changed hands many times after the war. Flown by the author in the mid-1950's, it was sold to Luke Murray, Columbus, Ohio, and was last registered to him. Photo was taken at old Milwaukee County Airport (now General Mitchell Field) in the winter of 1941-42.
(*Gregory C. Kohn*)

133   C17B   NC17078
Built 1937   Jacobs L-5, 285 hp

NOTES: Photo was taken by Caryl Lane at the old West Keene, New Hampshire airport in the Fall of 1941. Registered in 1966 to Larry Denton, Colfax, Washington. Supposedly owned by a Dupont when new, it ended up in northwestern U. S. on floats.
(*Caryl Lane*)

134   C17B   NC17079, NC47834
Built 1937   Jacobs L-5, 285 hp

NOTES: NC47834 registration may indicate this airplane was one of many civil impressments into military service in World War Two. Listed to Denzil Wright, Woodville, Ohio, 1964, powered by a Jacobs L-4 engine of 225 hp with a 1953 inspection date. Lee Willingham, Martinsville, Indiana, 1966, still a 1953 inspection date. Airplane probably being rebuilt.

135   C17B   NC17080
Built 1937   Jacobs L-5, 285 hp

NOTES: Hans Hoffman, Bogota, Colombia, 1939. No current listing.

131   C17B   NC17073
Built Mar. 4, 1937   Jacobs L-5, 285 hp

NOTES: Photographed at Boston, Massachusetts in 1941, this airplane is currently registered to Dennis K. Ward, Pease Air Force Base, New Hampshire.
(*Richard H. Howe*)

136   D17W   NC17081, BuNo 09776
Built Feb., 1937   Pratt & Whitney R-985-SC-G, 600 hp

NOTES: The first D17 model. It was equipped with the experimental P&W R-985-SC-G engine, and was reportedly built for Frank Hawks. Pratt and Whitney decided not to market the engine, and the airplane was converted to a Wright R-975 of 420 hp. By the beginning of World War Two, it had found its way to California, and the ownership of Ralph E. Myers who sold it to the Navy where it was carried as a GB-1, Bureau Number 09776. Evidently it did not survive the war.
(*Beech Photo*)

137   D17R   NC17082, NC51152
Built Mar., 1937   Wright R-975, 420 hp

NOTES: The first D17R, this airplane was later converted to the 450 hp P&W. Owned for the past several years by Lawrence Kakara of Miami, Florida, the airplane is registered as being disassembled.
(Warren D. Shipp)

138   E17B   NC17083, NC57839
Built Mar., 1937   Jacobs L-5, 285 hp

NOTES: First E17 model. Since the 1955 register it has shown a Jacobs L6MB of 330 hp which indicates it may have been used as a high altitude photo ship, but since 1955 it has been out of license with no current airworthiness inspection. Since the 1955 register it is shown registered to L. B. Strange, Tutwiler, Mississippi.   (Beech Photo)

139   E17B   NC17084
Built 1937   Jacobs L-5, 285 hp

NOTES: H. H. Bender, Toledo, Ohio, 1939. Not currently listed.
(E. C. Haney)

140   E17B   NC17085
Built 1937   Jacobs L-5, 285 hp

NOTES: Sold by Mouton and Clyde, Beechcraft dealers in San Francisco, California. Not currently listed.   (Peter M. Bowers)

141   E17B   NC16449
Built 1937   Jacobs L-5, 285 hp

NOTES: Photograph was taken at Union Air Terminal in Burbank, California on December 21, 1938. Airplane not currently listed.
(B. B. Deatrick)

142   E17B   NC17091, NC46293
Built 1937   Jacobs L-5, 285 hp

NOTES: Last registered on 1955 list to Joseph Buhmier, Westchester, Pennsylvania. Not on 1961 or any subsequent list. Photo taken by Bill Alston, supplied to author by James H. Harvey.   (James H. Harvey)

143   E17B   NC17092, NC50650
Built 1937   Jacobs L-5, 285 hp

NOTES: Not shown on the 1955 list; registered to Roland Maxon, Lakewood, California in 1961; then to Darrell A. Sausser of Twentynine Palms, California. Currently listed to Harlan Sheldon, Twentynine Palms with a current airworthiness inspection.   (Donald W. Sausser)

144   E17B   NC18025
Built 1937   Jacobs L-5, 285 hp

NOTES: This is the only photograph in this book made from an 8x10 negative—generously loaned by M. J. Woodhull, Jr., the photographer. The photo was taken around 1939 when the airplane was owned by W. D. Crook of Los Angeles, California. Not currently listed.
(M. J. Woodhull, Jr.)

145 E17B NC18026
Built 1937 Jacobs L-5, 285 hp

NOTES: S. B. Crabtree, Tyler, Texas, 1939. Not currently listed.

146 D17S NC18027, NC71, N67769
Built June, 1937 P&W R-985, 450 hp

NOTES: First D17S. Disassembled, the airplane is currently owned by Richard Stowe, Park Ridge, New Jersey. It will eventually be rebuilt.
(William Steeneck)

147 D17S NC18028
Built 1937 P&W R-985, 450 hp

NOTES: Registered to Aero Service Corporation, Philadelphia, Pennsylvania 1955, 1961, 1964; not currently listed. *(Peter M. Bowers)*

148 D17R NCJ8029
Built 1937 Wright R-975, 420 hp

NOTES: Photo taken in Galveston, Texas in December, 1938. Not currently listed.
(Thomas S. Cuddy II)

149 E17B NC18038
Built 1937 Jacobs L-5, 285 hp

NOTES: Not currently listed. *(Warren D. Shipp)*

150 E17B NC18039
Built 1937 Jacobs L-5, 285 hp

NOTES: Photographed in Boston, Massachusetts in 1938, this airplane is currently (1966 list) registered to Marcus L. Hill, Jr., Cisco, Texas, and has a current airworthiness inspection. *(Thomas S. Cuddy II)*

151 E17B NC18040, N48401
Built 1937 Jacobs L-5, 285 hp

NOTES: Hedge Flying Service, Hoxie, Kansas, 1955; Joseph Robison, Wichita, Kansas, 1961; Robert Raymond, Belleville, Illinois, 1964, 1966. Photo taken June 6, 1938 by William Yeager; supplied to author by Emil Strasser. *(Emil Strasser)*

152 E17B NC18041
Built 1937 Jacobs L-5, 285 hp

NOTES: W. Wheeler Farish, Perkinston, Miss., 1939. Not currently listed.

153   E17B   NC18042
Built 1937   Jacobs L-5, 285 hp

NOTES: Donald Provost, Teaneck, N. J., 1939. Not currently listed.

154   E17B   NC17066
Built 1937   Jacobs L-5, 285 hp

NOTES: Loffland Brothers Company, Tulsa, Oklahoma, 1939, 1940. Not currently listed.

155   E17B   NC17069
Built 1937   Jacobs L-5, 285 hp

NOTES: J. K. Kepley, Laredo, Texas, 1939. Not currently listed.

156   E17B   NC17071, NC48413, N17071
Built 1937   Jacobs L-5, 285 hp

NOTES: G. E. Parker, Jr., Port Arthur, Texas, 1955; Thomas Warlick, Lawndale, N. C., 1961; Algene Fuller, Brewer, Maine, 1964, 1966. Photo taken Fort Worth, Texas, Nov. 8, 1948. Airplane now has Jacobs L-4, 225 hp. Note non-standard exhaust stack, and poor fit of ring cowling.
(E. C. Haney)

157   E17B   NC18555
Built 1937   Jacobs L-5, 285 hp

NOTES: Charles L. Cox, Jr., Ruleville, Mississippi, 1955; Hays Maxwell, Omaha, Nebraska, 1961, 1964, 1966. The airplane now has a Jacobs L6MB of 330 hp. (See color pages for photo)

158   E17B   NC18556
Built 1937   Jacobs L-5, 285 hp

NOTES: Clarence Tarbet, Muncie, Indiana, 1939. Not currently listed.
(Leo J. Kohn)

159   E17B   NC18557
Built 1937   Jacobs L-5, 285 hp

NOTES: J. R. D. Moore, Laredo, Texas, 1939. Not currently listed.

160   E17B   CF-BHA, NC41852
Built Aug., 1937   Jacobs L-5, 285 hp

NOTES: Exported to Canada August 25, 1937. Noorduyn Aircraft, St. Laurent, P. Q., 1937; Merkley Air Service, Brockville, Ontario, 1939; back to Noorduyn in 1939 at Montreal; Hudson's Bay Company in Winnipeg, 1940; back to Noorduyn in Montreal in 1942; Tennessee Gas, Houston, Texas on March 27, 1944. Passed through several private owners in the U. S., now (1966) registered to Arthur H. McEwen Jr., Bangor, Maine. Now has Jacobs L-4, 225 hp. Photo shows airplane on skiis in Canada as CF-BHA.   (Beech Photo)

161   E17L   Unknown
Built Sept., 1937   Jacobs L-4, 225 hp

NOTES: First E17L. Sold into Argentina. Letter "R" on the rudder and number "343" on fuselage side do not relate to any known registrations. Not currently listed.   (Beech Photo)

162   E17B   NC18560
Built 1937   Jacobs L-5, 285 hp

NOTES: Registered since 1955 in the name of the late Earl Robinson, Wichita, Kansas. His sons, Edwin, and Dennis, supplied the above photo. The airplane has another owner, but the 1966 list did not show it. Probably not flying.   (Edwin A. Robinson)

163   E17B   NC2388
Built 1937   Jacobs L-5, 285 hp

NOTES: Owned by Connecticut State Department of Aeronautics before World War Two; reportedly given to U. S. Navy during the war. Not currently listed.

164　　D17W　　NX18562, NR18562, Army 42-107277
Built 1937　　P&W R-985-SC-G, 600 hp

NOTES: Standard D17 powered with special P&W engine. See s/n 136. This one was flown by Jacqueline Cochran, and set several speed and altitude records in the late 1930's. When it entered World War Two Army service it was converted to a Wright R-975 of 420 hp. The airplane crashed while in Army service, and was not rebuilt.

(Pratt & Whitney Photo)

168　　D17S　　NC18566, BuNo 09778
Built 1937　　P&W R-985, 450 hp

NOTES: The Beech Photo above carried this notation "Model D17W, August, 1937, Wasp Jr. SCG—525 HP", but it is carried on another Beech list as a D17S. In any event, it became a Navy GB-1 during World War Two. David Gray, Jr., Santa Barbara, California sold or gave it to the Navy. It was assigned to NAS Key West, Florida. Not currently listed.

(Beech Photo)

Serial Numbers 169 through 178 were Model 18's.

165　　D17S　　NC18563, BuNo 09777
Built 1937　　P&W R-985, 450 hp

NOTES: Sold by Wings Field, Inc., Ambler, Pennsylvania to the Navy in World War Two where it became a Navy GB-1. Not currently registered.

(Beech Photo)

166　　D17R　　NC400
Built 1937　　Wright R-975, 420 hp

NOTES: Chester Snow, Washington, D.C., 1939. Not currently listed.

179　　D17S　　NC18575
Built Aug., 1937　　P&W R-985, 450 hp

NOTES: Flown for years as a photo airplane for Aero Service Corporation in Philadelphia, Pennsylvania, it was sold to Major LaVerne Snowden, and rebuilt. Currently registered to Major Snowden (USAF Maintenance Officer) in Amarillo, Texas. Photo shows Major Snowden just after acquiring the airplane.

(John Howard)

180　　D17R　　NC18576
Built 1937　　Wright R-975, 420 hp

NOTES: Tom Potter, Kilgore, Texas in 1939. No current listing.

181　　D17R　　Unknown
Built 1937　　Wright R-975, 420 hp

NOTES: Republic of China. No current information.

182　　D17R　　Unknown
Built 1937　　Wright R-975, 420 hp

NOTES: Republic of China. No current information.

183　　D17S　　NC18579
Built 1937　　P&W R-985, 450 hp

NOTES: Carl F. Johnson, Lake Tahoe, Nevada, 1939. Not currently listed.

167　　D17R　　NC18565, NC46292, N35E
Built 1937　　Wright R-975, 420 hp

NOTES: Photographed in Columbus, Ohio in August, 1963, the airplane is currently registered (1966) to William Ruble, Newark, Ohio.

(Thomas A. Cooney)

184   D17R   NC18580
Built 1937   Wright R-975, 420 hp

NOTES: Electric Autolite Company, Toledo, Ohio, 1939. Photo taken on September 27, 1940. Not currently listed.   (Emil Strasser)

185   D17S   NC18581, BuNo 09780
Built 1937   P&W R-985, 450 hp

NOTES: To Barahona Co., Inc. in Central America. Impressed into Navy service in World War Two as a GB-1. Not currently listed.

186   D17S   NC18582
Built 1937   P&W R-985, 450 hp

NOTES: Cabot Carbon Company, Pampa, Texas, 1939. Not currently listed.

187   D17S   NC1324
Built 1937   P&W R-985, 450 hp

NOTES: Wallis C. Bird, Oyster Bay, Long Island, New York, 1939. Not currently listed.

188   D17R   NC18584
Built 1937   Wright R-975, 420 hp

NOTES: Tom Graham Oil Co., Corpus Christi, Texas, 1939. Not currently listed.

189   E17B   NC18585
Built 1937   Jacobs L-5, 285 hp

NOTES: Cavour Hartley, Duluth, Minnesota, 1939. Not currently listed.

190   E17B   NC18043, NC47458
Built 1937   Jacobs L-5, 285 hp

NOTES: Richard Card, Terre Haute, Indiana, 1939. Wilson Flying Service in Williams, Arizona, 1955. No further listing.

191   E17B   NC18044, NC48974
Built 1937   Jacobs L-5, 285 hp

NOTES: Howard Batt, Santa Monica, California, 1939; Bruce Dean, Los Angeles, California. Photo taken at Grand Central Air Terminal in Burbank on May 21, 1938.   (B. B. Deatrick)

192   E17B   NC18558
Built 1937   Jacobs L-5, 285 hp

NOTES: John K. Funk, Houston, Texas, 1939. Not currently listed.

193   E17B   NC18559
Built 1937   Jacobs L-5, 285 hp

NOTES: H. F. Wood, Birmingham, Alabama, 1939. Not currently listed.

194   E17B   NC18564
Built Nov., 1937   Jacobs L-5, 285 hp

NOTES: Not currently listed.

195   E17B   NC18577
Built 1937   Jacobs L-5, 285 hp

NOTES: Claude Gossett, Van Nuys, California, 1939. Note Curtiss P-40 in photo behind upper wing, and non-standard air scoop under engine cowl. Since 1955 this airplane has been listed with a 330 hp Jacobs L-6 engine. Mox-Air, Inc., Los Angeles, 1966.   (Leo J. Kohn)

196   E17B   NC18587, NC41663
Built 1937   Jacobs L-5, 285 hp

NOTES: Fred Comer, Tujunga, California, 1961 and later with a Jacobs L-6 of 330 hp. Photo shows current (1966) paint trim.   (B. B. Deatrick)

197   E17B   NC18588, NC57827
Built late 1937 or early 1938   Jacobs L-5, 285 hp

NOTES: Notations on photo: "Lockheed photo by J. H. Washburn, Please Credit", and handwritten note: "Hot on the trail. Shooting the 14 from the Beechcraft while the 12 tags along." "14" and "12" are Lockheed Models 12 and 14. William A. Wylam supplied the photo. Airplane was listed to Santa Maria Airlines, Los Angeles, California, 1939; no current listing.   (William A. Wylam)

198   E17B   NC18775, NC57829
Built Jan., 1938   Jacobs L-5, 285 hp

NOTES: Currently being restored by owner Donald J. Brown. Photo was taken in 1958.
(Donald J. Brown)

201   D17S   CF-BJD
Built Mar., 1938   P&W R-985, 450 hp

NOTES: Registered March 16, 1938 to E. O. Champagne in Canada. To E. F. McLean, Ltd. on June 20, 1938; Imperial Oil Ltd. in Toronto on August 16, 1939; Northern Wings, Ltd. at Seven Islands, P. Q. on June 25, 1948. Certificate lapsed and withdrawn from use on May 14, 1956, but the aircraft was not destroyed. Current status unknown.
(Robert Esposito)

199   D17S   NC18776, NC126, NC65297
Built 1938   P&W R-985, 450 hp

NOTES: Owned and raced by Ross Hadley, Los Angeles, California prior to World War Two, the airplane ended up with CAA, then through several owners to Robert V. Williams, an aerial photographer in San Antonio, Texas who still owns it.
(Peter M. Bowers)

202   D17S   NC18779
Built Mar., 1938   P&W R-985, 450 hp

NOTES: Owned by Charles W. Hansen, Uniondale, Long Island, New York, the aircraft burned on August 20, 1963, and may not be rebuilt. Current status unknown.
(Beech Photo)

200   D17S   NC18777
Built Mar., 1938   P&W R-985, 450 hp

NOTES: Reportedly flown by Jacqueline Cochran in the Bendix race in late 1930's, it was later owned by Hampden Wentworth. Later owned by Joe Shell in California. Registered to Robert Ward, Los Angeles, California on 1964, 1966 lists.
(Peter Berry)

203   D17S   CF-CCA
Built Apr., 1938   P&W R-985, 450 hp

NOTES: Sold into Canada on April 14, 1938 to Department of Transport. To Bradley Air Services, Ltd., Carp, Ontario on February 22, 1955; Spartan Air Services, Ltd., Ottawa on February 22, 1956; to I. Sanders, Ottawa on December 12, 1957. Certificate lapsed, withdrawn from use on December 7, 1958. Current status unknown.
(William T. Larkins)

204　E17B　NC18781
Built Jan., 1938　Jacobs L-5, 285 hp

NOTES: Ben Peterson, in above photo, bought the airplane from John Martenson of Los Angeles, California. It had been sitting for seven years, and was in a bad state of repair, but Ben hopes to eventually have it flying.　*(Ben Peterson)*

205　E17B　NC903, NC46493
Built 1938　Jacobs L-5, 285 hp

NOTES: Frank Battan, Wilmington, Delaware, 1939. Not current.

206　E17B　NC284Y
Built Apr. 21, 1938　Jacobs L-5, 285 hp

NOTES: Original owner was Max B. Miller and Company in New York City. Purchased in August, 1962 from Clifford Grover, Battle Creek, Michigan by the CDW Stagger Club, Inc., it began a restoration. Harry F. Wells is now the sole owner, and hopes to complete the restoration soon.　*(Harry F. Wells)*

207　E17B　NC18784, NC57831
Built 1938　Jacobs L-5, 285 hp

NOTES: J. G. Hammond, Inc., Fort Worth, Texas, 1939. Not current.

208　E17B　NC18785
Built April, 1938　Jacobs L-5, 285 hp

NOTES: Rebuilt by Edwin Burger, Sidney, New York several years ago, this airplane has been flown by him all over the United States, and into neighboring countries. Engine is now a Jacobs L-4 of 225 hp, and Mr. Burger reports it turns a cruise of 160 mph at 7200 feet using 75% power. Airplane is currently flying, and is still owned by Mr. Burger who was most helpful in supplying information for this book. *(Roger Besecker)*

209　E17B　NC40Y
Built 1938　Jacobs L-5, 285 hp

NOTES: State of Indiana, 1939. Not currently listed.　*(Leo J. Kohn)*

210　SE17B　NC18561
Built 1938　Jacobs L-5, 285 hp

NOTES: Operated as a seaplane by Mellor and Howard in New York City after World War Two, Robert Zullo of Schenectady, New York is the current owner.　*(William Mellor)*

211　F17D　NC18786
Built Apr., 1938　Jacobs L-6, 330 hp

NOTES: Agnes Pyno McLean, New York City, 1939. Not current.
　(Joe Juptner)

212   E17B   NC18787
Built 1938   Jacobs L-5, 285 hp

NOTES: Sold to Mouton and Clyde in San Francisco—photo was supplied by Mr. Clyde. Not currently listed.   (William H. Clyde)

213   E17B   NC18788
Built May, 1938   Jacobs L-5, 285 hp

NOTES: Mouton and Clyde, San Francisco. Monty Mouton on left, and inventor Henry Wolff on right. Airplane not currently listed.
(William H. Clyde)

214   D17R   NC18789
Built 1938   Wright R-975, 420 hp

NOTES: Photo taken by William Yeager on July 12, 1938. Emil Strasser supplied copy of photo to author. Airplane not currently listed.
(Emil Strasser)

215   D17R   NC18790
Built 1938   Wright R-975, 420 hp

NOTES: Manning and Martin, Denver, Colorado, 1939. Not current.

216   D17S   NC18791
Built 1938   P&W R-985, 450 hp

NOTES: Sold to Loffland Brothers Co., Tulsa, Oklahoma, and registered to them through 1940. Not currently listed.

217   D17R   Unknown
Built 1938   Wright R-975, 420 hp

NOTES: Republic of China, Chungking, China, 1939. Not current.

218   D17R   NC18793
Built 1938   Wright R-975, 420 hp

NOTES: Juan Serralles, Jr., Mercedita, Puerto Rico, 1939. Not current.

219   E17B   NC91, N91H
Built 1938   Jacobs L-5, 285 hp

NOTES: Shown as airworthy up through 1961, but now (1966) shown as disassembled, and registered to Samuel Urshan, Santee, California. Being rebuilt by Mr. Urshan.

Serial Numbers 220 through 224 were Model 18's.

225   F17D   NC285Y
Built 1938   Jacobs L-6, 330 hp

NOTES: Sold to the famous Colonel Elliot White Springs of the Springs Cotton Mills in South Carolina. Registered to him through 1940. Not currently listed.

226   F17D   NC2099
Built 1938   Jacobs L-6, 330 hp

NOTES: DuPont Airport, Wilmington, Delaware, 1939. Not current.
(Warren D. Shipp)

227   SE17B   CF-BKQ
Built June, 1938   Jacobs L-5, 285 hp

NOTES: Exported to Canada June 28, 1938; to J. E. Eaton, Toronto on July 4, 1938; to Spinwood Sportland Airways October 7, 1946; to R. G. Daniel, Toronto on July 1, 1947; to Aero Tool Works, Toronto on July 26, 1947; to R. R. Green, Red Lake, Ontario on January 29, 1953; to A. A. Mann and S. McDonald in Red Lake on February 22, 1955; certificate lapsed and withdrawn from use on August 31, 1955. Status of airplane unknown.
(Leo J. Kohn)

230   F17D   NC19466
Built 1938   Jacobs L-6, 330 hp

NOTES: William Yeager photo supplied by Emil Strasser. Taken on May 27, 1939. Airplane sold to Cleveland Pneumatic Tool Company, Cleveland, Ohio, and flown by Ephraim "Pop" Cleveland as "Miss Aerol No. 5". Owned by Victor Gelking, Minot, North Dakota for the past several years, it not flyable, but is being repaired.   *(Emil Strasser)*

231   E17B   NC19467
Built 1938   Jacobs L-5, 285 hp

NOTES: Registered to Raymond Porth, Sanborn, Iowa since 1955. Current status not known.

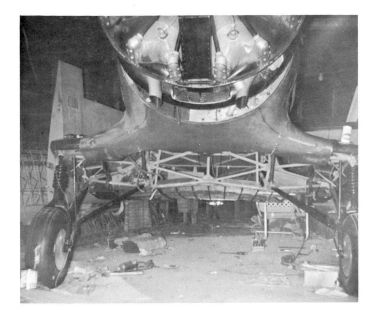

228   E17B   NC18570
Built July 8, 1938   Jacobs L-5, 285 hp

NOTES: John M. Wells July, 1938 to March, 1941 in Southbridge, Massachusetts; Max R. Heppenstall, Pittsburgh, Pennsylvania from March, 1941 to July, 1947; James Hoeveler, Jr., Allison Park, Penna. from July, 1947 to October, 1952; John Pullen and James Urquhart, Elmira, New York from October, 1952 to August, 1955; Ray Watson, Lindley, New York from August, 1955 to January, 1962; Charles F. Wilson, Horseheads, New York from January, 1962 to some date between then and 1966 on which date the airplane was sold to W. R. Gentry, Plainfield, Indiana, the 1966 owner. The airplane was grounded for rebuilding in 1948, passed through the various owners (being stored in a barn at one time), and now Mr. Gentry, and the airplane hasn't been rebuilt yet. Above data supplied by Mr Wilson, except for the date he sold it. That exact date is unknown. I do know Mr. Wilson began trying to sell it in late 1962, so perhaps Mr. Gentry bought it in late 1962 or early 1963.
(Charles F. Wilson)

232   E17B   VT-AKJ
Built 1938   Jacobs L-5, 285 hp

NOTES: First of a group of three E17B's sold to Indian National Airways, New Delhi, India. Crashed prior to World War Two.   *(Beech Photo)*

233   E17B   VT-AKK
Built 1938   Jacobs L-5, 285 hp

NOTES: See photo below. Second of the three E17B's sold in 1938 to Indian National Airways, and the only one to survive. The airplane has been lying in a hangar in Delhi since 1945.

229   F17D   PP-FAA
Built 1938   Jacobs L-6, 330 hp

NOTES: Sold to Brazil. Not currently listed.   *(Beech Photo)*

234   E17B   VT-AKL
Built 1938   Jacobs L-5, 285 hp

NOTES: Just barely visible as the last airplane in the above photo. VT-AKJ in the foreground with VT-AKK in the middle. Like VT-AKJ, this airplane (s/n 234) crashed prior to World War Two.   *(Beech Photo)*

235   D17R   Unknown
Built 1938   Wright R-975, 420 hp

NOTES: Republic of China, Chungking, China, 1939. Not current.

259   F17D   NC289Y
Built 1939   Jacobs L-6, 330 hp

NOTES: Standard Oil of New Jersey, New York City, 1939. Not currently listed.

260   F17D   Unknown
Built 1939   Jacobs L-6, 330 hp

NOTES: Harry Hammill, Austin, Texas, 1939. Not currently listed.

261   F17D   NC291Y, NC49704
Built 1939   Jacobs L-6, 330 hp

NOTES: Lammot DuPont Corporation, Wilmington, Delaware, 1939; Thor Solberg, New York City, 1955; Mid-County Construction Company, Manville, New Jersey, 1961, 1964; not listed on 1966 register.

262   F17D   NC19492
Built 1939   Jacobs L-6, 330 hp

NOTES: Muncie Aviation Corporation, Muncie, Indiana, 1939. Not currently listed.

271   F17D   NC20785, N50A
Built Mar. 24, 1939   Jacobs L-6, 330 hp

NOTES: Capt. Hans Hoffman, Bogota, Colombia, 1939. Owned by Allen W. Russell of San Antonio, Texas for years, it is now (1966) registered to Robert Keel, San Antonio, Texas. The airplane was converted several years ago to a P&W R-985 of 450 hp, and still uses that engine.
(Allen W. Russell)

263   D17S   NC19493
Built 1939   P&W R-985, 450 hp

NOTES: Robert LeSago, Dallas, Texas, 1939; William P. Thompson, 1955 to the present. Airplane is white with red trim.   (William P. Thompson)

272   F17D   NC238Y, N127J
Built 1939   Jacobs L-6, 330 hp

NOTES: Williams Gold Refining Company, Buffalo, New York, 1939. Gail Ebbutt, Crescent City, California, 1966.   (Robert H. Bell)

273   F17D   NC292Y
Built 1939   Jacobs L-6, 330 hp

NOTES: Wings Field, Inc., Ambler, Pennsylvania, 1939. Not currently listed.

274   E17B   VT-ALA
Built 1939   Jacobs L-5, 285 hp

NOTES: Indian National Airways, New Delhi, India. No current information.

264   D17S   NC19494, N36E
Built Mar., 1939   P&W R-985, 450 hp

NOTES: Texaco, New York City, 1939. Owned by A. D. Mallard, Shelley, Idaho for several years, it is now owned by Richard Stowe, Park Ridge, New Jersey who is rebuilding it, and converting it to G17S configuration.
(A. D. Mallard)

Serial Numbers 265 through 269 were Model 18's.

270   F17D   NC20787
Built Feb., 1939   Jacobs L-6, 330 hp

NOTES: Georgina Pope Yeatman, Philadelphia, Pennsylvania, 1939. Vics Flying Service, Somerset, Kentucky, 1955; no further listing.

275   F17D   NC20789, N53754
Built Mar., 1939   Jacobs L-6, 330 hp

NOTES: H. J. Mosser Oil Company, Alice, Texas, 1939. Registered to George Jensen on the 1964 list, he is a pilot in the U. S. Air Force, and supplied complete data on the airplane. On July 19, 1949 a Lycoming R-680-E3B of 300 hp was installed. At that time the airplane was owned by Tom Masterson Jr. of Truscott, Texas. In 1954 the airplane was sold to Harold Johnson, Fort Worth, Texas. In 1957 the engine was changed (another Lycoming R-680-E3B installed), and in 1958 the airplane was sold to Carroll B. Crane, then a Captain in the USAF. In 1963 he sold the airplane to George Jensen. On the 1966 list it is registered to Aircraft Conversions, Minot, North Dakota. The poor photo is a result of taking a picture in ten degree North Dakota weather with an instant-photo type camera.   (George Jensen)

276 F17D NC20790
Built 1939   Jacobs L-6, 330 hp

NOTES: Photo was taken on June 23, 1939 by William Yeager, supplied to me by Strasser. Registered to E. F. Dutro, Zanesville, Ohio in 1939, his name appears on fuselage just below forward side window. Not currently listed.   *(Emil Strasser)*

277 F17D NC20791
Built 1939   Jacobs L-6, 330 hp

NOTES: William Gladstone Green, The Seismograph Corporation, Tulsa, Oklahoma, 1939. Richard Hayes was the pilot. Not currently listed.

278 D17R NC20792
Built 1939   Wright R-975, 420 hp

NOTES: Loyal Penn, Binghamton, New York, 1939. Not currently listed.

279 SD17S NC20793
Built 1939   P&W R-985, 450 hp

NOTES: Rangeley Seaplane Service, Paterson, New Jersey, 1939. No current listing.

280 SE17B NC18778, PK-SAM
Built May 15, 1939   Jacobs L-5, 285 hp

NOTES: Story on this one appears elsewhere in this book. Sold to Christian and Missionary Alliance, it was used in missionary work in Borneo, and burned by the Dutch just before the Japs came in at the beginning of World War Two.   *(Reverend George Fisk)*

281 F17D NC2627
Built 1939   Jacobs L-6, 330 hp

NOTES: Socony-Vacuum Oil Company, New York City, 1939. Not currently listed.

282 F17D NC18792
Built 1939   Jacobs L-6, 330 hp

NOTES: Edgar McComb, Denver, Colorado in 1939. Not current.

283 F17D NC2626
Built 1939   Jacobs L-6, 330 hp

NOTES: Socony-Vacuum Oil Company, New York City, 1939. Richard Welsh, Palmdale, Pennsylvania, 1966. Photo was from Bernard Schureman who was probably the photographer, but it was supplied to me by Leo Kohn.   *(Leo J. Kohn)*

284 D17S NC19468
Built 1939   P&W R-985, 450 hp

NOTES: Firestone Tire and Rubber Company, Akron, Ohio, 1939. E. J. Quigloy was Firestone's pilot. Photo taken July 27, 1939. Owned by Hampden Wentworth in the late 1950's, it crashed on takeoff from a small strip at Reserve, New Mexico on February 2, 1960 causing fatal injuries to Mr. Wentworth and his wife.   *(Emil Strasser)*

285 D17S NC19470, NC42
Built 1939   P&W R-985, 450 hp

NOTES: Lone Star Elevators, Fort Worth, Texas, 1939. Photo was taken April 30, 1948 when CAA owned the airplane. Not currently listed.
            (E. C. Haney)

286 D17S NC20799
Built 1939   P&W R-985, 450 hp

NOTES: The Barahona Company, New York City, 1939 with Tex Anding as pilot. Not currently listed.

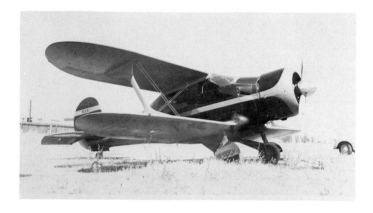

287 D17S NC20750, NC249E, N241, N241K
Built July 20, 1939   P&W R-985, 450 hp

NOTES: A. B. Cobb, Cut Bank, Montana, 1939. Photo taken at Livermore Sky Ranch, California on June 12, 1955. Registered to John Latta, Gustine, California, 1966.   *(Larry Smalley)*

288 D17S Unknown
Built 1939   P&W R-985, 450 hp

NOTES: Elizabeth Powell, Denver, Colorado, 1939. Not currently listed.

205

289 D17R NC20752, NC47939, N47D
Built 1939 Wright R-975, 420 hp

NOTES: Asa G. Candler, Atlanta, Georgia, 1939 with E. W. Hightower as pilot. Owned in the early 1960's by Oliver D. White, it is now registered to Aircraft and Engine Enterprises, Inc., Moore, Oklahoma on the 1966 list. *Oliver D. White, Jr.)*

Serial Numbers 290 through 294 were Model 18's.

295 YC-43(D17S) Army 39-139, DR628, NC91397, G-AMBY, VP-YIV
Built 1939 P&W R-985, 450 hp

NOTES: An airplane with a colorful history, it was originally purchased by the U. S. Army for use by Air Attachés, later is reported to have been given (or sold) to Prince Bernhardt of the Netherlands. It found its way back to the United States after the war to be registered as NC91397, then went to England in 1950 and was stored. In July, 1951 it came out of storage, and was registered as G-AMBY on July 27, 1951. On August 15, 1951 it went to Southern Rhodesia as VP-YIV. No current information. *(Beech Photo)*

296 YC-43(D17S) Army 39-140
Built 1939 P&W R-985, 450 hp

NOTES: To U. S. Army, same program as s/n 295. Not current.

297 YC-43(D17S) Army 39-141
Built 1939 P&W R-985, 450 hp

NOTES: To U. S. Army, same program as s/n 295. Not current.

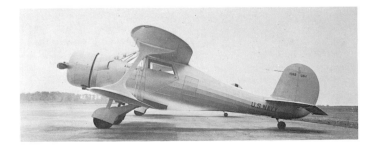

298 GB-1(D17S) BuNo 1589
Built 1939 P&W R-985, 450 hp

NOTES: To U. S. Navy. Not currently listed. Photo shows airplane was assigned to Anacostia in 1941. *(William T. Larkins)*

299 GB-1(D17S) BuNo 1590, N1189V, N16V
Built 1939 P&W R-985, 450 hp

NOTES: To U. S. Navy originally. Survived the war (World War Two), and existed until early 1960's, but not currently listed. *(Richard C. Seeley)*

300 GB-1(D17S) BuNo 1591
Built 1939 P&W R-985, 450 hp

NOTES: To U. S. Navy. Not currently listed.

301 GB-1(D17S) BuNo 1592, N9464H
Built 1939 P&W R-985, 450 hp

NOTES: To U. S. Navy. Existed until after 1955. No listing after 1955.

302 GB-1(D17S) BuNo 1593
Built 1939 P&W R-985, 450 hp

NOTES: To U. S. Navy. Not currently listed.

303 GB-1(D17S) BuNo 1594
Built 1939 P&W R-985, 450 hp

NOTES: To U. S. Navy. Not currently listed.

304 GB-1(D17S) BuNo 1595, N2422
Built 1939 P&W R-985, 450 hp

NOTES: To U. S. Navy. D. R. Simpson Jr., Hanford, California on 1966 list. *(William T. Larkins)*

305 D17A NC19453, NC50959
Built 1939 Wright R-760, 350 hp

NOTES: Aero Brokerage Service Company, Van Nuys, California in 1939. Impressed into military service in World War Two, Bill Woods of Boise, Idaho bought it in 1946, used it in flying into the Idaho primitive area. Sold it in 1958 to Bill Humphreys of Mackay Bar, McCall, Idaho who used it for the same purpose. The airplane is registered now (1966) to Frank Humphreys, Pacifica, California. *(Beech Photo)*

306   D17S   NC20768
Built 1939   P&W R-985, 450 hp

NOTES: Charles Gilbert, Detroit, Michigan, 1939. Photo taken September 2, 1939. Airplane, flown by William Maycock, came in sixth in 1939 Bendix Trophy Race. Not currently listed.   *(Emil Strasser)*

307   F17D   NC20769
Built 1939   Jacobs L-6, 330 hp

NOTES: William Morden, Bronxville, New York, 1939. Not currently listed.

308   F17D   NC20770, BuNo 09800
Built Aug. 2, 1939   Jacobs L-6, 330 hp

NOTES: J. A. Harris III, Philadelphia, Pennsylvania, 1939. Impressed into Naval service in World War Two, it is not currently listed.

309   *Unknown Model and Registration*

NOTES: Have absolutely nothing on this airplane. It probably was a serial number never assembled, or used for spares.

313   D17R   NC20776
Built Sept. 2, 1939   Wright R-975, 420 hp

NOTES: Mouton and Clyde, San Francisco, California, 1939. No current listing.   *(Leo J. Kohn)*

314   D17S   NC20777, PP-NAC, PT-BDL
Built Aug. 21, 1939   P&W R-985, 450 hp

NOTES: George F. Ryan, New York City, 1939. Not currently listed.

Serial Numbers 315 through 324 were Model 18's.

325   D17R   Unknown
Built 1939   Wright R-975, 420 hp

NOTES: Republic of China, Chungking, China. No current information.

326   D17R   Unknown
Built 1939   Wright R-975, 420 hp

NOTES: Republic of China, Chungking, China. No current information.

310   F17D   NC20772, NC50587
Built Aug. 7, 1939   Jacobs L-6, 330 hp

NOTES: Vanderburgh Johnstone, Santa Barbara, California, 1939. George Carpenter, Florissant, Missouri, 1955. No further listing. *(Peter M. Bowers)*

311   F17D   NC20773
Built Aug. 11, 1939   Jacobs L-6, 330 hp

NOTES: James Pierce, Jr., Charleston, West Virginia, 1939. Not currently listed.

327   D17S   NC21904, N114H
Built 1939   P&W R-985, 450 hp

NOTES: Hugh Drane, Corsicana, Texas, 1939. Willis M. "Bill" Woods, 1955 to present. Used extensively by Bill Woods for flying into Idaho's primitive area from Boise, Idaho, the airplane was recently rebuilt. Photo shows Bill Woods filling the fuselage tank.   *(Bill Woods)*

328   D17R   Unknown
Built 1939   Wright R-975, 420 hp

NOTES: Republic of China, Chungking, China. No current information.

329   D17R   Unknown
Built 1939   Wright R-975, 420 hp

NOTES: Republic of China, Chungking, China. Not current.

312   F17D   NC20774
Built Aug. 30, 1939   Jacobs L-6, 330 hp

NOTES: Louis Wasmer, Spokane, Washington, 1939. No current listing.   *(Leo J. Kohn)*

330   F17D   NC2663
Built 1939   Jacobs L-6, 330 hp

NOTES: Atlantic Aviation Sales, Inc., Garden City, New York, 1939. Then to Mr. John H. Wright, Jamestown, New York. Flown for him by Mr. Frederick C. Larson, the airplane suffered wing failure on May 19, 1940. It was recalled to the factory and rebuilt. Registered to George Holm, Ridgefield, Connecticut, 1966.   *(Frederick C. Larson)*

331 F17D NC19451
Built 1939 Jacobs L-6, 330 hp

NOTES: Yuengling Dairy Products, Pottsville, Pennsylvania, 1939. Not currently listed.

332 F17D N46296
Built Oct., 1939 Jacobs L-6, 330 hp

NOTES: Robert Foster, Robertson, Missouri, 1939. Original registration is not known; N46296 was probably assigned after World War Two when the airplane left military service. It was one of many civil airplanes impressed into military service during the war. Registered to Richard Miller, Ralston, Nebraska, 1966. (Leo J. Kohn)

333 F17D NC20798
Built 1939 Jacobs L-6, 330 hp

NOTES: Harry Homeyer, Overland, Missouri, 1939. Aluminum Siding Company of Virginia, Mount Crawford, Virginia, 1966 with an airworthiness inspection date of 1956. Probably disassembled or in dead storage. (Leo J. Kohn)

334 F17D XB-AGO
Built 1939 Jacobs L-6, 330 hp

NOTES: Purchased originally by Henry B. Hanson, San Francisco Mines of Mexico, Ltd., Chihuahua, Mexico, and owned by him to 1946. Registered in Mexico on December 14, 1939. Second owner, Mr. George Marvin, San Juan de Letran, Mexico. Third owner, C. Ricardo Crombé Menocal, Mexico City. Fourth owner was C. Fernando Pérez Lamadrid, Peubla, Mexico. Last report of the airplane was an accident in Pinotepa Nacional. Evidently it was destroyed. (Henry B. Hanson)

335 F17D NC48968, N385
Built 1939 Jacobs L-6, 330 hp

NOTES: Thomas Eastman, Hicksville, Long Island, New York, 1939. William Field, Riverside, California, 1966. (Bude Donato)

336 E17B VT-ALV
Built 1939 Jacobs L-5, 285 hp

NOTES: Indian National Airways, New Delhi, India. No current information. (Beech Photo)

337 F17D NC20771
Built Oct. 27, 1939 Jacobs L-6, 330 hp

NOTES: Reportedly delivered to David Peterson for charter work in Kansas. No current listing. (Beech Photo)

338 F17D Unknown
Built 1939 Jacobs L-6, 330 hp

NOTES: DuPont Airport, Wilmington, Delaware, 1939. No information on registration. Not currently listed.

339 F17D NC20780
Built 1939 Jacobs L-6, 330 hp

NOTES: No information. Appears on the 1939 list, but no owner is shown.

Serial Numbers 340 through 353 were Model 18's.

354 D17S PP-TGE
Built 1939 P&W R-985, 450 hp

NOTES: Senor Assis de Chateaubriand, Rio de Janeiro, Brazil, 1939. No further information.

355 D17S NC239Y, N334E
Built 1939 P&W R-985, 450 hp

NOTES: C. C. Cross, New York City, 1939. Harry Sorenson, Cleveland, Mississippi, 1961, 1964, 1966. Date of last airworthiness inspection shown as 1961.

356   D17A   NC21906
Built 1939   Wright R-760, 350 hp

NOTES: W. E. Brown, Jr., Tulsa, Oklahoma, 1939. Not currently listed.

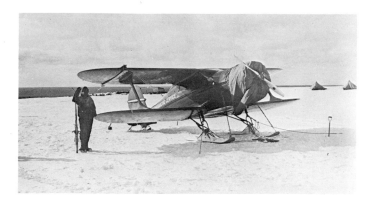

357   D17A   NC20778, A39-2, VH-AFP
Built Oct., 1939   Wright R-760, 350 hp

NOTES: Sold to Research Foundation of Armour Institute of Technology, Chicago, Illinois, and used in their Antarctic expedition. They brought the airplane back to the United States, and Beech offered it to Mr. E. J. Connellan of Alice Springs, Australia in a letter dated August 16, 1941. Evidently Mr. Connellan purchased the airplane, but before he could use it, the RAAF impressed it into service as A39-2. At the end of the war, the airplane was returned to him. One note in the file indicates the airplane was purchased directly by the RAAF from Beech, but notes relating to the transfer of the airplane from the RAAF to Connellan after the war indicate that he had more than a passing interest in it. In any event, he obtained it after the war, and owned it for most of its life. In the hands of a later owner the airplane crashed at Springton, Queensland on December 22, 1963 with fatal injuries to the pilot. The airplane was destroyed by fire.   (Beech Photo)

358   D17A   NC20788
Built Nov. 17, 1939   Wright R-760, 350 hp

NOTES: To Brazilian Navy. No current information.

359   D17A   Unknown
Built 1939   Wright R-760, 350 hp

NOTES: To Brazilian Navy. No current information.

360   D17A   DIBe 207
Built 1939   Wright R-760, 350 hp

NOTES: To Brazilian Navy. No current information.   (Beech Photo)

361   D17A   Unknown
Built 1939   Wright R-760, 350 hp

NOTES: To Brazilian Navy. No current information.

362   D17S   NC900
Built 1939   P&W R-985, 450 hp

NOTES: Frank Battan, Wilmington, Delaware, 1939. Not currently listed.

363   D17A   NC21905
Built 1939   Wright R-760, 350 hp

NOTES: Texaco, San Antonio, Texas, 1939. Owned by Deane Gill of Oklahoma City, Oklahoma for many years, it is registered now (1966) to Jackie Yoes, Stigler, Oklahoma with an inspection date of 1957 which may indicate the airplane is dismantled.   (Merle Olmsted)

Serial Numbers 364 through 374, and 381 through 384 were Model 18's. Serial Numbers 375 through 380 were Model M18R.

385   GB-1(D17S)   BuNo 1898
Built 1940   P&W R-985, 450 hp

NOTES: To U.S. Navy. Not currently listed.   (Joe Juptner)

386   GB-1(D17S)   BuNo 1899
Built 1940   P&W R-985, 450 hp

NOTES: To U.S. Navy. Not currently listed.

387   GB-1(D17S)   BuNo 1900
Built 1940   P&W R-985, 450 hp

NOTES: To U.S. Navy. Not currently listed.

388   E17B   NC293Y
Built 1940   Jacobs L-5, 285 hp

NOTES: Not currently listed.

389   F17D   NC47571
Built 1940   Jacobs L-6, 330 hp

NOTES: Not currently listed.

390   F17D   Unknown
Built 1940   Jacobs L-6, 330 hp

NOTES: Not currently listed.

391   F17D   NC21921
Built Mar. 11, 1940   Jacobs L-6, 330 hp

NOTES: Not currently listed.

392   F17D   N2801
Built 1940   Jacobs L-6, 330 hp

NOTES: James Derdick, Seattle, Washington, 1966.

393   F17D   NC21922
Built Mar. 25, 1940   Jacobs L-6, 330 hp

NOTES: Photo taken in 1940. Airplane not currently listed.
(William T. Larkins)

394   F17D   NC20786, NC46492
Built Feb. 2, 1940   Jacobs L-6, 330 hp

NOTES: Not currently listed.

397   D17R   NX20795, N20795
Built 1940   Wright R-975, 420 hp

NOTES: Wright Aeronautical Corporation. Engine cowling and exhaust arrangement is not standard. Registered Frank Grunder, Akron, Ohio, 1955; no further listing.   *(Thomas S. Cuddy II)*

395   D17S   NC20753
Built 1940   P&W R-985, 450 hp

NOTES: Photo taken August 17, 1957 at San Francisco airport. Note "Chief Hogumgas" painted on fuselage. To Ronald Horn, Hermosa Beach, California on 1966 list.   *(Larry Smalley)*

398   D17S   NC20779, BuNo 09774, N1190V
Built Feb. 12, 1940   P&W R-985, 450 hp

NOTES: Sold to the Navy by Lamont DuPont Copeland, Greenville, Delaware. Maynard Meyers, Salt Lake City, Utah, 1966.   *(E. C. Haney)*

399   D17S   VT-ALY
Built 1940   P&W R-985, 450 hp

NOTES: To Tata Sons, New Delhi, India. No further information.

400   D17S   NC20755, BuNo 09765
Built 1940   P&W R-985, 450 hp

NOTES: Not currently listed.

396   D17S   NC129M
Built 1940   P&W R-985, 450 hp

NOTES: General Tire and Rubber Company, Akron, Ohio, first owner. Flown by Ray Brown who was killed in World War Two. The airplane was sold by General Tire to the Navy in 1941 for one dollar, but I am unable to match it with a BuNo. Not currently listed.   *(Emil Strasser)*

401   D17S   NC21917, BuNo 09772
Built Feb. 27, 1940   P&W R-985, 450 hp

NOTES: Not currently listed.   *(Beech Photo)*

402   D17S   NC21918
Built Mar. 6, 1940   P&W R-985, 450 hp

NOTES: Not currently listed.

403   D17S   CF-DTE
Built 1940   P&W R-985, 450 hp

NOTES: Registered in Canada to Department of Transport, March 2, 1940. Cargair Ltd., Ste. Emilie de L'Energie, 1962, and noted as current.
(Beech Photo)

404   SD17S   CF-DTF
Built 1940   P&W R-985, 450 hp

NOTES: Registered in Canada to Department of Transport, March 8, 1940. Crashed one mile east, southeast of Northfield, Minnesota. Pilot parachuted to safety.
(Peter M. Bowers)

405   D17R   NC21919, NC48973
Built 1940   Wright R-975, 420 hp

NOTES: Mouton and Clyde, San Francisco, California first owners. Owned by Jack Hoke, Boise, Idaho for several years, he sold it in January, 1963. Aviation Enterprises Corporation, Glendora, California, 1966.
(Beech Photo)

406   D17S   NC240Y, BuNo 09766
Built 1940   P&W R-985, 450 hp

NOTES: Sold to Navy by James Dyer, Nashville, Tennessee in April, 1942. Not currently listed.

407   D17S   NX21920, BuNo 09773, N66282
Built June 10, 1940   P&W R-985, 450 hp

NOTES: Sold to Navy by George Fuller, San Francisco, California in February, 1942. Creed Aerial Spraying, Ralls, Texas, 1966.

408   D17S   Unknown
Built 1940   P&W R-985, 450 hp

NOTES: No information.

409   D17S   N1030
Built 1940   P&W R-985, 450 hp

NOTES: Currently being rebuilt by Dr. G. L. Smith, Cheyenne, Wyoming.
(Frank Hartman)

410   F17D   Unknown
Built 1940   Jacobs L-6, 330 hp

NOTES: No information.

411   E17B   NC114
Built 1940 or 1941   Jacobs L-5, 285 hp

NOTES: Owned by CAA at one time. Not currently listed.

412   F17D   NC21932
Built Aug. 21, 1941   Jacobs L-6, 330 hp

NOTES: Not currently listed.

413   F17D   NC21935, N59700, N1422T
Built Jan. 13, 1942   Jacobs L-6, 330 hp

NOTES: Stanley Trilip, Stockton, California, 1955; Fred Sorenson, Mountain View, California, 1961; Jack Amphlett, Vacaville, California, 1964, 1966.
(Ralph I. Brown)

414   SF17D   NC21931, NC133E
Built Apr. 4, 1941   Jacobs L-6, 330 hp

NOTES: Original owner probably Wiggins Airways in New England. Queen Shoals Coal and Elk Mining Company, Clay, West Virginia, 1955, no further listing.
(Thomas S. Cuddy II)

415   D17S   NC133
Built 1941   P&W R-985, 450 hp

NOTES: Not currently listed.

416   D17S   Unknown
Built 1941   P&W R-985, 450 hp

NOTES: No information.

417   D17S   Unknown
Built 1941   P&W R-985, 450 hp

NOTES: No information.

418   D17S   NC21926
Built Nov. 13, 1940   P&W R-985, 450 hp

NOTES: Not currently listed.

419   D17S   NC21930
Built 1941   P&W R-985, 450 hp

NOTES: Photo taken February 1, 1948, Fort Worth, Texas. Listed to Josephine Jones, Farmingdale, New York with an airworthiness inspection date of 1951.   *E. C. Haney)*

Serial Number 420 probably a Model 18.

421   D17S   NC21933, BuNo 09768
Built Sept. 2, 1941   P&W R-985, 450 hp

NOTES: La Brea Aviation Company, Los Angeles, California. They sold airplane to Navy. Not currently listed.

Serial Number 422 probably a Model 18.

423   D17S   NC213
Built 1941   P&W R-985, 450 hp

NOTES: To Civil Aeronautics Authority. Not currently listed. *(Beech Photo)*

424   D17S(G17S)   NC21936, NC21934, N34R
Built Jan. 1, 1942   P&W R-985, 450 hp

NOTES: NC21936 assigned and quickly withdrawn, then NC21934 assigned. NC21936 was never actually painted on the airplane. Built as a stock D17S, this airplane was the factory demonstrator, and was modified to the G17S configuration late in World War Two. William F. Krause, Ann Arbor, Michigan, 1966.   *(Joe Juptner)*

This ends what I refer to as "the three-digit serials" of Beechcraft 17 production. Except for the 20 G17S airplanes built in 1946, this might be said to be the end of the civil Beechcraft 17 production. From here on, only model 17 serial numbers will be listed. Omitted numbers were assigned to other models such as the military AT-10 and UC-45. So far as I have been able to determine, model 17 serials jump from s/n 424 to s/n 1013. This gap may be explained by an Army order for 1771 Beechcraft AT-10's in 1941.

All "four-digit serials," or military models, were the civil D17S powered by the P&W R-985 of 450 hp. Fahey's "*U.S. Army Aircraft, 1908-1946*" lists various other civil models, and Beech says some other civil types were built during World War Two, and this may be so, but I am inclined to believe that all four-digit model 17 serial numbers were military versions of the D17S only, and no other model.

All Navy models were GB-1's or GB-2's. All Army D17S airplanes (except for the 3 YC-43 aircraft of 1939) were either the UC-43 or the UC-43B.

Rather than list every four-digit serial individually as the three-digit serials are listed, runs of Beech serial numbers are shown with corresponding military serial numbers. There is some confusion in matching these numbers, particularly with U.S. Army serials. After having worked with this list for some six years, I believe the manner in which they are presented here is the most accurate. After these serial number lists, photographs of airplanes with four-digit serials are presented in choronological order with only the civil model number, and civil registrations shown.

Beech S/N	Army Serials	Navy Bureau Numbers
1014 to 1035	—	01625 to 01646
3090 to 3107	—	12330 to 12347
3108 to 3113	42-38665 to 42-38670	12348 to 12353
3114 to 3134	42-38671 to 42-38691	—
4791 to 4865	—	32992 to 33066
4866 to 4940	43-10818 to 43-10892	—
6669	44-67700	23657
6670 to 6672	—	23658 to 23660
6673 to 6677	44-67701 to 44-67705	23661 to 23665
6678 to 6682	—	23666 to 23670
6683 to 6690	44-67706 to 44-67713	23671 to 23678
6691	44-67714	—
6692	44-67715	23680
6693	44-67716	—
6694 to 6700	44-67717 to 44-67723	23682 to 23688
6701 to 6711	44-67724 to 44-67734	—
6712 to 6742	—	23695 to 23725
6743 to 6768	44-67735 to 44-67760	—
6869 to 6872	44-67761 to 44-67764	—
6873	44-67765	23679
6874	44-67766	23681
6875 to 6880	44-67767 to 44-67772	23689 to 23694
6881 to 6905	44-67773 to 44-67799	—
6906 to 6910	44-67800 to 44-67804	23727 to 23730
6911 to 6936	—	23731 to 23756

You will note overlap on many Beech serial numbers which are shown with both Army and Navy numbers. This is because the Army purchased aircraft for the Navy, and both services purchased airplanes for lend-lease to various foreign countries. Considering some of the countries who received the airplanes on lend-lease, it is difficult for me to understand how they contributed much to the war effort.

Navy Lend-Lease Airplanes: In the batch 01624 to 01646 of Navy BuNos, 6 were sent to Brazil in December, 1941. BuNo 01645 went to the Army to be sent to China under the Army Defense Aid program.

In the batch of BuNos (Bureau Numbers) from 23657 to 23756, the following BuNos went to Brazil: 23661 to 23665, 23677, 23678, and 23680. The following went to England: 23658, 23671 to 23676, and 23682 to 23688. BuNo 23745 went to the Goodyear Tire and Rubber Company for an unexplained reason.

Navy BuNos 85391 to 85458 were to have been assigned to a production order of 68 GB-2 airplanes, but they were cancelled.

Navy Civil Impressments: The following BuNos were from civil owners, and are shown in the three-digit serial listing. They are given here for cross reference.

BuNo	Beech S/N	BuNo	Beech S/N
09765	400	09774	398
09766	406	09776	136
09768	421	09777	165
09769	Unknown	09778	168
09770	Unknown	09780	185
09772	401	09800	308
09773	407		

Navy Three-Digit Serial Purchases: These are listed on the three-digit serial list, and are given here for cross-reference.

BuNo	Beech S/N
1589 to 1595	298 to 304
1898 to 1900	385 to 387

Army Three-Digit Serial Purchases: These are given here for cross reference.

Army Serial	Beech S/N
39-139 to 39-141	295 to 297

Army Civil Impressments: It has not been possible to match Beech s/n with Army serials on impressed airplanes. However, for the record, the Army serials are listed here.

	Army Serial	Number
UC-43A (D17R)	42-38226 to 42-38231	6 airplanes
	42-38245	1 airplane
	42-38282	1 airplane
	42-38357 to 42-38358	2 airplanes
	42-47383	1 airplane
	42-52999	1 airplane
	42-68339	1 airplane
UC-43B (D17S)	42-38232 to 42-38236	5 airplanes
	42-38281	1 airplane
	42-38359	1 airplane
	42-46905	1 airplane
	42-47384	1 airplane
	42-53002	1 airplane
	42-56085	1 airplane
	42-61097	1 airplane
	42-68340	1 airplane
UC-43C (F17D)	42-22246	1 airplane
	42-36825	1 airplane
	42-38237 to 42-38241	5 airplanes
	42-38243 to 42-38244	2 airplanes
	42-38246 to 42-38248	3 airplanes
	42-38283 to 42-38284	2 airplanes
	42-38361 to 42-38363	3 airplanes
	42-46635	1 airplane
	42-46906 to 42-46908	3 airplanes
	42-46914	1 airplane
	42-46916	1 airplane
	42-47385 to 42-47388	4 airplanes
	42-47449 to 42-47450	2 airplanes
	42-53510	1 airplane
	42-68337	1 airplane
	42-88636	1 airplane
	42-97048 to 42-97050	3 airplanes
	42-97411	1 airplane
	42-107411	1 airplane
	42-107414	1 airplane
UC-43D (E17B)	42-43845	1 airplane
	42-46636	1 airplane
	42-46909 to 42-46910	2 airplanes
	42-46915	1 airplane
	42-47442 to 42-47448	7 airplanes
	42-49070	1 airplane
	42-53000 to 42-53001	2 airplanes
	42-53005	1 airplane
	42-53007 to 42-53008	2 airplanes

	42-53013	1 airplane
	42-53021	1 airplane
	42-53508 to 42-53509	2 airplanes
	42-53511	1 airplane
	42-53516 to 42-53517	2 airplanes
	42-56087	1 airplane
	42-68359 to 42-68360	2 airplanes
	42-94124	1 airplane
UC-43E (C17R)	42-47389	1 airplane
	42-78039	1 airplane
	42-97417	1 airplane
	42-97424	1 airplane
	42-97431	1 airplane
UC-43F (D17A)	42-49071	1 airplane
UC-43G (C17B)	42-53006	1 airplane
	42-68855	1 airplane
	42-88620	1 airplane
	42-88628 to 42-88629	2 airplanes
	42-88634	1 airplane
	42-97415	1 airplane
	42-97426	1 airplane
	42-97427	1 airplane
	42-97428	1 airplane
UC-43H (B17R)	42-68856	1 airplane
	42-94137	1 airplane
UC-43J (C17L)	42-94133	1 airplane
	42-97413	1 airplane
	42-97420	1 airplane
UC-43K (D17W)	42-107277	1 airplane

It is possible that some of the above airplanes (particularly the UC-43C and UC-43D) were 1941 and 1942 military production airplanes, but if this is so, it has not been possible to positively identify them on the four-digit serial list.

Army serial numbers 44-76029 to 44-76091 (63 airplanes) were possibly not assigned. This may have been the 63 airplane batch purchased at one time for the Navy by the Army.

British Military Beechcraft 17's: Some 105 military Beechcraft 17's (included in the four-digit Army and Navy airplanes) went to the British Empire on lend-lease. British serials were FL653 to FL670, FZ428 to FZ439, and FT461 to FT535. A very shaky matching with Beech serial numbers runs about as follows;

Beech S/N	British S/N
3117 to 3134	FL653 to FL670
4918 to 4925	FZ428 to FZ435
4932 to 4935	FZ436 to FZ439
6682 to 6686	FT461 to FT465
Unknown	FT466 to FT472
6699 to 6711	FT473 to FT485
Unknown	FT486 to FT515
6888 to 6903	FT516 to FT531
Unknown	FT532 to FT535

Four-Digit Serial Listing: The following list of four-digit serial number Beechcraft 17's is not complete. It is composed only of those airplanes for which I have a photo, or known civil registrations, or about which some interesting comment can be made. The format is the same as the three-digit serials with some abbreviations—only the Beech serial number, and civil registrations are shown. Military serials can be obtained from the lists just given. Date built is not shown as all of these airplanes were built in 1941, 1942, 1943, or 1944. The model is not shown as this can be obtained elsewhere in this book for military models, and civil model is assumed to be the D17S. Engine installed is not shown because it is the P&W R-985 of 450 hp, or some variant of that basic engine. The first number shown is the Beech serial number. All other numbers and/or letters shown are civil registrations.

1013   N74584, CF-GPO

NOTES: To Canada in 1951 from Grubb Oil Company, Lexington, North Carolina. Evidently still current in Canada, last registered to H. O. Thomas, Victoria, British Columbia.

1014   N9115H

NOTES: Overturned at Tucumcari, New Mexico February 15, 1962, it has been rebuilt. Registered to Billie Hodges, Vega, Texas, 1966. He owned it in 1962 when it was damaged at Tucumcari.   *(Leo J. Kohn)*

1015   N163, N163E

NOTES: One of many military models turned over to CAA after the war, later sold to a private owner. A Betsy Davis Cross owned it from 1953 to 1957, and cracked it up at Black Mountain, North Carolina. It was rebuilt, and eventually sold to J. H. Cunningham, Jr. of Cunningham Brick, Thomasville, North Carolina. On August 31, 1961, Cunningham and his wife, and Mr. and Mrs. W. R. Boothe were killed when the airplane crashed on takeoff from a small field near New Castle in Craig County, Virginia.   *(Leo J. Kohn)*

1016   N1213V

NOTES: Listed to Neigel Engineering Company, Glen Rock, New Jersey with airworthiness inspection date of 1956. Note unusual markings in photo, missing wheel fairings, removed engine accessory cowling.
(Richard C. Seeley)

1017   N1038M

NOTES: Shown on 1966 list to R. I. Bromschwig, Minneapolis, Minnesota with airworthiness inspection date of 1960. Letters to Mr. Bromschwig were returned.

1024   N67445

NOTES: Photo taken Oakland Airport, California on October 27, 1941. Listed in 1966 to Lavera Lovell, Las Vegas, Nevada with an airworthiness inspection date of 1954. *(Peter M. Bowers)*

1025   N2832D

NOTES: 1966 owner is Earl Moore, Shelton, Washington. Has current airworthiness inspection.

1019   N75554

NOTES: Not currently listed. Photo shows the airplane in standard Navy markings. *(Beech Photo)*

1029   N1254N

NOTES: Photo taken at same Fly-In as s/n 1020 above. This airplane is carried on FAA lists as s/n 01640 which, of course, is the Navy BuNo. Lloyd Cohoon, Lone Pine, California on 1966 list. *(William T. Larkins)*

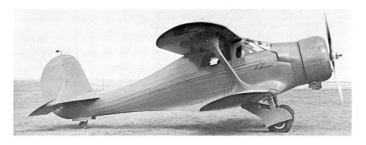

1674   NC20786

NOTES: Info taken from back of the above Beech photo shows the airplane is an F17D sold to H. Homeyer. Not currently listed. Not carried or shown on any list of military serial numbers. *(Beech Photo)*

1020   N79091

NOTES: Photo taken at Merced, California, May, 1962 Antique Airplane Association Fly-In. Airplane in background is s/n 6669. 1966 owner of s/n 1020 is Jack Raines, Inglewood, California. *(William T. Larkins)*

2685   N9376H

NOTES: Photographed at Love Field, Dallas. Texas on November 3, 1951. Not currently listed, and not on any military serial lists. A D17S model. *(Mitch Mayborn)*

2718   PP-DDH

NOTES: No information.

3081   PT-ADT

NOTES: None. Note Staggerwing and DC-3 in background.   (Peter Berry)

3086   N75728

NOTES: Formerly owned by John Evans, listed in 1966 to Richard Gillespie, Riverside, California with 1963 airworthiness date.
(John J. Evans)

3088   N75544

NOTES: Listed to C. F. Henderson, Hackensack, New Jersey on 1966 list. Current airworthiness inspection.   (Tom Cuddy)

3090   No civil registration known

NOTES: Photographed at Chicago-Midway Airport, Chicago, Illinois in 1946. Not currently listed.   (Robert L. Taylor)

3091   N9885H

NOTES: 1966 list shows Duke Holdcroft, Yakima, Washington with a current airworthiness inspection.   (Leo J. Kohn)

3093   N67734

NOTES: Currently owned by Robert C. Ellis, Cartagena, Columbia. He purchased it in 1963 from Paul Rennard, Moosic, Pennsylvania.
(Robert T. O'Dell)

3094   No civil registration known

NOTES: Photo was taken in 1946. Not currently listed.(William T. Larkins)

3096   No civil registration known

NOTES: Photo taken 1946. Not currently listed.   (William T. Larkins)

216

3097 N65594

NOTES: M. B. Waddle, Franklin Park, Illinois, 1966 with a current air-worthiness inspection.

3098 N9595H, CF-FEQ

NOTES: Entered Canada in 1962. Owned by Ben Keillor of Hamilton, Ontario, it is now in Goderich, Ontario, present owner unknown.
(Leo J. Kohn)

3100 N69267, N69217

NOTES: Owned right after World War Two by Henry Line in Carlisle, Pennsylvania, it went through several hands to end up with Jack B. Sellers, Drumright, Oklahoma in 1961. Sold later to J. M. Fly, Victoria, Texas, and currently registered to Mr. Fly. *(Jack B. Sellers)*

3101 No civil registration known

NOTES: None. *(Beech Photo)*

3102 N397

NOTES: None. See s/n 3108.

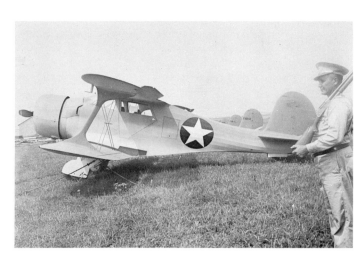

3103 No civil registration

NOTES: Photo taken prior to delivery at Beech factory. No current listing.
(Beech Photo)

3105 No civil registration known

NOTES: None. *(Roger Besecker)*

3108 N397, N1532M

NOTES: S/n 3102 was originally registered as N397, and this registration was later given to s/n 3108, which later became N1532M. Listed in 1966 to Goetz Oil Company, Sherman, Texas with airworthiness inspection date of 1959. *(E. C. Haney)*

3109 N52950

NOTES: On 1966 list to Willis Leek, Salem, Oregon with an airworthiness inspection date of 1957.

3110   N67197

NOTES: Owned by Strafford Wentworth from 1950 to 1956. It was ground looped at Guaymas, Mexico, January of 1956, hauled to Nogales, Arizona, and sold to the mechanic there. Listed in 1961 to Strafford Wentworth, Palermo, California, and no further listing. Mr. Wentworth sold it to the mechanic at Nogales in 1956 who evidently never changed the registration. Airplane probably not in existence now.
(Peter M. Bowers)

3114   N1015M

NOTES: Joe Marrs, Hollywood, Florida on 1955 list. No further listing.

3118   FL654   *No civil registration known.*

NOTES: Shipped to Suez, March, 1943. Note Spitfire in background behind nose. FL654 is British military marking just barely visible on aft fuselage side.
(Peter Berry)

3119   OO-TAX, LX-TAX F-BEEK

NOTES: No current information.

3121   F-BDRX

NOTES: No current information.

NOTE: Serial Numbers 3123 through 3134 were lost on the S.S. Agurmonte which was sunk on June 10, 1943.

3179   N236E

NOTES: Richard Leaver, Schererville, Indiana, 1966 with a current airworthiness inspection.
(Thomas A. Cooney)

3181   N75729

NOTES: Roy Rock, Roseville, Michigan, 1955. No further listing.

3184   N322H

NOTES: Formerly owned by Dr. Ben Meckel, Burwell, Nebraska, registered on 1966 list to Smitty's Aircraft Service in Burwell.
(Michael Haynes)

3186   CF-HSK

NOTES: Owned by A. M. Hubbard, Seattle, Washington in early 1950's. Registered in Canada to Pacific Western Airlines, Vancouver, British Columbia on June 30, 1954. Sold to the Tri-Tyro Syndicate on July 28, 1955. Damaged on hitting dock while taxiing at Whitehorse on the Yukon River (the airplane was on floats). Certificate lapsed on September 27, 1960, no current information.

4793   F-BEXA

NOTES: No current information.

4794   N1503M

NOTES: Ernest Webb, Charlotte, N. C. on 1964 list. Dismantled.

4798   N61208

NOTES: Steven Sharkey, Mishawka, Indiana, 1961. No further listing.

4801   N2625

NOTES: George Brinckerhoff, College Park, Maryland, 1955. No further listing.

4803   N9405H

NOTES: Robert Lee, Minneapolis, Minnesota, 1966 with a current airworthiness inspection. Photo taken at Love Field, Dallas, Texas around 1952.   *(Mitch Mayborn)*

4807   N9724H

NOTES: Registered to Eby Campbell, Dayton, Ohio, 1966. Has current airworthiness inspection. Letters to owners failed to produce a photo, so my friend Don Roetman chased the airplane down, finally photographed it in crowded hangar with above results.   *(Don E. Roetman)*

4804   N66300

NOTES: Note unusual paint trim. Listed to Precision Realty Company, Paterson, New Jersey on 1966 list with an airworthiness inspection date of 1965.   *(Warren D. Shipp)*

4808   N9936H

NOTES: Grafton Insurance Agency, Inc., Grafton, Wisconsin, 1966 with a 1961 airworthiness inspection date.   *(Leo J. Kohn)*

4806   N75614

NOTES: Stephen D. Kost, Roswell, New Mexico, 1966 with a current airworthiness inspection. Photo taken at NAS Alameda, California on March 6, 1946.   *(William T. Larkins)*

4810   N480

NOTES: John Robert Gravance, Palmdale, California, 1966 with a current airworthiness date. Photo taken June 22, 1953.   *(Ken A. McLean)*

4811   N65596

NOTES: Jerald Baker, Angleton, Texas, 1966 with current airworthiness inspection. Photo taken Wichita Falls, Texas on June 14, 1962.
(E. C. Haney)

4812   F-BEXK

NOTES: No current information.

4813   N1020M, CF-EKA

NOTES: Sold into Canada in 1952 from Fort Lauderdale, Florida. Passed through several hands ending up owned by Ron Uloth who recently completed overhaul on the airplane. Photo was taken early this year (1966). Note unusual placement of bird trim on engine cowling rather than on forward side of fuselage. Ron Uloth lives in St. Laurent, Quebec.
(Ron Uloth)

4815   N52941, N787MD, N113Q

NOTES: W. E. Freeman, Stone Mountain, Georgia, 1966; the airplane is dismantled. Parts of it are being used to build up G17S, s/n B-5, also registered to W. E. Freeman.

4816   N67783

NOTES: Dean Curtis, Eugene, Oregon, 1966 list with an airworthiness inspection date of 1953.

4817   N67714

NOTES: Photo taken late in World War Two. Shown on 1966 list to John Besson, Paso Robles, California with a current airworthiness inspection.
(E. C. Haney)

4818   N63476

NOTES: Chet Smith Trucking Company, Daly City, California, 1966 with a current airworthiness inspection.   (Ralph Nortell)

4819   Civil registration unknown.

NOTES: Originally owned by Joe Dyer of Winston Salem, North Carolina. It crashed at Avon Park, Florida in 1949 while being flown by some of Mr. Dyer's friends. Alan G. Phillips purchased the remains from Mr. Dyer and sold it for parts. All that remains today is the nameplate, which Mr. Phillips still has.

4821   N161K

NOTES: C. C. Fisher, Huntington, Indiana, 1966 with an airworthiness inspection date of 1957. Crashed in West Virginia around 1958, now in storage pending repairs.

4822   N67430

NOTES: Sylvan Vick, Stockton, California, 1966 with a 1956 airworthiness inspection date.   (Joe Christy)

4823   N9113H

NOTES: Donald R. Quinn, Wichita, Kansas with a 1964 airworthiness inspection date. Quinn is (or was in 1963) a Captain on active duty with the USAF.   (Leo J. Kohn)

4824   NC65044

NOTES: The end of a Gallant Lady—the junk heap at Vest Aircraft, Denver Sky Ranch, Denver, Colorado, June 22, 1955. Quo Vadis?
(Mitch Mayborn)

4825   N52996

NOTES: William Trilling, Farmingdale, New York, 1955. No further listing.

4827   N17643

NOTES: Had not flown in five years when Ed Eisler rebuilt it in 1958. He has owned it since, and lives in Youngwood, Pennsylvania now. Photo was taken when Ed was at Fort Rucker, Alabama. Note unusual, but attractive, paint trim.   *(Edward I. Eiseler)*

4829   N1255N

NOTES: Pictured above on the Three See Ranch airstrip just outside her hangar, the airplane is owned by veteran Western Air Lines Captain Jack Crall who keeps the ship on his Elizabeth, Colorado ranch for personal transportation. He also uses it for ranch work as it is a little faster for checking pastures than a horse would be. Has a current airworthiness inspection.   *(Jack K. Crail)*

4830   *No civil registration known.*

NOTES: No information.   *(Leo J. Kohn)*

4831   N839

NOTES: Norman Wheeler, Fresno, California, 1966 with a 1952 airworthiness inspection date.

4833   N52931

NOTES: Vest Aircraft and Finance Company, Denver, Colorado, 1966 with a 1958 date of airworthiness inspection.

4835   N230

NOTES: After Navy service in World War Two, the airplane went to the CAA, eventually to Mr. B. B. Duncan, a retired Navy Commander who bases it at Shannon Airport, Fredricksburg, Virginia. Mr. Duncan works for the FAA in Washington, flies the airplane for pleasure.
(B. B. Duncan)

4836   N5734N

NOTES: Leslie George, Rock Springs, Wyoming, 1966 with a current airworthiness inspection.

4837   N52832

NOTES: Edward Ferguson, Tacoma, Washington, 1966 with a 1963 airworthiness inspection date.   (Leo J. Kohn)

4838   XB-LIF

NOTES: Owned by Ing. Luis Struck, Mexico City, 1963, and dismantled in his hangar. Rebuilt and sold to a Dr. Pelaez in Veracruz, it later crashed somewhere near Coatzacoalcos, and was completely destroyed.

4839   N9873H

NOTES: Note broad stripes used on the bird paint trim. C. G. Purinton, Phoenix, Arizona, 1964 with a 1963 airworthiness inspection date. No later listing.   (Mitch Mayborn)

4840   N9597H

NOTES: Compare bird paint trim in this photo to s/n 4839. Registered on 1966 list to Steven Zuzow, Detroit, Michigan with a current airworthiness inspection.   (Robert T. O'Dell)

4841   N67717

NOTES: D. A. Nienstedt, Pasadena, California, 1966 with a 1957 airworthiness inspection date.

4846   N9370H

NOTES: Photo taken Chino, California on October 22, 1963. Denzel Marshall, Pasadena, California, 1966 with a 1962 airworthiness inspection date.   (Tom Cuddy)

4847   N67747

NOTES: Photo taken Fairbanks International Airport, Fairbanks, Alaska, June 30, 1963. Note wheel fairing doors removed, engine accessory cowling partially removed. Registered to Arvid Neslund, Fairbanks, Alaska, 1966. Airworthiness date shown as 1957.   (Bernard Robar)

4848   N67736

NOTES: On 1966 list to R. E. Dickenson, Santa Paula, California with current airworthiness inspection.   (Russell R. Hiatt)

4850   N49788

NOTES: William Fauth, Columbus, Ohio on 1966 list with date of 1961 for last airworthiness inspection.

4858   N1256N

NOTES: Kenmore Air Harbor, Inc., Kenmore, Washington, 1955. No further listing.   (Peter M. Bowers)

4865   N1609

NOTES: Photo taken August 21, 1952. Owned for many years by Fred Johnson, Atlanta, Georgia, it is still actively being flown by him.
(Ken McLean)

4859   N61278

NOTES: Richard Denaple Jr., Fullerton, California, 1966 with a 1964 airworthiness inspection date.   (Leo J. Kohn)

4867   N60149

NOTES: Photo taken February 9, 1952. Registered to Peter Bowen, Denver, Colorado on 1966 list with 1964 airworthiness inspection date.
(Leo J. Kohn)

4860   No civil registration known.

NOTES: Evidently photographed just after production roll-out, airplane serial number is still marked on windows and engine cowling. No current listing.   (Beech Photo)

4870   N1027M, N7778B

NOTES: R. T. Stingley, Anchorage, Alaska, 1966 with a 1963 airworthiness inspection date.   (Leo J. Kohn)

4871   *No civil registration.*

NOTES: Photo taken at Beech factory after an evident mishap. No current listing.   *(Beech Photo)*

4875   N5447N

NOTES: Photo taken at Fort Worth, Texas on April 6, 1949. Owned by Aero Service Corporation in Philadelphia, Pennsylvania for several years, it is now (1966) listed to Paul Rennard, Moosic, Pennsylvania with a current airworthiness inspection.   *(E. C. Haney)*

4876   N59719

NOTES: Lou Foote, Lancaster, Texas, 1955. No further listing.

4872   N60148

NOTES: Photo taken at the 1964 EAA Fly-In at Rockford, Illinois. Registered to Stagger Wing, Inc., Scottsbluff, Nebraska, 1966 with a current airworthiness inspection.   *(Tom Cooney)*

4877   N61862

NOTES: Note unusual paint trim. Owned by famed Staggerwing pilot, Strafford Wentworth, Palermo, California from 1956 through 1962, the airplane is shown on the 1966 list to Geoda Manufacturing Company, Salinas, California with a 1961 airworthiness inspection date.
                                                          (Leo J. Kohn)

4874   N51444, CF-GKY

NOTES: Sold into Canada in 1951 to OK Construction and Supply Company in Edmonton, Alberta. They flew it for several years, sold it in 1958 to E. G. Bowhay, and J. Burroughs in Edmonton. In 1959 it went to Northern Air Service Company at Fort Nelson, British Columbia, then to Trans Aircraft Company in Calgary, Alberta in 1961, and from them to C. W. Simmons, Prince George, British Columbia in 1962. No later information.   *(Osborne R. Love)*

4878   N333E

NOTES: Selmer Thomas, Port Lauaca, Texas, 1966 with a 1957 airworthiness inspection date.   *(Peter Berry)*

4879   PP-FER

NOTES: No information.

4880   N1502, N15021

NOTES: Portions of airplane in foreground are of an ex-Navy Grumman TBF being used in spray operations. It was really the subject of the photo—photographer Cuddy just happened to get s/n 4880 in the photo. Airplane not currently listed.   (Thomas S. Cuddy II)

4886   N51745

NOTES: Donald Payne, San Francisco, California, 1966 with a current airworthiness inspection.   (Frank Hartman)

4882   N52686

NOTES: Photo taken at AAA Fly-In, Ottumwa, Iowa in 1963. Bingham Motors, Inc., Redding, California, 1966 with current inspection.
                                                          (James H. Harvey)

4888   N264, N264E

NOTES: Photo taken August, 1946 when CAA owned the airplane. Noel Goursolle, Jr., Sacramento, California, 1966 with 1963 airworthiness inspection date.   (William T. Larkins)

4883   NC368

NOTES: Note military star on fuselage side partially painted over. Military data stencilled on fuselage side under pilot's window had not yet been painted out. No current listing.   (Leo J. Kohn)

4885   ZS-CLM, N1591V

NOTES: No information on the ZS-CLM registration. Aero Service Corporation, Philadelphia, Pennsylvania, 1955. No further listing.

4890   N51746

NOTES: A working Staggerwing, this one is flown by its owner, L. G. McCarley, Blackfoot, Idaho on charter flights into the Idaho Primitive Area. He has owned the airplane for many years, and currently is flying it. Photo shows the airplane over the Idaho Primitive Area.
                                                          (L. G. McCarley)

4891   N46810

NOTES: Owned by M. E. Park, La Mesa, California for several years, it has a 1964 airworthiness inspection date. Upon close examination, one can see that the engine cowling has been extended back against the accessory cowling. A cowl flap similar to the G17S model cowl flap was installed.   (M. E. Park)

4893   N46431

NOTES: Photo taken at Merced, California AAA Fly-In on May 19th and 20th, 1962. On 1966 list to Carl Ott, Napa, California with a 1961 airworthiness inspection date.   (William T. Larkins)

4896   N69H

NOTES: Legal Eagle, Inc., Hialeah, Florida, 1966 with a 1964 airworthiness inspection date.   (Leo J. Kohn)

226

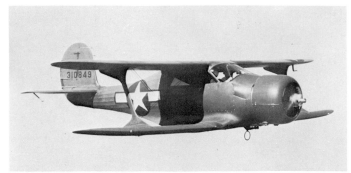

4897   No civil registration known.

NOTES: No current information.   (Russell Hiatt)

4898   N51969

NOTES: Examine this photograph carefully. The fuselage is metal covered! Edward Harris, Eglin AFB, Florida on 1966 list with current airworthiness inspection.   (Charles Lucas)

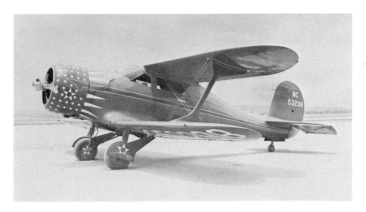

4900   NC53298

NOTES: Photo taken Montebello, California on May 21, 1946. Second Staggerwing owned by Ross Hadley, racing pilot. Note the unusual markings, and compare to s/n 199, his first airplane. Dr. John Moore, Kirkwood, Missouri on 1966 list with current airworthiness inspection.
(William T. Larkins)

4902   N51120

NOTES: Texas Aviation Corporation, Tyler, Texas, 1961. No further listing.

4903   N663

NOTES: Registered to CHH and W, Lubbock, Texas, it is owned by four people (Bill Cantrell is one of them), and is currently being rebuilt. Photo shows airplane as of April 8, 1966.   (Bill W. Cantrell)

4906   N54657, N477FT

NOTES: Frank Thera, St. Paul, Minnesota, 1966 with a current airworthiness inspection. Photo above was taken several years ago.

(Leo J. Kohn)

4907   No civil registration known.

NOTES: No current information.   (William T. Larkins)

4914   N51121

NOTES: Henry Line, Carlisle, Pennsylvania, 1966 with a current airworthiness inspection. He has owned the airplane for several years.

(Henry Line)

4915   N80024

NOTES: Open access door on engine accessory cowling in photo is oil service door. Murphy Foster, Franklin, Louisiana, 1966 with a current airworthiness inspection.   (Leo J. Kohn)

4916   N239E

NOTES: Sky Service Corporation, Richmond, Virginia, 1966 with a 1948 airworthiness inspection date. Letters to the owner were returned. I believe the aircraft no longer exists.

4917   N79484

NOTES: Photographed at Van Nuys, California in February, 1963. Don Neely, Burbank, California, 1966 with a current airworthiness inspection.   (Richard S. Allen)

4918   No civil registrations known.

NOTES: FZ428. To Suez, October, 1943.

4919   No civil registration known.

NOTES: FZ429. Crashed before delivery.

4920   OO-VIT, SE-BRY, HB-UIH

NOTES: Lars Erik Lundin supplied the information that this airplane was brought to Sweden in 1951, and made a trip to the Sudan in that same year. Upon its return it was given a complete overhaul (rebuilt, evidently), and for the next seven years it was flown sporadically by a former Luftwaffe officer, Herr Schulze. In April, 1958 the airplane was sold to Mr. Bjorn Hjelme Lundberg of Huskvarna, Sweden. In April, 1960 the airplane was sold to Monsieur Louis Bill, La Chaux de Fonds, Switzerland, and registered as HB-UIH.   (Lars Erik Lundin)

4921   G-AJLD, N6402N

NOTES: Registered in England by D. W. Conner on April 2, 1947. Left England October 6, 1948. Photo above was probably taken in France, date unknown. No current information.   (Peter Berry)

4922   G-AJJJ, VH-MJE

NOTES: First registered in England April 11, 1947. In December, 1952 it went to Australia where it has remained. Registered up through at least 1964, and probably still current. Owned by J. W. Morton, Bundoran, Nonda, Queensland through 1961, and probably still owned by him.   (John Hopton)

4923   F-BCJY

NOTES: No current information.   (Peter Berry)

4925   G-AJJE, VP-YIT

NOTES: First registered in England May 8, 1947. Went to Southern Rhodesia in August, 1951. No further information.

4935   G-AJLA, HB-KID, F-DADL

NOTES: Registered in England by Daphne Miller on March 27, 1947. Left English register on December 31, 1948. No further information.

4937   VR-HEE, F-OABR

NOTES: No current information.

4940   N265E

NOTES: Fred Naegele, Helena, Montana, 1966 with a current airworthiness inspection.   (Leo J. Kohn)

6669   N9451H

NOTES: Photo taken at Compton, California on October 21, 1963. Cyril Mehling, Kingspark, New York, 1966 with current airworthiness inspection.   (Thomas S. Cuddy II)

6670   N9470H

NOTES: Dr. Roy G. Larson, Thousand Oaks, California, 1966 with a 1964 airworthiness inspection date. Bird insignia on fuselage side of this airplane is as near standard factory bird markings as one is likely to find.
(Roy G. Larson)

6671   N420E

NOTES: Photographed at Fort Worth, Texas on October 17, 1963. Registered to E. Fike, Jr., McAllen, Texas, 1966, and shown as being dismantled.
(E. C. Haney)

6672   N162, N3775C

NOTES: Lady in the photo is Mrs. Sidney Smith, wife of Doctor Sidney Smith who purchased the airplane as a gift for her in 1961. It is still registered to her in Bradenton, Florida with a 1961 airworthiness inspection date. An earlier owner was Truman Miller who flew the airplane for twelve years, and visited Mexico and Canada frequently in the airplane.
(Sidney Smith)

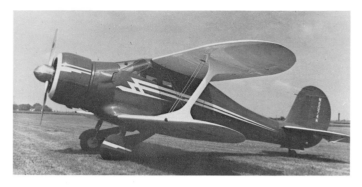

6680   N5074N

NOTES: R. E. McPhaul, San Rafael, California, 1966 with a current airworthiness inspection.
(Richard C. Seeley)

6681   F-BEXJ

NOTES: First registered in France on May 30, 1950. No current information.

6682   N4688N

NOTES: Carl King, Atlanta, Georgia, 1966 with an airworthiness inspection date of 1954. Being rebuilt, and at this writing almost ready to fly.

6684   N1112M

NOTES: F. A. Conner, Miami Springs, Florida, 1966. Photo illustrates the worse possible end for an airplane—being allowed to sit out in the weather and deteriorate. Photo was taken at San Juan International Airport, and the airplane—or what is left of it—is still sitting there.
(Jaime Serra)

6685   N40E

NOTES: Photo taken at Merced Municipal Airport, California on May 19, 1962. Now registered to Alan Gerard, Seattle, Washington with a current airworthiness inspection. Alan flies the airplane for pleasure.
(Larry Smalley)

6686   G-AHXJ

NOTES: First registered in England on February 17, 1947. Damaged beyond repair at Ypenberg on June 24, 1947 in ground collision with a Tiger Moth.
(William T. Larkins)

6691   NC156, N3776C

NOTES: Formerly owned by Truman Miller, on 1966 list to William Weasner, Pennington, New Jersey with a 1964 airworthiness inspection date. The airplane is registered by its Navy BuNo, 23679, and there is some doubt as to its exact Beech s/n. All authorities are agreed, however, that it is either s/n 6691 or s/n 6873. The difficulty is in matching Beech s/n with Navy BuNo, and 23679 just happens to be one of the few controversial Navy Bureau Numbers. In any event, the photo and data are given here with s/n 6691 although the airplane might easily be s/n 6873.
(Merle Olmsted)

6687   N9455H

NOTES: Allen Gunn, St. Louis, Missouri, 1966 with a 1957 airworthiness inspection date.
(Keith A. Abbott)

_98   N33, N33H

NOTES: Photo taken at Long Beach Municipal, California on August 11, 1957. Richard Gerry, San Francisco, California, 1966 with a 1963 inspection date.
(Larry Smalley)

6688   N9466H

NOTES: James Almand, Jr., Grand Prairie, Texas, 1966 with a 1964 airworthiness inspection date.
(Leo J. Kohn)

6689   No civil registration known.

NOTES: None.

6699   LN-HAK, G-ALNN, F-OACT, F-BATL

NOTES: First registered in Norway, then transferred to England in April, 1949. Shortly thereafter, it went to France as F-OACT. Was seen at Toussus-le-Noble in 1951 as F-BATL. Last note indicates it was at Nice in December, 1961. No further information.
(Peter Berry)

6700   N9459H

NOTES: Richard Musser, Ekalaka, Montana, 1966 with a current airworthiness inspection.   (Paul L. Parker)

6704   N1183V

NOTES: R. S. Gimblin, Colusa, California, 1966 with a 1957 airworthiness inspection date.   (Ralph Nortell)

6705   N9454H

NOTES: Raydoe Wood, Fort Lauderdale, Florida, 1966 with an inspection date of 1957.

6701   N1193V

NOTES: Formerly owned by Ed Smith it is on the 1966 list to Paul Thiessen, Houston, Texas with a 1964 airworthiness inspection date.   (Ed Smith)

6706   N1181V

NOTES: Photo taken in 1954. Listed in 1955 to L. R. Edminster, Portland, Oregon (no further listing). See s/n 6765.   (William T. Larkins)

6703   N1196V

NOTES: Note unusual paint trim. William Reefe, Cleveland, Ohio, 1966 with a 1964 inspection date.   (George Gosney)

6712   N75620

NOTES: Photo taken at Love Field, Dallas, Texas June 23, 1951. Not currently listed.   (Mitch Mayborn)

6714   N75512

NOTES: On 1955 list to Leo Lamberson, South Bend, Indiana. No further listing. Shown on the 1955 list with Navy BuNo 23697 as s/n rather than 6714.   (Leo J. Kohn)

6715   N68916

NOTES: On 1955 list to M. R. Clarke, San Lorenzo, California. Robert C. Ellis reports the airplane is rotting away at Merida, in western Venezuela.   (Leo J. Kohn)

6717   N67550

NOTES: John Dickenson, Santa Paula, California, 1966 with current inspection.

6718   N66426

NOTES: Shown on 1966 list to the late Carl Hughes of San Antonio, Texas with an inspection date of 1955. Current status of the airplane is unknown.

6720   N63477

NOTES: Jack Robins, Salt Lake City, Utah, 1966 with a 1955 airworthiness inspection date.

6723   N68113, N192H

NOTES: Owned by Charles F. Hanna of Houma, Louisiana for several years. A long-time friend of the author, Mr. Hanna traded a Waco for this Beechcraft. Current airworthiness inspection.   (Charles F. Hanna)

6724   N67677

NOTES: Mike Des Marais, Phoenix, Arizona, 1966 with a current inspection date.   (Leo J. Kohn)

6725   No civil registration.

NOTES: Photo taken at the factory before delivery. No current listing.   (Beech Photo)

6726   N9290H

NOTES: Pennsylvania Aerial Surveys, Inc., New Cumberland, Pennsylvania, 1966 with a current inspection date.

6727   N4574N

NOTES: Pictured above is the late Jim Phillips and his son, Martin. Photo was taken in 1965; Jim Phillips was fatally injured in a non-flying accident in October, 1965. His widow still owns the airplane, and is a lifetime member of the National Staggerwing Club, to which Jim belonged.   (James L. Phillips)

6728   N1341V

NOTES: Photo taken in St. Louis, Missouri on June 22, 1963. George Tregre, Fort Worth, Texas, 1966 with 1964 airworthiness inspection date.
(Ralph I. Brown)

6732   N68104

NOTES: Pacific Air Industries, Long Beach, California, 1955. No further listing.
(Leo J. Kohn)

6729   N63549

NOTES: Noel Goursolle, Sacramento, California, 1966 with a 1964 inspection date.
(Bude Donato)

6733   N67716

NOTES: Photo taken at Oxnard, California, 1958. Dr. Joseph Higgins, Oxnard, California, 1966 with current inspection date.
(Ken McLean)

6731   N838

NOTES: David R. Cummock, Jacksonville, Arkansas, 1966 with 1964 inspection date. He has sold the airplane since the list was made up. Present owner unknown.
(Rhodes F. Arnold)

6734   N1120V

NOTES: Mrs. B. C. Ferguson, Wayside, Mississippi, 1966 with an airworthiness inspection date of 1960.
(Leo J. Kohn)

6735　　N67487, XB-YOE

NOTES: Note bird insignia on both left wingtips. Also note unusual bird trim insignia on fuselage. James Baird, Seattle, Washington, 1955. No information on Mexican registration.　　(Bude Donato)

6741　　N65590

NOTES: Curtis Sky Ranch, Bryan, Texas, 1966 with 1961 date of airworthiness inspection.　　(Leo J. Kohn)

6745　　N9456H
NOTES: No information.

6746　　N1185V

NOTES: H. L. Mears, Santa Paula, California, 1966 list with a current airworthiness inspection.

6747　　N1175V

NOTES: Hagan Glass Drilling Company, Austin, Texas, 1955. No further listing.

6736　　No civil registration known.

NOTES: No information.　　(Robert T. O'Dell)

6737　　N4512N

NOTES: U.S. Oil of Louisiana, Inc., Houston, Texas, 1966 with a current airworthiness inspection.

6748　　N1184V, XB-JUI, N1184V

NOTES: Harry Golding, Long Beach, California sold the airplane into Mexico in 1948. The government of North Lower California owned the airplane initially, then sold it to C. Ruiz Gonzalez of Tijuana. On August 13, 1953 the airplane was sold back into the United States, and on the 1966 list it is shown to Morton Clark, Torrance, California with a current inspection.　　(William T. Larkins)

6738　　XB-LEQ, N4926V

NOTES: Photo taken in Mexico City, 1954. Owned by Manuel Cubillas, Hermosillo, Sonora, Mexico. Sold back to the U.S. prior to 1955, and shown on 1966 list to Vern Hongola, Manhattan Beach, California with a 1963 inspection date.　　(Ing. Jose Villela, Jr.)

6749　　N1195V

NOTES: Formerly owned by Dr. Zinschlag, it is now (1966) registered to Robert Jones, Reynoldsburg, Ohio with a 1957 airworthiness inspection date.　　(Edward N. Zinschlag)

6750   NC22, N5099N, N722MD

NOTES: Photo taken August, 1963 at Smithfield, Rhode Island. Currently (1966) owned by Dr. Ashby Woods, Bainbridge, Georgia. Suffix letter M in N722MD is part of registration, suffix letter D is not, but FAA aircraft registration branch allows two suffix letters to be used on aircraft.
(Thomas S. Cuddy II)

6753   N1182V

NOTES: Photo taken Love Field, Dallas, Texas March 3, 1952. Registered to Balsam and DeFrance, Miles City, Montana on 1955 list, no further listing. Suspected to be at Clover Field, Santa Monica, California in dismantled condition.
(Mitch Mayborn)

6751   N79996, N787MD

NOTES: Formerly owned by National Staggerwing Club president, William C. Yarbrough, it is now (1966) owned by Dr. William Compton, Lithonia, Georgia with a 1961 airworthiness inspection date.
(Photo by Author)

6758   LN-HAI

NOTES: Owned by Kare Sekkelsten, Grefsten, Norway. Crashed on April 21, 1949 after takeoff from Fornebu airport. Engine quit, went down in fifteen fathoms of water.
(Peter Berry)

6752   N1335V

NOTES: Milky Way Hereford Ranch, Phoenix, Arizona on 1955 list. No further listing. At that time, they also owned s/n 4829, N1255N. Photo taken Oakland Airport in February, 1958, but airplane does not appear on 1961 list.
(Larry Smalley)

6759   N50E

NOTES: William Deacon III, Kaycee, Wyoming, 1955. No further listing.
(Merle Olmsted)

6760   N9461H, N28A

NOTES: Purchased in 1950 by Pennsylvania Aerial Surveys, Miami, Florida, it was used by them in aerial photo work as high as 35,000 feet. Recently sold, it is shown on the 1966 list to Gordon Warren, Gunnison, Colorado with a current airworthiness inspection.   *(Faye Works)*

6762   N58, N58E

NOTES: Neal Foster, Nome, Alaska, 1955, no further listing.

6763   LN-HAH, VH-MLC, VH-BBL

NOTES: Photo taken Moorabbin, Victoria, Australia, November, 1961. Note unusual engine cowling and exhaust. At some point in the airplane's history the P&W R-985 was removed and a Wright R-975-E3 was installed, hence the odd cowling and exhaust stack. Originally owned by Vingtor Luftveier, Oslo, Norway. Sold into England in 1951, then to Australia. The airplane is shown on the Australian register with s/n 67755 which is a contraction of its U.S. Army s/n 44-67755. Sometime around 1962 the registration was changed to -BBL from -MLC. The airplane is still currently registered.   *(John Hopton)*

6764   N9450H

NOTES: Springfield Feeder Lines, Inc., Springfield, Massachusetts, 1966 with a 1953 inspection date.   *(Roger Besecker)*

6765   NC16, N16M

NOTES: Can't determine if the blob on the vertical fin is actually on the film, or on the airplane. If it's on the airplane, somebody must have thrown a can of paint at the vertical fin—and hit it! L. R. Edminster, Portland, Oregon, 1966 with a 1964 date of inspection.   *(Leo J. Kohn)*

6766   N5653N

NOTES: Woltz Aerial Surveys, Des Moines, Iowa, 1964 with a 1955 inspection date. No further listing. A letter from Woltz indicates they sold the airplane around 1955 or 1956. Evidently the new owner has never processed the registration papers.

6767   N5400N

NOTES: Don Hubby, Boone, Iowa, 1966 with a 1964 airworthiness inspection date.   *(Leo J. Kohn)*

6768   CR-LBF, ZS-BBZ

NOTES: CR-LBF is a registration in the Portuguese Colonies. Transferred to Union of South Africa, date unknown. No current information.   *(William N. Fleming)*

6869   N18, N18V

NOTES: Laurence Johnson, Hailey, Idaho, 1966 with current airworthiness inspection. Photo shows airplane when it was owned by CAA.
(Leo J. Kohn)

6874   N4612N

NOTES: Charles Harley, Davenport, Iowa, 1966 with a 1964 inspection date.
(Leo J. Kohn)

6870   N9458H

NOTES: Blanche Bowles, East Brentwood, Long Island, N.Y., 1966. Airworthiness inspection date shown as 1960.
(George Gosney)

6875   N39392

NOTES: Harold Chittim, Kalispell, Montana, 1966 with a 1955 date of inspection.
(Leo J. Kohn)

6871   N248E

NOTES: Owned by Clarence L. Baker, and Richard Marvin, Trona, California, 1966 with a current inspection date.
(Clarence L. Baker)

6873   See s/n 6691.

6876   N67555

NOTES: Darrell Pearson, Los Angeles, California, 1966 with a current airworthiness inspection.
(Peter M. Bowers)

6878   N67494

NOTES: Calair Dusters, Madera, California, 1955. No further listing.
(Peter Berry)

6879   N9169H

NOTES: Don Tillett, Elkhorn, Wisconsin, 1966 with a current airworthiness inspection.

6880   N52962

NOTES: Dwight Cross, Huntersville, North Carolina, 1966 and shown as dismantled.
(Leo J. Kohn)

6881   NC25, N25K

NOTES: Photo taken in 1948 when CAA owned the airplane. Owned by A. S. Wikstrom, the airplane was dismantled and stored in 1956 or 1957. It will eventually be rebuilt.
(Leo J. Kohn)

6883   N27E

NOTES: Purchased in February, 1954 by John Fadler, Jr., Boyertown, Pennsylvania, and currently owned by him. The airplane is now in dead storage, but Mr. Fadler plans to put it in flying condition sometime in the future.

6884   N1192V

NOTES: Formerly owned by Caryl Lane, East Swanzey, New Hampshire, he sold it in 1963 to H. Goetz, Middletown, Ohio. The airplane has a current airworthiness inspection.
(Caryl Lane)

6885   LN-HAG, OH-VKN, BC-2

NOTES: Used (as BC-2) as the personal transport of the Commander-in-Chief of the Finnish Air Force from 1951 to 1960, and sold as scrap in 1960.

6886   N52414

NOTES: Formerly owned by H. A. Houseman, Wayland, Michigan who had a large store of Beechcraft 17 parts. Around 1964-65, Houseman sold out to James C. Henning, Kalamazoo, Michigan. Photo above was taken in 1965. Mr. Henning plans to rebuild the airplane.
(James C. Henning)

6888   N30E

NOTES: William Mock, Decatur, Alabama, 1955. No further listing.
(Leo J. Kohn)

6890   N1334V, XB-HAY

NOTES: Photo taken Love Field, Dallas, Texas August 11, 1956. Transferred to Mexico in late 1950's, and still flying there. It is probably still owned by Captain P. A. Manuel Alarcon of Mexico City. *(Mitch Mayborn)*

6894   N1333V

NOTES: John Drew, Inc., Broadview, Illinois, 1966 with a 1955 inspection date.   *(Leo J. Kohn)*

6892   N1174V

NOTES: Note the unusual paint trim. Registered to Carrol Gresham. Covina, California with a 1964 inspection date, Mr. Gresham has been in the process of rebuilding the airplane.   *(Carrol Gresham)*

6897   N1336V

NOTES: R. P. Rice, Kennett, Missouri, 1966 with a 1961 inspection date.   *(Peter Berry)*

6893   N1172V

NOTES: A. N. Manucy, Jr., Mount Pleasant, South Carolina, 1966 with a 1964 inspection date.   *(Charles W. Martin)*

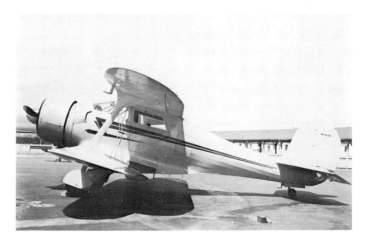

6898   N9465H

NOTES: Norman Wilson, Little Rock, California, 1966 with a 1957 airworthiness inspection date.   *(Peter Berry)*

239

6900   N9463H

NOTES: Howard McWhorter, Selfridge Air Force Base, Michigan, 1966 with a current airworthiness inspection. (James C. Henning)

6904   N1180V, XB-PAN

NOTES: Owned by Quinn G. Boyd of El Paso, Texas, and Hacienda de Carretas, Via San Miguelito, Sonora, Chihuahua, Mexico, he has now registered the airplane in Mexico, and uses it on the ranch, Hacienda da Carrestas. Photo is at the northern end of the ranch headquarters landing strip. (Quinn G. Boyd)

6905   G-AIHZ

NOTES: Registered in England January 27, 1947. Sold out of England to South Africa, June, 1948. No further information.

6907   N75606

NOTES: Photo taken Torrance, California May 21, 1957. Note "Chief Burnumgas" painted on fuselage near pilot's side window. Evidently reflects the sentiments of the owner about the P&W R-985 fuel consumption rate which runs 20 to 25 gallons per hour at cruise settings. Registered to Min Snide, Los Angeles, California, 1966 with a 1964 airworthiness inspection date. (Larry Smalley)

6908   N67543

NOTES: Photo taken at San Fernando Valley Airport, Van Nuys, California at AAA Fly-In, January 31, 1965. Note unusual paint trim. Registered to J. C. Roberts, Long Beach, California, 1966 with 1964 inspection date. (B. B. Deatrick)

6910   N9886H

NOTES: Smitty's Aircraft Service, Burwell, Nebraska, 1966 with 1963 inspection date. (Leo J. Kohn)

6911   N17679

NOTES: Photo taken May, 1961 when Mr. Henley owned the airplane. On 1966 list to Clifton Hood, Blytheville, Arkansas with current inspection date. (W. B. Henley)

6912   N2623

NOTES: Streckert Manufacturing Company, Abbotsford, Wisconsin, 1955. Reportedly overturned in 1966 and reduced to spares. No listings after 1955.

6913   N67198

NOTES: Photo taken 1955. Phillip Action, Fortuna, North Dakota, 1966 with 1963 inspection date.   (William T. Larkins)

6914   N67737, CF-GLL

NOTES: Photo taken Calgary, Canada in 1953. Sold into Canada in 1951, and last noted in 1958 belonging to F. McCarvill, Vancouver, British Columbia, and current at that time. No later information.   (E. C. Haney)

6915   N75922, CF-GCJ, CX-AQG

NOTES: Sold into Canada in 1961 to J. H. Lucas. In 1953 to Canadian Javelin Foundries and Machine Works, Montreal, then sold to O. Witbeck, Santiago, Chile in June, 1955, and in October, 1955 flown to Montevideo, Uruguay, and registered there as CX-AQG. No current information.   (Gary G. Kuhn)

6916   N67426

NOTES: Photo taken by Bob Bell when he owned the airplane. Except for curled prop tips, and minor belly damage, the airplane was unhurt, and quickly repaired. Shown on 1966 list to William Johnson, Jr., Philadelphia, Pennsylvania with a current inspection.   (Robert H. Bell)

6917   N1178V

NOTES: Donald Wagher, Victoria, Illinois, 1966 with a 1964 inspection date.

6918   N1054M

NOTES: Photo taken Rockford, Illinois August, 1963 at the EAA annual Fly-In. Note unusual paint trim. C. H. McLendon, Coral Gables, Florida, 1966 with 1964 airworthiness inspection date.   (Tom Cooney)

6919   N4626N

NOTES: Lieutenant Commander Paul deTamble, St. Louis, Missouri, 1966 with a 1961 inspection date. The airplane is reportedly being rebuilt.   (Leo J. Kohn)

6920   N1359V

NOTES: Paul Peterson, Altoona, Pennsylvania, 1955. No further listing.

6922   N44561

NOTES: Photo shows landing gear fairing doors removed. Jewell Jones, Redwood City, California, 1966 with current airworthiness inspection.
(Leo J. Kohn)

6923   N44562

NOTES: Dave McComas, Norwalk, California, 1966 with a 1956 inspection date.

6925   N44564

NOTES: Transferred to Goodyear Tire Company by the Navy. It was evidently given to Goodyear to fly executives of the company in support of military contracts during the war. James Leslie, Hutchinson, Kansas, 1966 with a 1960 inspection date.
(E. C. Haney)

6926   NC1367M, YS-83, N4008B

NOTES: Photo taken at Fort Worth, Texas, August, 1956. Converted to civilian status on April 18, 1947 by Mississippi Aircraft Service, Clarksdale, Mississippi. Owned by P. F. Good and John Jager, Athens, Ohio until 1950 at which time it was flown to San Salvador, El Salvador, and evidently registered there as YS-83. James Morgan, Jr., and Ricardo Krieste, Jr. picked the airplane up in New Orleans on November 2, 1950, and flew via Brownsville, Texas, Tampico and Veracruz, Mexico to El Salvador. On June 2, 1952 the airplane returned to New Orleans for resale by TACA, the United States consignee. It was purchased in September, 1953 by the son of the president of TACA, Thomas Bridges. The registration was changed at that time to N4008B, and the aircraft was overhauled. In February of 1956 the airplane was sold to K. Florence, Fort Worth, Texas, then to Dick Carrol of Aledo, Illionois in July of 1961. American Air Lines Captain Marty Pettigrew bought it from Mr. Carrol October 15, 1961, and still owns it. Captain Pettigrew has flown the airplane on extensive tours of the Western Hemisphere. (E. C. Haney)

6927   N4607N

NOTES: Photo taken Love Field, Dallas, Texas, September 6, 1951. R. P. Scaling Fort Worth, Texas, 1966 with an airworthiness date of 1964.
(Mitch Mayborn)

6929   N63599

NOTES: Delivered to Marine Corp Air Station, El Centro, California July 12, 1944. Transferred to MCAS El Toro, California on April 17, 1945. To Naval Air Station San Diego on August 26, 1946. Declared surplus and delivered to War Assets Administration, Concord, California on February 25, 1947. Secretary in an office there gave William T. Larkins advance notice of arrival of the airplane, so he was on hand to photograph it, and meet the secretary. She later became Mrs. Larkins. Dr. T. M. Toler, Washington, Louisiana on 1955 list; no further listing. (William T. Larkins)

6933   N164E

NOTES: Sam Anest, Spokane, Washington, 1966 with an airworthiness inspection date of 1959. Reportedly being rebuilt. (Ralph Nortell)

6935   N67735

NOTES: "Droopy" look in photo was due to a poor landing at Detroit City Airport on July 12, 1962. Evidently the airplane was repaired as it now carries an inspection date of 1964. Registered to Lloyd Berry, West Melbourne, Florida, 1966.   *(Robert F. Pauley)*

8443   N368

NOTES: See s/n 4883 for photo. There is no current listing for s/n 4883, but s/n 8443 is listed to Gilbert Trudeau, Las Vegas, Nevada, 1966 with a 1963 inspection date. I think this s/n (8443) is incorrect, but it is the one carried on the U.S. civil register. However, matching military serials with Beech s/n gives s/n 4883 for this aircraft. The difference may be due to a typographical error dating back twenty years, and now impossible to trace.

For those interested in such things, the four-digit serials were built in the following years;

1000 Series 1941
3000 Series 1942
4000 Series 1943
6000 Series 1944

B-1   NC80302, CU-463

NOTES: Called the "Cuban Dominican Beechcraft," the airplane was originally registered as NC80302, probably later became CU-463. No current information. Reportedly delivered to a sugar company in the Dominican Republic, and flown by Eddie Burgin, but there is no record of the airplane on the Dominican Republic aircraft register. Possibly the airplane was registered in Cuba and flown out of the Dominican Republic.   *(Beech Photo)*

B-3   NC80304, N44G

NOTES: Owned for several years by National Staggerwing Club president, William C. Yarbrough, this is perhaps the most elaborate Beechcraft flying. A deep maroon and red, Mr. Yarbrough tagged her "Big Red," and flies her mostly for pleasure. He intends to own the airplane permanently.   *(Photo By Author)*

B-2   NC80303

NOTES: First flown as NX80303 awaiting final certification of the radio equipment, the airplane was purchased originally by the Sweetbriar shops in Denver, and rolled out of the factory June 28, 1946. Pilot Bob Woodard flew the airplane for Sweetbriar. Known as "Sally Sweetbriar II," the above photo was the result of an attempted flight from Denver to Grand Junction, Colorado in March, 1948. The weather closed in, and pilot Woodard set Sally down on the highway at Wheeler Flats near Dillon, Colorado. In 1948 Sally was sold. She does not appear on the 1955 or any subsequent list.   *(Robert H. Woodard)*

B-4   N80305

NOTES: Photographed by Villela at Mexico City Central Airport in 1958, the airplane is registered (1966) to John Stowers, Corona Del Mar, California with a 1964 airworthiness inspection date.   *(Ing. Jose Villela, Jr.)*

B-5   NC80306, N333, NC80306

NOTES: Purchased by General Petroleum Corporation, Casper, Wyoming, and flown by Robert H. Woodard. The original owner may have been a Mr. Christie of Wichita Falls, Texas, from whom General Petroleum purchased the airplane. They sold the airplane in 1951 to Vest Aircraft in Denver. It went through several owners, and was finally crashed in a weather accident on the east coast. The pilot and his passengers walked away from it, and the remains were purchased by Delta Air Lines Captain William Freeman of Stone Mountain, Georgia who is in the process of rebuilding the airplane. When finished it will probably be the most elaborate Beechcraft flying.   (Leo J. Kohn)

B-8   NC80309
Built 1946   P&W R-985, 450 hp

NOTES: Crashed early in its career, and stored in a barn, the remains were recently purchased by William C. Yarbrough. The airplane will eventually be rebuilt.   (Beech Photo)

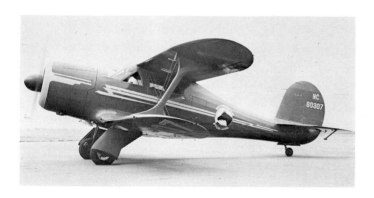

B-6   NC80307
Built 1946   P&W R-985, 450 hp

NOTES: Sold August, 1946 to Coldstream Stud, Inc. Not currently listed.
(Beech Photo)

B-9   N291Y

NOTES: Currently owned by Richard Hotaling, Atlanta, Georgia. Has current airworthiness inspection.   (Beech Photo)

B-7   NC80308

NOTES: Owned by Clayton Carriveau, Franksville, Wisconsin for several years, it is in the process of being rebuilt.   (Ralph Nortell)

B-10   VT-CIT

NOTES: Purchased originally by Tata Iron and Steel Company in India. In 1960 they sold the airplane to Simon Carves Limited. In July, 1962 Associated Airworks, Calcutta, India purchased the airplane for air charter and company flying. Still currently flying.   (D. Ghosh)

245

B-11   NC80312, N70E

NOTES: Major Arthur W. Laughton, Merced, California, 1966 with current airworthiness inspection.
(John W. Church)

B-14   NC80315

NOTES: Darwin C. Fenner, Atlanta, Georgia, 1966 with current airworthiness inspection.
(Leo J. Kohn)

B-12   NC80313, N911

NOTES: Clayton Carriveau, Franksville, Wisconsin, 1966 with 1963 date of airworthiness inspection. But, the record does not always keep up with the actual events. Early in 1965 the airplane was sold to Mr. H. H. Holloway, Jr., Baton Rouge, Louisiana. Mr. Holloway is presently having the airplane completely refitted.
(Leo J. Kohn)

B-15   NC80316, N262C

NOTES: Owned for years by Fuller Longley of Tom Cat Overalls, Chattanooga, Tennessee, it is now (1966) registered to Robert Coleman, Knoxville, Tennessee with a current airworthiness inspection.
(William C. Yarbrough)

B-13   CF-ESU, N4710V

NOTES: Purchased by Page Aviation of Canada for A. E. dePalma of Toronto. Registered in Canada December 14, 1946. Transferred to Mr. dePalma's wife on May 21, 1948. Back to Mr. dePalma on June 29, 1951. Sold to C. W. Millard of Toronto on April 6, 1953 for export to the United States to J. J. Conner, Tucson, Arizona. Samual Dunlap III, New Canaan, Connecticut, 1966 with current airworthiness inspection.
(Beech Photo)

B-16   N8464A, NC80317

NOTES: Photo taken at Fort Worth, Texas, 1953. Airplane is currently registered to John Church, Alameda, California with a current inspection. Mr. Church just recently completed a refitting program to place the airplane in first class condition. Sold to Richard F. Durant, Albuquerque, N.M. late in 1966.
(E. C. Haney)

B-17   N8485A

NOTES: Original owner unknown. File removed from United States register on May 25, 1949 and cancelled.

B-18   N8589A

NOTES: Registered to O'Keefes, Inc., San Francisco, California, 1966 with airworthiness date of 1962. On February 17, 1963 the airplane landed at Half Moon Bay airport wtih the landing gear retracted. Evidently pilot William F. O'Keefe touched down a little hard as a fuel tank obviously ruptured, and the airplane was almost entirely consumed by fire.   *(Leo J. Kohn)*

B-19   N8590A, N700N

NOTES: Originally owned by Hampden Wentworth. Photo taken at San Francisco, California, August, 1957. In 1958 it was owned by Inland Container Corporation of Indianapolis, Indiana. In late 1959 or early 1960 the Roscoe Turner Aeronautical Corporation of Indianapolis was hired to restore the airplane. Before they completed their work, the airplane was sold to Don Engel of Wichita, Kansas. Mr. Engel continued the rebuilding job, but didn't finish it. In the Spring of 1964 the airplane was sold to Harvey Rosen and George Stevens of Wichita, and Melvin Porth of Clay Center, Kansas was hired to complete the restoration of the airplane. In September of 1964 Mr. Porth had completed the work, and the late Larry Bangiola test flew the airplane. He flew it for Rosen and Stevens until the winter of 1964-65 at which time it was sold to L. B. Maytag, Jr., president of National Air Lines who currently owns it.
(Larry Smalley)

B-20   NC80321

NOTES: Donald Lumis, Bakersfield, California, 1966 with an inspection date of 1933. To Conlan Carter, Woodland Hills, California, Dec. 31, 1966.
(Leo J. Kohn)

All G17S models were built in 1946, and were powered with various models of the P&W R-985 engine. The original production order called for 30 airplanes, but this was later reduced to 20, and all were built in 1946, but not all were assembled that year. They were assembled as purchased. Some sources say the last three airplanes were purchased as parts by a company in Texas and assembled by them. In any event, the last G17S was probably assembled in 1948 or 1949.

CURRENTLY REGISTERED AIRCRAFT

By studying the serial number lists, the reader can learn exactly which individual airplanes are currently flying. Based on a list compiled as of February 18, 1966, the following tabulation was made;

Total Beechcraft 17's registered in U.S. 254
Number with a 1964 airworthiness inspection date 53
Number with a 1965 airworthiness inspection date 78
Number probably active 131

From the above tabulation, it can be seen that about half of the airplanes on the civil register are not currently licensed. They vary from airplanes completely dismantled, and almost worthless, to airplanes that are sitting intact in the rear of someone's hangar, and just a few years out of license.

— End —

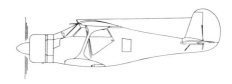

INDEX TO PART I